# CHARACTERISTIC

# MATERIA MEDICA.

BY

W. H. BURT, M.D.,

OF LINCOLN, ILL.,

AUTHOR OF

"A MONOGRAPH ON POLYPORUS OFFICINALIS, POLYPORUS PINICOLA, AND USTILAGO MADIS."

MULTUM IN PARVO.

PHILADELPHIA:

A. J. TAFEL.

1869.

CAXTON PRESS OF SHERMAN & CO., PHILADELPHIA.

TO

HENRY N. GUERNSEY, M.D.,

PROFESSOR OF OBSTETRICS AND DISEASES OF WOMEN AND CHILDREN,

IN THE

HOMŒOPATHIC MEDICAL COLLEGE OF PENNSYLVANIA,

The originator of the Characteristic or "Key-note System" for the choice of remedies in disease, brought out in your "Treatise on Obstetrics," the most valuable work ever written on the science of medicine.

In consideration of the great benefit I have derived from your labors, I would most respectfully dedicate to you this, my humble effort, with gratitude.

THE AUTHOR.

# PREFACE.

The following work is neither a "Text-book," nor an "Epitome;" much less is it offered as a substitute for the Materia Medica.

But from all the sources within my reach, including pretty much the entire range of our English and American Homœopathic literature, I have endeavored to collect those symptoms, which, whether originally pathogenetic, or clinical only, have come to be regarded as "Characteristics," and as "Key-notes," by reason of their own prominence, or from the frequency of their mention by the best authorities.

Very many of the symptoms comprised within this book, have been expressly set forth as "Key-notes," and "Characteristics," by Drs. Guernsey, Hering, and numerous others. To all of whom due credit has been given in every instance. These symptoms, thus approved, as having been tried and verified, *ex usu in morbis*, I have, with great labor, collected and arranged, in such a manner as to render them at the same time more accessible to the junior members of the profession, and more convenient for their use.

And in order the better to facilitate the study of

the remedies which these symptoms represent, I have adopted a method of grouping, arranging by themselves those remedies which produce similar physio-pathological and pathogenetic symptoms. In forming such groups, I have availed myself of the labors of Dr. Hale and Dr. Hughes. The method here pursued, differs from that of Teste, who based his groups upon the pathogenesis alone. His plan appears to me to be both unscientific and insufficient; since, in order to apply our remedies successfully, we must understand their pathological relations, as well as their pathogenetic symptoms.

It is for this reason that I have also attempted, in a few words, to point out the several organs and tissues for which each particular remedy has a special affinity; and also the nervous spheres through which it primarily acts upon the system.

In the next place is stated the particular kind of pathological influence which the remedy exerts upon each tissue and important organ.

Then follow what I have allowed myself to term the Grand Characteristics of the remedy.

And here it is proper that I should refer to the sources from which these latter are derived, although it would seem superfluous to give a full catalogue of the numerous works consulted; and the more especially, since, wherever practicable, an authority has been subjoined to each individual "Characteristic," or "Key-note." And while I have endeavored to render this work representative of the practical experience of the whole profession, rather than that of a single man, I cannot here refrain from making especial mention of Professor H. N. Guernsey's work on Obstetrics. Upon this, as will appear, I have depended more for Characteristics, than upon any other.

The initial G. stands, therefore, for Prof. Guernsey; H., for Prof. Hering; and F., for Prof. Frost. The names of other authorities being given in full. The symptoms credited to Prof. J. S. Douglas, were from my notes of his lectures.

In the absence of any fixed and absolute rule for grouping, I have been obliged to depend upon my own judgment; and whether from my own inability, or the natural difficulties of the undertaking, it is no doubt as true that others may prefer a different classification, as that I found it impossible to confine certain remedies exclusively to any particular groups.

And from being alone, and thus obliged to depend upon my own judgment only, in regard to what symptoms should be selected as characteristic, and what rejected, it also follows, most undoubtedly, that many persons will look in vain in these pages, for symptoms which *they know to be characteristic*, from having successfully applied them for years in their practice. This being the *first attempt* to collect together the characteristic symptoms, it must be regarded only as a beginning, and, therefore, necessarily imperfect.

It is believed that the present work will be found of especial use to the profession, from its presenting the most important symptoms and indications of some new and valuable remedies, many of them contained in Dr. Hale's Materia Medica of the New Remedies; not to mention my own humble contributions of Polyporus and Ustilago madis: the latter of which Dr. J. B. Woods reports (Hahnemannian Monthly, Apr., 1869), "having used with good success in cases of uterine hemorrhage," &c. In other respects, I have made use of my own experience in writing and compiling this work, which, I trust, may richly repay my labor, by proving itself acceptable and useful to the profession.

A few inaccuracies which have crept into the text, are here noted; since, while not in themselves of much importance, they mar the sense.

In page 165, the paragraph (beginning Dry, husky, scaly skin;) should be understood as a portion of the next one, or symptom quoted from D. R. Gardiner; the quotation-marks were unfortunately omitted.

A similar omission of quotation-marks occurs also on page 175, where the whole of the paragraph on Lycopodium in Typhoid fever, should have been credited to Prof. Frost.

In page 297, in the sixth line from the top, instead of hydropho*bia*, read hydropho*binum*.

In the list of Group V, page 229, insert *Arum tri.;* and omit "Potassium, in its various compounds," which latter had their place in Group IV.

# LIST OF GROUPS.

## GROUP I.

Aconitum napellus,
Veratrum viride,
Cactus grandiflorus,
Gelseminum semp.,
Bryonia alba,
Rhus tox.,
Rhus rad.,
Rhus vernix,
Digitalis,
Cimicifuga,
Tartar emetic,
Antimo. tart.,
Veratrum alb.,
Arnica montana,
Colchicum,
Senega,
Baptisia,
Chelidonium.

## GROUP II.

Belladonna,
Hyoscyamus,
Stramonium,
Opium,
Alcohol,
Chloroform,
Ether,
Glonoine,
Agaricus,
Cicuta vir.,
Gymnocladus,
Camphora,
Zizia aurea,
Cuprum,
Cannabis ind.,
Coffea,
Tabacum,
Solanum nig.,
Aethusa,
Lachnantes,
Ailanthus.

## GROUP III.

Nux vomica,
Strychnine,
Ignatia,
Cocculus,
Conium,
Curare,
Angustura,
Æsculus hip.

## GROUP IV.

Sulphur,
Calcarea carb.,
Lycopodium,
Silicea,
Hepar sulph.,
Phosphorus,
Cistus can.,
Sarsaparilla,
Sanguinaria,
Kali carb.,
Kali hyd.,
Causticum,
Rumex crispus,
Carbo veg.,
Carbo an.,
Alumina,
Stannum,
Juglans cinerea,
Graphites,
Thuja,
Magnesia,
Dulcamara,
Corallia rub.,
Psorin,
Kali bichromicum,
Electricity.

## GROUP V.

Mercurius, and its various preparations,
Iodine, and its compounds,
Chlorine, and its compounds,
Bromine, and its compounds,
Arum triphyllum,
Ammonium,
Podophyllum,
Iris versicolor,
Phytolacca,
Arsenicum alb.,
Sepsin,
Leptandria,
Stillingia,
Aloes,
Argentum,
Spongia,
Baryta carb.,
Croton tig.,
Aurum.

## GROUP VI.

Ipecacuanha,
Antimonium crud.,
Tartar emetic,
Bismuth,
Lobelia,
Robinia,
Euphorbia,

## GROUP VII.

Ferrum met.,
Manganese,
Zincum,
Helonias dioica,
Hypophosphites.

## GROUP VIII.

Lachesis,
Crotalus,
Hydrophobinum,
Naja tripujians,
Theridion curass.,
Tarantula.

## GROUP IX.

Cantharides,
Apis mel.,
Chimaphila,
Terebinth.,
Copaiva,
Cubebs,
Hydrastis,
Kali chloricum,
Borax,
Cannabis sat.,
Erigeron,
Apocynum can.,
Asparagus,
Urtica urens,
Petroleum,
Erechthites,
Mitchella,
Euphrasia,
Helleborus,
Sambucus,
Uranium,
Eupatorium purpur.,
Sticta,
Zingiber.

## GROUP X.

Colocynth,
Dioscorea,
Collinsonia,
Plumbum,
Jalapa,
Scammonium,
Mezereum,
Gummi guttæ,
Elaterium,
Rheum.

## GROUP XI.

Asafœtida,
Valeriana,
Valerianate of Zinc,
Scutellaria,
Ambra grisea,
Nux moschata,
Platina,
Moschus,
Chamomilla,
Castoreum,
Cypripedium,
Agnus castus,
Mephitis.

## GROUP XII.

| | |
|---|---|
| Cina, | Cucurbita pepo semen, |
| Santonine, | Teucrium, |
| Spigelia, | Artemisia, |
| Filix mas, | Staphysagria. |
| Kousso, | |

## GROUP XIII.

| | |
|---|---|
| China, | Gelseminum, |
| Quinia, | Chanchalagua, |
| Ostrya vir., | Capsicum, |
| Polypori, | Salix alba, |
| Eupatorium perf., | Cornus florida, |
| Natrum mur., | Ptelea, |
| Cedron, | Nux v., |
| Arsenicum, | Carbo v., |
| Ipecacuanha, | Sulphur. |

## GROUP XIV.

| | |
|---|---|
| Secale cornutum, | Crocus, |
| Ustilago madis, | Thlaspi, |
| Pulsatilla, | Senecio aureus, |
| Sepia, | Cinnamonum, |
| Sabina, | Millefolium, |
| Kreosote, | Caulophyllum, |
| Hamamelis, | Tanacetum, |
| Trillium, | Gossypium. |
| Cyclamen, | |

## GROUP XV.

| | |
|---|---|
| Acidum sulphuricum, | Acidum hydrocyanicum, |
| Acidum nitricum, | Acidum fluoricum, |
| Acidum phosphoricum, | Acidum benzoicum, |
| Acidum muriaticum, | Acidum oxalicum. |

CHARACTERISTIC

# MATERIA MEDICA.

---

## GROUP I.

| | |
|---|---|
| Aconitum napellus, | Cimicifuga, |
| Veratrum viride, | Tartar emetic, |
| Cactus grandiflorus, | Veratrum alb., |
| Gelseminum semp., | Arnica montana, |
| Bryonia alba, | Colchicum, |
| Rhus tox., | Senega, |
| Rhus rad., | Baptisia, |
| Rhus vernix, | Chelidonium. |
| Digitalis, | |

Aconitum napellus, and its analogous remedies, are our true antiphlogistics. All produce physio-pathological states, which, if not identical, are very similar; all reduce the activity of the circulation, quiet nervous excitement and excessive action of the heart and arteries, and prevent congestion and inflammation.

Primarily, they all produce paralysis of sensation; voluntary and involuntary motion; venous congestion of the brain and its membranes; the lungs, heart, and all the abdominal viscera. The blood becomes dark and coagulated, the heart loses its contractility, and serous exudations, asphyxia, and death result.

Secondarily, they produce arterial excitement, congestion, inflammation, spasms, tremors, general irritation, &c.

## ACONITUM NAPELLUS.

*Wolfsbane.*

Aconite especially affects that portion of the ganglionic nervous system which presides over the action of the heart and arteries; the posterior portion of the spinal cord, that which presides over sensation; the serous membranes, muscles, joints, and digestive organs.

The great sympathetic or ganglionic system of nerves, is deeply invaded by the poisonous principle of Aconite; the heart and arterial capillary vessels are so paralyzed as to produce violent congestion and inflammation in any and every organ and tissue in the body that contains capillaries; the parts become swollen, red, hot, and painful, with all the constitutional symptoms of phlegmonous inflammation; such as high fever, hard, bounding pulse, violent thirst, great anxiety, restlessness, &c.

Thus we find that Aconite expends its poisonous principles especially upon those delicate arterial capillary vessels, and so paralyzes their action as to produce congestion and inflammation.

Meyer says: "Aconite's sphere of action is manifested principally in the ganglionic system, and exercises here its special influence upon the nerves of the capillary vessels, exciting fevers, congestions, and inflammations."

Grusselich says: "Its operation on the arterial system is unmistakable; its reaction upon the nerves and lymphatic vessels easily substantiated from physiological principles."

Diez says: "Aconite corresponds to the first stage of inflammation; as such, and apart from its various modifications, it occupies the foremost rank among all the medical plants that have been proved up to the present time."

*Cerebro-spinal System*, or nervous system of animal life.—This includes the brain, spinal cord, with the nerves connected with them, and the ganglia seated upon these nerves.

First, the Brain. The arterial capillary vessels of the brain are so paralyzed as to produce violent cerebral congestion, as shown by the swollen face, blue lips, violent pain in the head, stupor, partial insensibility, trembling of the head, mania; at times singing and laughing, and then weeping and moaning; filled with hope or great despair; pain in the head, as if it was filled with hot water or encircled with a hot iron; excessive anxiety; restlessness; dread of death; whizzing in the ears; loss of sight; vertigo, with partial loss of consciousness; loss of memory, &c.

*Nerves of Motion.*—Aconite sometimes produces convulsions, but more generally paralysis of the muscular system. It does not irritate the motor nerves of animal life directly, like Nux vomica.

*Nerves of Sensation.*—These are more powerfully

acted upon by Aconite, as shown by the numbness, tingling, prickling, crawling, and creeping sensations throughout the body. "This sensation arises from its depressing action upon those ganglionic or vaso-motor nerves which follow the bloodvessels to their most minute ramifications, and preside over their functions." This congestion, by pressing on the sentient nerves, arrests the nervous circulation and produces a state similar to that when a limb is said to go to sleep; consequently the neuralgia Aconite is homœopathic too, is secondary, from pressure of the congested vessels surrounding the nerve. When the nerve alone is involved we must look to other remedies that directly affect the nerves.

*Muscular System.*—Aconite especially affects the muscular system, also the tendons and the fibrous tissues of the joints; producing in them congestion and inflammation of a rheumatic character. For inflammatory rheumatism of the joints and fibrous tissue, in any part of the body, no known remedy is equal to Aconite. If the fibrous tissue is the seat of the disease, the pains are tearing and aching. If it is in the serous membranes, the pains are sticking, or sore and stinging. If in the mucous membrane, the pains are burning. If in the muscles, the pain from sudden movement is extremely great.

*Serous Membranes.*—The most accurate and best authenticated cases of poisoning by Aconite establish the fact that it affects especially the capillaries, and this through a direct impression upon the retinæ of ganglionic and vaso-motor nerves supplied to them. This power to influence the whole or any portion of the capillary system, renders it a polychrest *par excellence.* Its field of operation is the ganglionic nervous system, which it affects primarily. This primary impression is communicated to the vaso-motor filaments which regulate the circulation in all the vessels. The changes which occur in the circulation of a tissue brought under its (Aconite's) influence are believed to be very similar to those indicated by Dr. Bennet as peculiar to the congestive process.

Dr. Prevost found that if Aconite, much diluted by water, was brought in contact with the web of a frog's foot, contraction and afterwards dilatation of the capillary vessels ensued.

The congestive stage of inflammation in serous membranes most frequently commences with a chill, followed by dry heat, &c. Inflammation in serous membranes does not generally go on to ulceration, sloughing and gangrene; but the fluid that is thrown out in the second stage takes on what is termed "adhesive inflammation," the fluid effused undergoes such an organizing process as to glue the opposing surfaces of the serous membranes together. As soon as the second stage, that of effusion, takes place in serous membranes, the usefulness of Aconite ceases, and Bryonia or some other remedy must be chosen, but up to the stage of effusion, Aconite is the remedy *par excellence.*

Most examples of serous inflammation are believed to be more or less rheumatic in character. This again shows us why Aconite is so useful in serous inflammation, for the inflammation caused by Aconite is rheumatic in character.

*Mucous Membranes.*—Mucous membranes are highly vascular, and the millions of arterial capillary vessels found in them become the centre for the action of Aconite; acute congestion and inflammation in this tissue are at once produced under its influence.

*Lymphatic System.*—Lymphatics have three coats. 1. Internal epithelial and elastic fibre; 2. Middle, smooth, muscular, and fine elastic fibres; 3. External, areolo-fibrous, areolar tissue, intermixed with smooth muscular fibre. Arteries are distributed to their outer and middle coats, and in these two coats, Aconite produces congestion and inflammation.

### *Grand Characteristics.*

The grand sphere for Aconite is found in all diseases of a congestive, inflammatory, or rheumatic character, with full bounding pulse, much heat, dry, burning skin, agonized tossing about, violent thirst, red face, shortness of breath, and great nervous excitability.

"Great fear and anxiety of mind, with great nervous excitability."—G.

"He is afraid to go out, to go where there is any excitement or many people, or to cross a street. His life, in fact, is rendered miserable by this all-pervading fearfulness. The countenance exhibits strong and unmistakable expression of fear."—G.

"Fear of death—predicts the day he will die."—G.

"If the patient sits up in bed, he immediately falls over in consequence of vertigo, and he is afraid to rise again, lest the same trouble should recur."—G.

"Extreme congestion and inflammation of the parts. She dreads too much activity about her."—G.

"She is alarmed, and sure she will die, although there is no occasion for alarm."—G.

"Chill and synochal fever, from dry cold air. Everything except water has a bitter taste."—G.

"Sensation as if the hairs of the head were standing on end; the scalp is sensitive to the touch."—G.

"The child has a dry, hot skin, sleepless, restless, cries much, bites its fist, and has a green, watery diarrhœa."—G.

"Child has much pain; feverish, constant restlessness, and biting its hands."—G.

Agony; has to sit straight up; can hardly breathe; pulse thread-like; very sad.

Active hemorrhages, with fear of death, and great nervous excitability.

"Inflammation; the parts burn as from hot coals."

"Excessive sensibility to the least touch."

"She complains much of her head, with anguish and great fear of death."—G.

Vertigo, when rising from a recumbent position, with fainting and pale face.

"So giddy cannot sit up in bed."—G.

Headache, as if everything would press out of the forehead, with vertigo on rising.

Burning sensation, extending from the stomach all the way to the mouth, and along the dorsum of the tongue, with tingling in the lips, tongue, fingers, and spine. Everything tastes bitter except water; has great thirst for cold water.

Bitter, bilious vomiting, with anguish and cold perspiration.

"Sharp, shooting pains in the whole abdomen, which is very tender to the touch."—G.

"Abdomen swollen after scarlet fever."—HEMPEL.

"Green, watery diarrhœa, like chopped spinach."—G.

Watery, dark-colored stools.

"Bilious diarrhœa of infants, with colic, which no position or circumstance relieves." —G.

Dysentery, with high synochal fever; great fear and restlessness.

Inflammation of the bowels; high synochal fever; great fear and restlessness.

"Cutting, lancinating, burning and tearing pains in the abdomen, with anguish and fear." —G.

"Retention of urine from cold, particularly in children, with much crying and restlessness." —G.

"Aconite often restores the menses of plethoric women, after their suppression from any cause."—G.

Suppression of the menses after a fright.

"Catamenia too profuse."—LIPPE.

"If a pregnant woman has fright, and the fear remains, and she cannot seem to get over it, she must take Aconite at once."—G.

"Suppression of the lochia, or too scanty discharge, soon after confinement, with distress in the abdomen, chest and head."—G.

"Puerperal peritonitis."—LIPPE.

Breasts hard and knotted, with hot dry skin; much thirst and fear.

"The mammæ are congested, burning hot; hard, and distended, with little or no milk." —G.

"*Os uteri*, dry, tender, and undilatable; with distress, moaning and restlessness during every pain."—G.

"Cannot bear the pain, nor bear to be touched or uncovered."—G.

"When the patient, during pregnancy, is

distressed between twelve and three, A. M., having to get up to urinate. Has no affection for any one."—J. C. M.

Great fear during pregnancy that the child will be deformed, or that she never can give it birth.

"Desire to urinate accompanied with great fear, anxiety and distress."—G.

Bright red and hot urine.

"Retention of urine with stitches in the kidneys."—G.

"Difficult and scanty emissions of urine."—G.

"First stages of croup, with cough and loud breathing during expiration, but not during inspiration; every expiration ends with a hoarse hacking cough."—G.

"The child has much oppression of the chest; anxiety; can scarcely cough, the suffering is so intense."—G.

"Child grasps at the throat with every coughing fit."—G.

"Croupy cough, awaking in first sleep, particularly with children, after dry cold west winds."—G.

"After violent chill, dry heat, with difficult breathing, and lancinating pain through the chest."—G.

"Blood spitting; the blood comes up with

an easy hawking, hemming, or some coughing, either after mental excitement, after drinking wine, or exposure to dry cold air."—C. HERING.

"Stitches in the chest, hindering respiration; cannot breathe freely in consequence of a sensation, as if the lungs would not expand."—G.

"Stinging pains in internal organs."—LIPPE.

"Burning in internal organs."—LIPPE.

"Numbness in left arm; can scarcely move the hand."—C. HERING.

At night the pains are insupportable, with fear, anxiety, and great restlessness.

Adapted to people of full, plethoric habit, especially young girls, of sanguine temperament and sedentary life; and to acute diseases brought on by dry, cold west winds.

## VERATRUM VIRIDE.

*Green Hellebore.*

Acts especially upon the portion of the sympathetic nervous system which presides over the action of the heart and arteries, the base of the brain, cervical portion of the spinal cord, and pneumogastric nerve.

The action of Veratrum viride upon the great sympathetic differs widely from that of Aconite; the latter produces congestion and inflammation in any and every organ and tissue in the body, while Veratrum viride produces congestion and inflammation only in the thoracic viscera, base of the brain, upper portion of the spinal cord, and stomach. Its action on the organic nervous system much resembles that of cholera, but it does not so profoundly affect the functional power of the mucous epithelial glands of the intestinal canal. No remedy in the materia medica will so quickly and surely produce congestion and inflammation of the lungs as the Veratrum viride.

*Nerves of Motion.*—The sedative action of Veratrum viride upon these nerves is most profound. Sometimes it irritates them so as to produce convulsions, but generally the muscular system is completely paralyzed, so that the patient or animal cannot stand or walk, and the breathing nearly ceases. We have much to learn yet about its action on the cerebro-spinal system.

*Nerves of Sensation.*—It produces pain and hyperæsthesia.

Upon the pneumogastric nerve it has a most powerful effect, irritating the filaments of that portion of the nerve which is distributed to the stomach and lungs, so as to produce violent nausea and vomiting, and asthmatic breathing. The secretions of the stomach and lungs are greatly increased.

### *Grand Characteristics.*

In all diseases where Veratrum will be found indicated, there will be more or less gastric irritability, congestion and inflammation of the lungs, with nausea and vomiting and high fever, nausea and frequent vomiting of glairy mucus, bile, and blood, with hiccough and a sensation as though a ball was rising in the œsophagus.

Constant burning distress in the cardiac region, with high fever.

Frontal headache, with nausea, vomiting, and fever.

Complete loss of vision and hearing when rising from a recumbent position, accompanied with hiccough, nausea, vomiting, dilated pupils, green circles around the eyes.

Tongue feels as though it had been scalded, with intense burning in the fauces.

Cold sweat on the face, hands, and feet.

Skin shrivelled up.

Spasms of an opisthotonic character with Hippocratic face.

Chorea.

Neuralgia.

Especially adapted to gastric, catarrhal, and pulmonary diseases and chorea.

## CACTUS GRANDIFLORUS.

*Night-Blooming Cereus.*

Acts especially upon the heart and arteries, also the lungs. The results of its action on the system resemble rheumatism.

*Grand Characteristics.*

In diseases that call for the use of Cactus, there will always be found more or less derangement of the heart. The patient will be greatly reduced in flesh, with great nervous excitability.

"Feeling as though an iron band was around the heart, preventing its normal motion."

Palpitation of the heart in debilitated patients; worse when lying on the left side; when walking, and at night, with great melancholy.

"Chronic bronchitis, with profuse rattling of mucus in the lungs."

Difficulty of breathing.

Arterial pulsation in the scrobiculus.

Nervous consumption.

Adapted to hypertrophy of the heart; palpitation of the heart; rheumatism of the heart; acute and chronic carditis and rheumatism.

And also to acute inflammation of the diaphragm.—F.

## GELSEMINUM SEMPERVIRENS.

*Yellow Jessamine.*

This remedy depresses and paralyzes the action of the sympathetic and cerebro-spinal nervous system in a remarkable manner. "The most prominent of all the effects of Gelseminum is to induce a profound and intense prostration of the whole muscular system. Its effects are first manifested on the voluntary muscles and then on the involuntary. This action is caused by impairing the vitality of those nerves which supply it with life." —HALE.

*Nerves of Sensation.*—Its action on these nerves is not direct; but the excess of sensitiveness is probably caused by its action on the organic nerves, or by the "cramp-like contractions of muscles" which are presided over by the motor nerves, which it so powerfully influences.

*Vascular System.*—The congestion produced by Gelseminum differs from that of Aconite or Veratrum viride. The congestions caused by the two latter tend to inflammation, but the congestion of Gelseminum much resembles that of malarious affections, which go on to inflammation. The action of the heart is at first greatly paralyzed; but afterwards it becomes quick and full.

### *Grand Characteristics.*

Especially adapted to nervous, excitable, hysterical females. Sensitive people and little children; to male and female onanists.

Hysteria, with spasms; palpitation of the heart and great nervous excitability.

Nocturnal emissions and sexual dreams, followed the next day by great languor and irritability of mind.

Involuntary emissions of semen, with or without erections, with much flaccidity and coldness of the genital organs, accompanied with great languor and depression of spirits.

"A feeling as though the heart would stop beating in a moment, if she did not walk incessantly, with a feeling of impending death." —HALE.

Irritative, remittent, and intermittent fevers in very sensitive people and children, with excessive irritability and nervous erethism, with no gastric, hepatic, or visceral complications.

Confusion of the mind.

Great depression of spirits in onanists, accompanied with excessive languor.

Intense congestion of the brain in children during dentition.

Nervous headache; the pain commences in the cervical portion of the spinal cord, and then spreads over the whole head. (See Sanguinaria.)

Great heaviness of the eyelids; it is impossible to keep them open.

Dilatation of the pupils, with blindness and vertigo.

Dimness of vision.

Diplopia.

Amaurosis from masturbation.

Paralysis of the sphincter muscles of the bladder.

Rigid os uteri in labor, in nervous or hysterical females.

*Nervous chills* with shivering and chattering of the teeth; depending upon an irritated condition of the nerves of motion in very sensitive, hysterical subjects; these chills may appear from fear or fright in healthy subjects; they often attend relaxation of the os uteri in labor.

"*Fever without thirst;* wants to lie still and rest; particularly with inflamed tonsils beginning on the right side."—J. B. BELL.

"Fever, with shooting pressive pains through the temples and nasal sinuses, with brilliancy of eyes and loquacity."—C. H. W.

"Cannot get to sleep on going to bed at night, on account of thinking, which she cannot control; in sensitive people."—J. C. M.

Intense passive congestion of both veins and arteries, in which irritation of the congested organ sets in.

Congestive stage of pneumonia.

Feeling of lightness in the body from spinal exhaustion, in onanists.

Paralytic condition of the lumbar and sacral muscles in onanists.

Congestive facial neuralgia; the pains are grumbling or shooting; worse on pressure.

## BRYONIA ALBA.

*White Bryonia.*

No remedy affects the serous membranes more

powerfully than Bryonia. Its greatest field of action is upon parenchymatous organs, inclosed in serous membranes; but it has the greatest influence over the pleura and lungs: the next organ most influenced is the brain; then the synovial membranes and muscular fibre. Over the liver it has a powerful influence; and, lastly, the kidneys and mucous membrane of the large intestines.

Noack and Trinks say: "Bryonia excites both the peripheral nerves and capillary vessels, thus giving rise to symptoms intermediate between inflammation and nervous irritation. Bryonia has striking relations with the secretory organs of bile and with the uterus, likewise with the serous membranes, and is especially suitable in hyperæmia of the latter. Bryonia is especially indicated in affections where reabsorption is required: in typhoid infiltrations, serous effusions, and sanguineous exudations. It is especially efficacious in affections where the catarrhal, pituitous, and rheumatic character prevails, or when synochal symptoms pass into the nervous stage."

Hempel says: "Bryonia is particularly adapted to inflammations of a torpid character, when developing themselves from a rheumatic base; or in acute inflammations, which threaten to pass into the stage of exudation or paralysis, with a small, soft, or even compressible and somewhat accelerated pulse."

"It is particularly in inflammatory affections of the respiratory organs, the lungs, and their enveloping membrane, that Bryonia has been found eminently useful; not, however, in the first invasion of the disease, but after the synochal form has been subdued by Aconite, we shall find Bryonia particularly useful."—HEMPEL.

Prof. R. Ludlam says: "As a rule, Bryonia is more serviceable in inflammations of the synovial capsules and the pleura, than in peritonitis or pericarditis."

In rheumatic and arthritic inflammations, no remedy can supersede Bryonia. "Its powerful influence over serous and synovial membranes and muscular fibre, with its fever and sour sweats, point unmistakably to rheumatism."—HUGHES.

"Most examples of serous inflammation are believed to be more or less rheumatic" in character, and this again shows us why Bryonia is so useful in those diseases.

### *Grand Characteristics.*

Stitching, tearing pains; greatly aggravated by motion; relieved by rest; worse at night.

The sovereign remedy for all inflammations that have advanced to the stage of serous effusion. This action extends over all the serous membranes.

Exceedingly irritable; everything makes him angry. Headache as if it would split open; greatly aggravated by motion, opening the eyes or stooping; relieved by pressure and closing the eyes.

"Lips parched, dry, and cracked."—G.

"Constipation of hard, dry stools, as if burnt."—G.

"Frequent bleeding from the nose, when the menses should appear."—G.

Sitting up in bed causes nausea and fainting.—G.

"Desire for things that cannot be had, or which are refused, or not wanted when offered."—G.

People with choleric temperament, bilious tendency, dark hair and complexion, with firm, fleshy fibre.

Fear of the future.

Congestive headache, as if the forehead would burst open, with epistaxis.

Eyes very sore, and feel as if they would be pressed out of the head.

Shooting pains in the teeth.

Tongue coated grayish, or thickly yellowish, with lips dry and cracked.

"The mouth is unusually dry with thirst."—G.

"Motion more or less constant, of the jaws, as if chewing something; lips dry and cracked."—G.

"Cannot sit up from nausea and faintness."—G.

"Food is thrown up immediately after eating, with constipation, and lips dry and cracked."—G.

Everything tastes bitter.

Nausea when rising up.

Pressure in the pit of the stomach as if there was a stone in it; goes off with much eructation.

Sour vomiting.

Stomach becomes extremely sensitive to the touch or pressure.

"Diseases caused by cold drinks in warm weather, after cold."—HERING.

Food is vomited immediately after eating, with constipation, and the lips dry and cracked.

Diarrhœa in the morning.

Burning diarrhœa. The disease is worse in warm weather.

"Diarrhœa worse every spell of hot weather."—G.

"Diarrhœa from cold drinks in hot weather."—H.

Constipation; stools dry and hard, as if burnt.

"During colic, must keep very still; with stools hard and dry, as if burnt."—G.

Stitches in the liver.

"Tensive burning pains in the region of the liver, which is swollen and sore."—HEMPEL.

Peritonitis, with stinging, burning pains; abdomen very sore to the touch, with constipation, especially if in a rheumatic subject.

Urine hot, red, and diminished in quantity.

"Menses too early, too profuse, worse on motion."—G.

"Frequent bleeding at the nose when the menses should appear."—G.

"Pinching and uneasiness in the abdomen, as if the menses should appear."—G.

"During the menses has tearing pains in the legs; worse on motion."—G.

"Stitching pains in the ovaries on taking a deep inspiration; can hardly bear the least touch on the affected parts; worse on motion."—G.

"Menses too early, too profuse; of dark red blood, with pain in the back, and aching in the head, as if it would split open; worse on motion."—G.

"Nausea, relieved by keeping quiet; desires to keep still, with splitting headache."—G.

"Her breasts have a stony hardness in them; they are hot and painful, but not very red."—G.

"Lochia suppressed, with headache, as if it would burst open, greatly aggravated by motion."—G.

"Eruptions do not fully make their appearance, with much dyspnœa and quick breathing."—G.

Shortness of breath; a full inspiration produces stitching pain in the chest.

"Cough worse after drinking, with respiration much oppressed."—G.

"Dry cough, with brickdust-colored expectoration; worse on motion.

"Pleuro-pneumonia, with stabbing pains; frequent respiration; bloody expectoration; high fever; bursting headache; worse on motion, and deep inspiration.

"Inflammation of the first and second divisions of the bronchi, with an irritative, shaking, dry cough; heat; pain, and soreness behind the sternum; worse daytimes and by motion."—HUGHES.

Articular and muscular rheumatism, greatly aggravated by motion; the pains are tensive and tearing; sour perspiration.

"The child cannot bear to be moved, the least movement so greatly increases its suffering; with dry, parched lips and constipation."—G.

Fever, with dry, burning heat, mostly internal, as if the blood was burning in the veins.

"Intermittent fever; chills begin on the lips and on the tips of the fingers and toes; great thirst during all stages."—R. GARDNER, M.D.

Colds, with a feeling as if the body had been pounded all over.

In typhoid fevers, with the above symptoms, it is the best medicine in the materia medica.

## RHUS TOXICODENDRON.

*Poison Oak.*

Under this heading I will note the particular effects of Rhus tox. only. The characteristics of the other two, Rhus rad. and vernix, not being known. They both have characteristics peculiar to themselves, and demand a careful study by the profession.

Rhus tox. affects that portion of the ganglionic nervous system that presides over the skin, fibrous tissues, fascia, sheaths of nerves, tendons, ligaments, muscles and mucous membranes, producing nervous irritation and inflammation of a rheumatic character.

Also affects the cerebro-spinal system, including the cerebral, sentient and motor nerves, producing depression and paralysis.

This drug must have some hæmatic properties, it being found so useful in low grades of typhoid fever. Rheumatism is greatly controlled by this remedy.

### *Grand Characteristics.*

"Particularly suited to very rheumatic persons, worse before a storm, and in damp weather."—G.

"Cannot lie long in one position, but must shift about, to obtain relief; the relief lasts but a short time, when the patient must move again."—G.

The pains are greatly aggravated by rest;

worse after midnight and before storms; relieved by motion; has to toss about constantly to get relief.

"Worse at night, particularly after midnight."—G.

"Restless at night; must turn often to find a few moments' rest."—G.

"The child always gets particularly worse after midnight; has more colic; more diarrhœa, and more restlessness."—G.

Bad effects from severe wetting in rain, when heated.

Bad effects from strains.

Eyelids present a bladder-like appearance.

Burning and redness over large cutaneous surfaces, which soon swell up and become covered with watery vesicles, accompanied by almost intolerable itching, with a tendency to invade large surfaces, rather than to penetrate deeply in the tissues.

Slow fevers; tongue dry and brown; sordes on the teeth; bowels loose; great weakness; powerlessness of the lower limbs; can hardly draw them up; with great restlessness after midnight; has to move often to get relief.

Headache relieved by motion.

General unhappiness of temper.

"Corners of the mouth sore and ulcerated, or chafed around the genitals."—RAUE.

"Putrid taste; after the first mouthful has no appetite."—G.

"Pain between the shoulders when swallowing."—G.

"Soreness as if beaten in the hypochondriac region, and still more in the abdomen; worse in the side on which he lies; worse when turning, and more when beginning to move."—L.

"Diarrhœa, with tearing pains down the legs; at every stool the pain streaks down the legs, which are powerless."—G.

Great pain before stool, which is greenish, and contains jelly-like globules, or flakes; jelly-like stools.

Involuntary stools, with great exhaustion; bloody stools at night.

Constant tenesnus, with nausea and tearing pains in the intestines; is rheumatic, and has to change his position often to get relief.—G.

Sense of constriction in the rectum, as though one side had grown up.

Cholera infantum, typhoid type; the child is very restless at night; has to be changed often to get relief.

Urine red and scanty.

Involuntary irritation during rest.

Snow-white sediment in the urine.

Bloody urine discharged in drops.

"Intense itching and burning of the mons

veneris, with watery vesicles, and stitching pains in the vagina."—G.

"The menstrual discharge causes a violent pain in the vulva."—G.

"Menorrhagia from a strain; in rheumatic females, worse at night; must change positions often to get relief, and aggravated on change of weather."—G.

"Membranous dysmenorrhœa in rheumatic females."—G.

"Is particularly indicated where repeated drenchings in the rain have deranged the uterine functions."—G.

"After labor, a vitiated discharge continues from the vagina, with shooting upwards in the parts, with a bursting sensation in the head."—G.

"For weeks after delivery, has much pain in the right limb, with numbness from the hips to the feet."—G.

"The lochial discharge lasts too long; is thin, offensive, and occasionally bloody."—G.

"Abortion from a strain; pains worse in the last part of the night; very restless; has to change often to get relief."—G.

"The breasts are painfully distended, red in streaks, with a rheumatic condition of the whole body."—G.

Ichorous, or yellow discharge from the nose.

"Terrible cough, which seems as if it would tear something out of the chest."—G.

"A dry, teasing cough, coming on first before the chill, and continuing during the chill."—DUNHAM.

"Putting the hand out of the bed brings on the cough."—H.

"For weeks after delivery, has a terrible cough, which seems as if something would be torn out of the chest."—G.

Tickling under the sternum, that excites cough.

"Acute catarrh; the nasal, laryngeal, tracheal, and bronchial passages seem stuffed up; commencing at about sunset, with sneezing, and dry, hard, tickling cough, continuing very severe until midnight, when all the sufferings are relieved. Renewed next morning."—C. W. BOYCE.

Expectoration of brickdust or bloody sputa, raised with great difficulty, with high fever.

Rheumatoid pains, that affect every part of the body, all aggravated by rest and relieved by motion.

Rheumatic paralysis.

"Pains as if sprained; ailments from spraining or straining, lifting; particularly from stretching arms high up to reach things."—H.

"Lameness and stiffness, and pain on first

moving after rest, or on getting up in the morning; relieved by continued motion."—H.

"Stiffness of the limbs before a storm."—G.

A light edge of inflammation surrounds every portion of the eruption, with much itching and vesicular inflammation.

"Rubbing the affected parts increases the eruption."—G.

Vesicular eruptions on any part of the body.

"Aching in the left arm, with disease of the heart."—Raue.

"Swollen around the ankles after sitting too long, particularly in travelling."—H.

## DIGITALIS PURPUREA.

*Purple Foxglove.*

Digitalis acts especially upon the muscular tissue of the heart and arteries, paralyzing their action to a great degree. Hughes says, "We conclude that Digitalis acts directly upon the muscular tissue of the heart, which it weakens even to the extent of paralysis; that the increased frequency of the pulse, which results from small doses, depends mainly upon cardiac debility—Nature endeavoring to make up by greater frequency for decreasing power; and that the retardation of the heart's action, which is caused by large doses, is due to an influence transmitted through the vagi. The irregularity and intermission of the pulse so characteristic of the drug, we also ascribe to the cardiac debility it induces." "The researches of M. Claude Bernard show that Digitalis is one of the poisons which act directly upon the muscular tissue, paralyzing and killing it. It affects that portion of muscular tissue which constitutes the heart earlier than any other, so that in cold-blooded animals (as frogs) the heart's action may cease for four hours before general death ensues, producing a dead heart in a living body. *Rigor mortis* sets in exceedingly early; and, on opening the thorax immediately after death, the heart is found contracted, rigid, motionless, and totally empty. A farther examination discloses remarkable chemical and electrical changes in the heart and other muscles. The muscular juice is acid instead of alkaline, and the external surface is electrically negative to the cut surface, instead of (as normally) positive. The immediate cause of this phenomenon has been shown to be the change of the muscular juice from alkaline to acid; and this very change is involved in the destructive action of the drug upon the integrity of the muscular tissue."

Digitalis also affects the pneumogastric nerve, mucous membrane of the stomach and descending colon, kidneys, and brain.

### *Grand Characteristics.*

In all diseases for which Digitalis will be found useful, the heart will be more or less involved, accompanied with irregular or intermittent pulse.

The least movement produces violent palpitation of the heart.

"A sensation as if the heart would stop beating if she moved, with fear of impending death."—HALE.

Frequent stitches in the heart.

Short, hurried respiration.

Desponding and fearful, with great apprehension of the future.

Excessive desire to be alone.

Stools, very light-colored and loose.

Œdema of the feet and legs.

Bloating and paleness of the face.

Hissing before the ears.

Objects seem paler than they really are, and have a greenish look.

Profuse flow of frothy saliva.

Stinging in the throat between the acts of deglutition.

"Nausea, as if she would die; more in the morning."—G.

"Motion produces vomiting and great faintness."—G.

"Smell of food excites violent nausea, with clean tongue, thirst for water, and absence of all fever."—G.

"Tendency to nausea without real nausea."—RAUE.

Feeling of goneness in the stomach, as if he would die, with deathly nausea and vomiting.

"Stools in the evening, passing great quantities of ascarides."—G.

"Ash-colored stools."—HUGHES.

This color of the stools is probably caused by a depraved secretion of the follicles of the colon, and not from hepatic disease.

Obstinate constipation for several weeks.

Frequent and painful emission of small quantities of burning urine of a dark, cloudy color.

Profuse and frequent emission of clear, pale urine.

"Dropsy consequent on organic disease of the heart, and in anasarca following scarlatina."—MARCY and HUNT.

Given in large doses, it is getting quite a reputation for delirium tremens.

## CIMICIFUGA RACEMOSA.

*Black Cohosh.*

Acts upon the ganglionic and especially upon the cerebro-spinal system, the muscular system, ligaments of the vertebra, and the female generative organs.

*Nerves of Motion.*—It causes nervous tremors resembling chorea. Dr. T. C. Miller says, "Fifteen years' observation and experience have proved this agent to be one of the most remarkable in all diseases of the ganglio-spinal system, particularly when the motor side is excited; and yet, in the whole, prevails as an atony in the muscular and nervous system."

*Nerves of Sensation.*—Dr. Hale says, "It seems to exercise considerable control over this system, independently of its action on the vascular system. It cures many of those purely neuralgic pains to which females are liable."

*Muscular System.*—Dr. Hale says, "One of the first of the series of primary effects of this drug is to cause relaxation of the muscular system. This leads directly to painful conditions of muscles, or *myalgia.* Under this head are to be found the burning, cramping, stitching pains which affect these structures. Cimicifuga is pre-eminently a muscle remedy. Hence its efficacy in myalgia and its varieties, as pleurodynia."

In muscular rheumatism and myostitis caused by cold, nervous exhaustion, or over-exertion, this will be found a valuable remedy. Dr. Ludlam uses it when "rheumatism affects the belly of a muscle."

*Upon the uterus* it has a most powerful action, producing a rheumatic, neuralgic state of the uterus and ovaries; amenorrhœa; dysmenorrhœa and abortion; accompanied with hysteria; nervousness; irritability; sleeplessness; sensitiveness and low-spirited.

### *Grand Characteristics.*

Nervous and muscular irritation, of a rheumatic, neuralgic, or gouty origin, especially in delicate hysterical females, who are afflicted with more or less diseases of the generative organs.

Neuralgic, rheumatic dysmenorrhœa, and after-pains, with great mental and nervous irritability; sleeplessness; low-spirited and very sensitive.

Choreic affections in nervous, hysterical, rheumatic females, from irritations of the generative organs.

Rheumatic or neuralgic irritation of the ligaments in the lumbar region, producing lumbago or crick in the back.

Uterine rheumatism.

Obstinate insomnia.

Great wakefulness, imagining strange objects in the room, on the bed, &c.; with dilated pupils; tremor of the limbs.

Incessant talking; roaring in the head.

Pains in every portion of the head, but more in the vertex and occiput; often extending to the shoulders and down the spine; of a pressing and throbbing nature, accompanied with delirium.

" Sensation as if the top of the head would fly off, with a sensation as if the cerebrum was too large for the skull, pressing outwards and upwards."

"All the pains in the head are from within outwards."—HALE.

Headache of drunkards and students.

"Intense and persistent pains in the eyeballs, of a dull, aching, sore nature."

Pupils dilated.

Dry pharynx, with dysphagia and frequent inclination to swallow.

*Nausea* and vomiting due to cerebral or nervous sympathetic irritation.

Sinking sensation at the stomach.

Neuralgic pains in the abdomen.

Urine pale and abundant.

Leucorrhœa in hysterical and rheumatic females.

Nervous irritation of the ovaries, producing amenorrhœa, dysmenorrhœa, and menorrhagia in rheumatic females.

Rheumatic and neuralgic affections of the uterus.

Threatened abortion in rheumatic hysterical females, with much excitement.

Affects the motor nerves of the uterus as well as the sentient, as so beautifully shown in after-pains.

Dry cough from irritation, and tickling in the lower part of the larynx.

Reflex nervous pains.

Urticaria from menstrual or rheumatic disorders.

Weakness, trembling, and spasmodic action of the muscles, as shown in choreic affections.

Its influence over the spinal cord renders it capable of curing many diseases arising therefrom.

## ANTIMONIUM TARTARICUM.

*Tartar Emetic.*

The three great spheres of Tartar emetic are, first, upon the pneumogastric nerve; second, upon the respiratory mucous membrane; and third, upon the skin. Also acts upon the base of the brain and medulla oblongata, and the blood becomes liquefied.

The action upon the pneumogastric nerve causing vomiting, is sympathetic or nervous, not gastric. Hughes says, "The emetic influence of tartarized antimony appears to be purely neurotic in its *modus operandi.* The numerous muscular movements, whose harmonious play produces the complex act called vomiting, are under the control of the nervous centres at the base of the brain, and in the medulla oblongata, and are especially affected through the medium of the pneumogastric nerves. That Tartar emetic acts directly on these centres and through these nerves, is shown positively by the fact that it causes vomiting when injected into the veins or rectum, or rubbed into the skin, as well as when introduced into the stomach, and in the latter mode of administration is emetic in doses too small to irritate the mucous membrane ; *negatively*, by the experiment of dividing the vagi on both sides, when neither antimony nor any other remedy will act."

*Mucous Membranes.*—It produces a pustular inflammation in the mouth, throat, œsophagus, stomach, and small intestines. Upon the respiratory mucous membrane the inflammation is of a catarrhal character, though pustules have been seen in the larynx.

"The nares escape untouched, but the inflammation beginning in the larynx becomes intense in the trachea and bronchi. In the lungs the pneumonia induced never goes beyond the second stage (*i. e.*, that of red hepatization); that it is always accompanied by bronchitis; and that the inflammation of the bronchial tubes is observed in cases where the animals die, before the pneumonia has time to be developed."—HUGHES.

*Skin.*—Upon this tissue it produces an eruption very similar to variola and ecthyma. This pustular ulceration can be produced by vaccination or internal administration.

### *Grand Characteristics.*

Large collections of mucus in the bronchial tubes; expectorated with great difficulty; indicating approaching paralysis of the pneumogastric nerve.

"When the patient coughs, there appears a large collection of mucus in the bronchial tubes, and it seems as if much would be expectorated, but nothing comes up."—G.

"Much nausea and vomiting day and night, with drowsiness."—G.

"Colliquative diarrhœa, with meteorism." —G.

Vomiting of large quantities of mucus, which is a nervous and sympathetic rather than a gastric effect.

"Vertigo, with drowsiness."—H.

"Cannot keep his eyes open; irresistible sleepiness, and deep, stupefied sleep; when awake, hopelessness and despair, or chill and fever, or vomiting of food."—H.

"The head trembles, particularly when coughing, with an inward trembling; teeth chattering, and drowsiness, more in the evening and in warmth."—H.

"Tongue coated thinly white, with reddened papillæ; red edges, particularly with whooping-cough."—H.

"Nausea and vomiting of large collections of mucus."—G.

The child wants to be carried, and cries if any one touches it.—LIPPE.

Painful urging to urinate; scanty discharge; dark red, or the least bloody, with stitches in the bladder and burning in the urethra.

"Leucorrhœa of watery blood; liable to occur in paroxysms; worse when sitting."—G.

"Catarrhal and pustular inflammation of the mucous membranes."—HUGHES.

"The pustular inflammation occurs in the œsophagus, mouth, throat, larynx, stomach, and small intestines."—HUGHES.

"Upon the respiratory mucous membrane the influence of Tartar emetic is almost purely catarrhal, although pustules are said to have been found in the larynx."—HUGHES.

"The nares escape untouched; the inflammation, beginning in the larynx, becomes intense in the trachea and bronchi."—HUGHES.

In broncho-pneumonia, second stage, with bronchi loaded with mucus, it is specific.

Paralysis of the lungs, with great dyspnœa and fits of suffocation.

"Rattling or hollow cough; worse at night, with suffocation; throat full of phlegm; sweat on forehead; vomiting of food."—H.

"Coughing and gaping constantly, particularly children, when crying or dozing, and twitching in the face."—H.

Acute œdema of the lungs.

"Cough, when we have partial paralysis of the pneumogastric nerve; short, hoarse, weak, nearly suffocating breathing, with whistling noise; thorax expands with great difficulty;

head thrown backwards, with great anxiety and prostration; face livid and cold; forehead and sometimes the whole body covered with cold perspiration; pulse feeble and accelerated."

Fever of dentition.

"Beating and throbbing through the whole body, particularly in the belly or pit of stomach, with great concern about the future."—Raue.

Variola, vomiting, viscid mucus clogging the air-passages; pustules in the larynx, mouth, throat, and digestive organs.

"Ecthymatous eruptions."—E. Wilson.

## VERATRUM ALBUM.

*White Hellebore.*

Veratrum alb. acts especially on the great sympathetic system, on the cerebro-spinal axis, pneumogastric nerve, and the special senses.

The great sympathetic "fills two great offices in the animal economy. It regulates the metamorphosis of tissue, the basis of all secretion and nutrition; and, by its infinitesimal ramifications on the coats of the bloodvessels, it gives tonicity to every part of the vascular system, and especially to the capillaries. When its function fails, secretion stops, and the watery elements of the blood exude through the relaxed tissues. The acid secretions of the stomach, and the alkaline secretions of the intestines, are perhaps the first arrested. Then that great emunctory, the liver, becomes dormant, and the stools are grayish, or foamy and limpid. If not relieved here, the patient will sink rapidly; the kidneys will soon stop secreting, the metamorphosis of tissue everywhere will cease, and rapid emaciation, collapse, with unquenchable thirst (watery diarrhœa), and death closes the scene."—W. H. Holcombe, M.D.

Now this is just the effect of Veratrum alb. on the ganglionic system. It strikes down the functions of the ganglionic system that preside over the vascular capillary system of the intestinal mucous membrane, causing serous diarrhœa, which is a genuine sweating of the mucous membrane of the bowels. This watery element is mainly derived from the innumerable follicles in the intestinal tract. The choleraic and Veratrum album poison both affect the great sympathetic system so nearly alike, that in cholera times no man is able to tell one from the other.

The powerful influence it has upon the pneumogastric nerves to produce such violent nausea and vomiting, shows that the nervous centres at the base of the brain, and in the medulla oblongata, are especially affected.

Upon the brain it produces a "sudden sinking of innervation, causing loss of power to control one's movements; staggers about; feels dizzy; vision becomes obscure, and complete extinction of nervous power is going on at a fearful rate."—HEMPEL.

Hughes says, "The picture presented by acute Veratrum poisoning is decidedly choleraic. There is general coldness, with prostration going on to collapse; embarrassed circulation; copious watery vomiting and purging; and severe spasmodic colic. The more recent experiments of Schroff have further proved that these evacuations do not depend upon gastro-enteritis, as Veratrum causes no inflammation, but at most a transient hyperæmia of the parts it touches. If its action be more intensified, it causes a rapid degeneration of the gastric mucous membrane, but no gastro-enteritis."

### *Grand Characteristics.*

Exhausting diarrhœa, with cold sweat, especially on the forehead.

"Cold sweat upon the forehead."—G.

"Leaden color of the face, with frequent nausea and vomiting, with great exhaustion."—G.

"Very exhausting diarrhœa; excessively weak after every stool; with cold sweat on the forehead."—G.

"Terrible colic; the suffering causes a cold sweat to stand upon the surface, especially on the forehead."—G.

"Cramps of the limbs, with cold sweat."—G.

"Thirst, with craving for the coldest drinks." —G.

Anguish; fear of death.

"Despair about his position in society; feels very unlucky."—H.

"Headache causing delirium; demented; and cold sweat upon the forehead."—G.

Wanders about the house; is very taciturn.

"Sudden paroxysms of a sinking of cerebral innervation, characterized by sudden loss of power to control one's movements; feels dizzy; staggers about; vision becomes obscured; the pulse is depressed; and complete extinction of nervous power is going on at a fearful rate."—HEMPEL.

Puerperal mania and convulsions, with violent cerebral congestion; bluish and bloated face; protruded eyes; wild shrieks, and disposition to tear.

Excessive mirthfulness; collapse of pulse; cold extremities; cold sweat on the forehead; expression of fright; anxiety; and stertorous breathing.

"Sensation as if a lump of ice was on top of the head."—RAUE.

"Attacks of pain, with delirium, or driving to madness."—H.

"Disposed to talk about faults of others, or

silence; but, if irritated, scolding, and calling names."—H.

Nervous headache at each menstrual molimina.

Vertigo in drunkards, opium-eaters, or those who use tobacco, characterized by sudden fainting, collapse of pulse, loss of vision, cold sweat on forehead.

Cold, collapsed face; pinched-up bluish nose; dry and cracked lips; lock-jaw; grating of the teeth.

"While in bed, face is red; after getting up it becomes pale."—H.

"Neck too weak to hold the head up, particularly children with whooping-cough."—H.

Tongue cold.

Voice feeble.

Cold breath, with great prostration, and cold perspiration on the forehead.

"Frequent nausea and vomiting, with leaden color of face, and cold perspiration, especially on the forehead."—G.

Violent retching; wants everything cold.

Least quantity of liquid excites vomiting.

Motion excites the nausea.

Terrible colic, with violent nausea and vomiting.

Unquenchable desire for cold drinks.

Vomiting, with diarrhœa and great prostration.

Burning and oppression in the epigastrium.

Colicodynia, with sensation as though the bowels were tied up in knots.

"Irritation of the cœliac plexus, with fainting, great prostration, cold perspiration, nausea and vomiting, Hippocratic countenance, loss of vision, and cold extremities."—HEMPEL.

Burning in the bowels, as from hot coals.

Copious watery diarrhœa, with violent nausea and vomiting.

"Watery diarrhœa expelled in a forcible gush, with little or no griping."—RAUE.

Involuntary watery stools without the patient's knowledge.

"Dysmenorrhœa, with vomiting and purging, or exhausting diarrhœa with cold sweat." —H.

Nymphomania, from unsatisfied passion or mental causes.

Fevers, with great coldness externally, and violent internal heat; pulse thread-like; great craving for cold drinks.

Spasmodic cough, with blue face, suffocation; retching.

Asthma; with great suffocation, anguish, and oppression about the heart.

"Difficult walking; first the right then the

left hip-joint feels paralytic (or, in other patients, first left then right)."—H.

Disease caused by cold drinks in warm weather.

Adapted to young people and women of a sanguine or nervo-sanguine temperament; also to people who are habitually cold and deficient in vital reaction, gay dispositions, fitful mood, and who have not been exhausted by long excesses or starvation.

## ARNICA MONTANA.

*Leopard's Bane.*

Arnica acts upon the muscular system, fasciæ and tendons; on the capillary system of the veins and arteries; on the dermoid and cellular tissue; on the lymphatic system; and upon the nervous system. No remedy can equal Arnica for those "muscular pains which are so apt to occur in the weakly invalid; these pains may occur wherever there are voluntary muscles, or their tendinous prolongations; the trunk is more commonly attacked than the limbs; the abdominal walls more than the thoracic, and the legs more constantly than the arms; they are generally mistaken for the pains of neuralgia, hysteria, spinal irritation, indigestion or disease of some internal organ. The tendinous parts are more frequently the seat of the pain than the muscular, for every muscular fibre terminates at each end in tendinous fibre, and these are inserted into the bones; hence, whenever a muscle contracts, there are four strains upon the tendinous fibre, viz., one at each end of the muscle, and one at each of its insertions into the bone; hence, these pains are four times as numerous as all the muscles in the body. When the gastrocnemius muscle of the leg has been overstretched or overstrained, the pain is confined almost exclusively to the origin and insertion of the tendo-Achillis. When delicate females first attempt to sit up, after a severe fit of illness, they are apt to get a severe pain in the aponeurosis of the trapezius, and occipital insertion of the same muscle. The severe and unusual strain thrown upon the erector muscles of the back, while leaning over a table to cut out dress patterns; the immense muscular exertion required in the birth of the child, &c., &c. This muscular ache often reaches a high pitch of severity, so as to cause a burning pain between the shoulders for many hours. When the pain is seated in the muscle, it is aching; when it has been severely strained it is a burning ache; when in the tendons, it is described as pain. The more feeble the patient, the more apt they are to have these myalgic pains."

*On the Capillaries.*—The capillaries may be divided into those of secretion and nutrition. Arnica affects more particularly the capillaries of secretion; hence, its usefulness in hemorrhages, perspirations, mucous fluxes, dropsical effusions, &c. The capillaries are tubular continuations of the arteries, and the commencement of the veins. This accounts for the great power of Arnica to produce absorption, in extravasations of blood, effusions of serum, such as occur after falls, blows, &c.

*On the Dermoid and Cellular Tissue*, Arnica has a powerful influence, producing a pustule very painful to touch, with a red inflamed base, resembling boils; also a vesicular eruption. The extravasation of blood into the cellular tissue while in a fluid state, Arnica causes the venous capillaries and absorbents to quickly take up. The lymphatics are not so much influenced by Arnica as the venous capillaries are.

*Nervous System.*—Affects the motor more than the sentient nervous system, as shown in paralysis from mechanical injuries, where there is more or less extravasation of blood, lymph, &c.

### *Grand Characteristics.*

Diseases of a traumatic origin; the muscular fibre is chiefly involved; the pains are sore and aching.

"The bed or couch on which he lies feels too hard; complains constantly of it, and keeps changing from place to place."—RAUE.

"Inflammation caused by a bruise or concussion; a bruised, sore feeling remaining." —G.

"Sore and bruised feeling all through the patient, as if from a bruise."—G.

Hemorrhages from mechanical injuries.

Sensation of soreness in the stomach; and belchings, tasting like rotten eggs.

Especially adapted to sanguine plethoric persons, with lively complexions.

Acts feebly upon people that are greatly debilitated, with soft flesh and impoverished blood.

Is very sensitive, with anxiety and restlessness.

Stitches in the head, especially in the temples and forehead.

Bad effects from concussion of the brain.

Traumatic ophthalmia.

"The face or head alone is hot, while the body is cool."—RAUE.

"Dry heat of the face, with coldness of the nose."—H.

"Swelling of the cheek, with throbbing and twitching pains; swollen lips, and heat in the head."

"Hard, tensive, shining red swelling of the left cheek."—MARCY and HUNT.

Cracked lips, with formication as if they would go to sleep.

"Bleeding from the nose."—G.

"Contusive pain in the nose from above downwards; same in the ears."

"Toothache; the roots of the teeth feel as

if they had been scraped; face and cheek hot and swollen."—HEMPEL.

"Putrid eructations, as if from rotten eggs." —JAHR.

"Feeling of nauseous repletion after eating."—G.

"Vomiting of dark clotted blood."—HEMPEL.

Myalgia of the stomach.

"The pain comes on immediately, even during eating; the patient is weak and lax of fibre, and often has myalgia elsewhere."—HUGHES.

Brown urine, with brick-red sediment.

"Cannot walk erect on account of a bruised sore feeling in the uterine region."—H.

After severe labor, great soreness of the parts.

Traumatic injuries of the testicles.

"Nipples itch, and are sore, as if bruised." —G.

Emissions of flatus from the anus, smelling like rotten eggs.

Stools of mucus, blood, and pus, where the muscles of the rectum are involved.

Sensation of soreness of the muscles of the chest.

"Myalgia of the intercostal muscles after great exertions, with a sensation as if all the ribs were bruised; short breath; pain in the chest; with anxiety."—RAUE.

"Pleurisy, when the exudation consists of coagulable lymph or serous exudation."—HUGHES.

"Typhoid fever; with the greatest indifference; putrid breath; and red spots, like suggilations, on the body."—H.

"Gout; with the greatest fear of being struck by persons coming towards him across the room."—H.

"Tendency to small boils; ecchymoses on various parts of the body."—H.

Bad effects from strains, falls, bruises, concussions, and all mechanical injuries.

C. Hering, M.D., says: "Arnica is more apt than Aconite to spoil a case. Arnica makes a much more profound impression upon the system than Aconite. Its real culminating action is similar to typhus fever. Brilliant results have frequently been obtained with it in the worst forms of typhus. No Arnica should be used except such as is made from the root."

## COLCHICUM AUTUMNALE.

*Meadow Saffron.*

Acts especially upon the cerebro-spinal centres, and terminates in a violent inflammation, of a choleraic character, in the mucous membrane of the gastro-intestinal canal. The ganglionic centres are most powerfully influenced, as shown by the effects it has upon the vaso-motor nerves of the alimentary canal. The next organ most influenced is the kidneys. It also affects the liver, lungs, heart, and salivary glands.

### *Grand Characteristics.*

Arthritic or rheumatic diathesis.

"Sudden sinking of the vital forces; if the patient is raised up, the head falls backwards; the mouth opens to its widest extent."—Raue.

Arthritic or neuralgic inflammation of the intestinal canal, where the mucous membrane is principally involved.

"Sero-mucous vomiting and rice-water stools, thrown off with great force; with cramps of the abdominal muscles, flexors of the arms and feet; and shrunken features."

"Cold surface, tongue and breath; mottled skin and bluish nails."

"Great flatulent distension of the stomach."

"Stools like jelly, or bloody mucus, with spasms of the sphincter ani."

Dropsy of the uterus, from suppression of the menses.

"Urine dark and scanty; discharged in drops, depositing a whitish sediment."

Dry, hacking cough, with burning and feeling of constriction across the chest.

" Rheumatic pericarditis and rheumatism in the small joints; rheumatic pains, that frequently change about; they are of a tearing nature, and are generally in the muscles."

Gout; this is the real specific for this painful disease: "The pulse is slightly irritated; affected parts exceedingly painful; skin looks rose-colored, and leaves a white spot under the pressure of the fingers."

More strongly called for if there is more or less irritation of the gastro-intestinal canal.

" In warm weather these tearing pains are principally felt at the surface of the body; as the air grows colder, they seem to penetrate the deeper tissues and bones."—TESTE.

## SENEGA.

*Snake-root.*

Acts especially on the mucous membranes of the respiratory organs, the fibrous tissue, eyes, and digestive organs.

### *Grand Characteristics.*

Its main sphere of usefulness is in diseases of the respiratory mucous membrane.

" In subacute or chronic exudations of the pleura, and in catarrhal pleuro-pneumonia, where Bryonia has failed."—HALE.

"Irritating, shaking, dry cough; in chronic bronchitis, especially in old people."—HUGHES.

Severe pains about the chest.

"Soreness of the walls of the chest on moving the arms, particularly the left."—J. B. BELL.

"Burning pain about the heart."—J. B. BELL.

"Sensation of trembling, with no visible trembling."—J. B. BELL.

"It has been administered with great success in hydrothorax, ascites, and anasarca, after primary or secondary albuminuria."—E. M. HALE.

"Iritis and specks on the cornea."—HUGHES.

Watery diarrhœa, with griping pains in the bowels, nausea, and vomiting.

"Frequent emissions of urine with greenish tinge, depositing a cloudy sediment."

"Urine at first mixed with mucous filaments; afterwards it becomes thick and cloudy."

## BAPTISIA TINCTORIA.

*Wild Indigo.*

Acts especially upon the ganglionic and cerebro-spinal nervous system as a sedative; producing paralysis both of sensation and motion, very closely resembling that of typhoid fever, for which it is such a *specific*.

*Mucous Membranes.*—Has a special effect upon the mucous membrane of the buccal cavity and lower portion of the intestinal canal, producing ulceration "having a fetid odor and a sanious, excoriating character."—HALE.

*Vascular System.*—Baptisia causes "a condition of the blood similar to the typhus crasis, and a state of the fluids of the body nearly identical with that occurring in low fevers."—HALE.

*Glandular System.*—Baptisia has an irritating effect upon the lymphatic and glandular system, producing swelling and enlargement of the tonsils and inguinal glands.

### *Grand Characteristics.*

"Discharges from mucous surfaces, having a fetid odor and a sanious, excoriating character."—HALE.

Typhoid diseases, with "delirious stupor; face dark red, with a besotted expression; eyes injected; diarrhœa; tongue coated brown, dry, particularly in the centre; very offensive breath; sordes on the teeth; fetor of the urine and stools."—SMALL.

Very fetid and exhausting diarrhœa.

Dysenteric stools of blood and mucus, with severe tenesmus and colicky pains in the hypogastrium, before and during stool, without much fever.

"She cannot go to sleep because she cannot get herself together. Her head feels as though scattered about, and she tosses about the bed to get the pieces together."—J. B. Bell, M.D.

Dull stupefying headache.

Stupor and delirium at night.

Confusion of ideas.

"While answering a question, falls into a deep sleep in the middle of a sentence."

Head feels too heavy, with numbness.

Excitement of the brain, especially at night.

"Face dark red, with a besotted expression."—Small.

Confusion of sight.

"Soreness of the eyeballs; they feel as if they would be pressed into the head."

Tongue dry and red, as if burned.

"Tongue coated brown, and dry, particularly in the centre."—Small.

"Pasty tongue, heavily furred."—Hale.

"Putrid, offensive breath."—Hale.

"Putrid ulceration of the buccal mucous membrane, with salivation."—Hale.

"The sweat, urine, and stools are all extremely fetid."—Small.

"Very fetid, exhausting diarrhœa."

Dysenteric stools of scanty, bloody mucus.

"Violent colicky pains in the hypogastrium before and during stool."

Great tenesmus, with stools of mucus and blood without fever.

"Soreness of the flesh and whole body, with chilliness."—DOUGLASS.

"Limbs tremble and are very weak."—DOUGLASS.

Restless nights, with delirium and frightful dreams.

Patient must go to the door for fresh air.

## CHELIDONIUM MAJUS.

*Great Celandine.*

Acts through the ganglionic system upon the lungs, liver, digestive organs, kidneys, and skin. Also powerfully irritates the sentient nervous system.

*Upon the lungs* it produces congestion and inflammation, sometimes going on to hepatization; the mucous membrane is also involved, producing broncho-pneumonia.

*The liver* is powerfully affected by this remedy. Dr. Bachmann's proving gives us the following symptoms: "Pain, both acute and dull, and tenderness of the liver; pain in the right shoulder; stools either soft, or bright yellow, or whitish and costive." Deeply tinged urine appeared in all the provings. "In three, the skin became yellow or dark; and in one, regular jaundice set in." It has cured numerous cases of jaundice, gall-stones, acute and chronic hepatitis.

*Upon the kidneys* the renal irritation is so great that in "one case an examination of the urine showed the presence of tube-casts of increased uric acid, and diminished chloride of sodium. The mischief in this case was so considerable that œdematous swellings of the extremities occurred."—HUGHES.

It also acts upon the diaphragm.

### *Grand Characteristics.*

"Constant pain under the lower inner angle of the right shoulder-blade."—G.

Loose rattling cough, remains a long time.

Nausea causes great heat of the body.

"Stools like sheep's dung."—G.

Very apt to have hepatic disease, with jaundice and pain in the right shoulder.

Deeply-tinged green urine.

Retarded menstruation, but when the menses do come on, they continue too long.

Severe neuralgia of the head and eyes.

Acts best in melancholic, choleric temperaments.

Adapted to neuralgias, inflammations, and infectious diseases, as whooping-cough.

Sallow, jaundiced complexion.

Burning and redness of the face.

"Must close the eyes, and is alleviated thereby, without photophobia."

White or yellow coating on the tongue.

Loathing of food.

Gastric or bilious diarrhœa, stools slimy, grayish-yellow, or watery.

"Stools like sheep's dung."—G.

Urine scanty, deep yellow, and sour.

Bloating in the region of the liver, stomach, and spleen, with hardness and painfulness on pressure.

Acute and chronic hepatitis.

Gall-stones, with hepatodynia and general jaundice.

"Pain in the whole region of the liver, relieved by eating.

"Pinching and spasmodic pains in the inner border of the right scapula, with a kind of drawing, pressive shooting from the left side of the occiput to the forehead."

Violent, spasmodic, straining cough, with profuse lachrymation; comes in paroxysms, with burning, shooting pains.

Constant tickling and desire to cough in the larynx.

Spasmus glottidis.

Long-continued cough, with rattling mucus.

Bilious or gastric pneumonia, with lungs full of mucus, from paralysis of the pneumogastric nerve; cheeks dark red.

## GROUP II.

| | |
|---|---|
| Belladonna, | Gymnocladus, |
| Hyoscyamus, | Camphora, |
| Stramonium, | Zizia aurea, |
| Opium, | Cuprum, |
| Alcohol, | Cannabis ind., |
| Ether, | Coffea, |
| Chloroform, | Tabacum, |
| Glonoine, | Solanum nig., |
| Agaricus, | Aethusa, |
| Cicuta vir., | Lachnantes. |
| Ailanthus, | |

THE above group represent our true cerebral stimulants or narcotics. They all cause, *primarily*, active congestion and inflammation of the brain and its membranes; furious delirium, spasms, and an excited circulation.

*Secondarily*, paralysis of the voluntary and involuntary muscles; coldness of the surface; prostration; coma; asphyxia, and death.

*Pathological Conditions.*—Arteries of the brain highly engorged; effusions of serum; extravasation, and a liquid state of the blood.

Notwithstanding this similarity, each remedy produces physio-pathological states peculiar to itself, "differing from each other as much as they differ in their symptomatic manifestations." But their general similarity defines the group.

## ATROPA BELLADONNA.

*Deadly Nightshade.*

The great centre of action for Belladonna is upon the cerebro-spinal nervous system, especially affecting the cerebrum, producing active congestion of the whole encephalic mass; delirium, mania, insomnia, sopor, exhaustion, and active inflammation of the brain, with flushed face and violent throbbing of the carotid arteries.

The medulla oblongata, and the nerves that arise from it, are powerfully irritated by the Belladonna poison, as shown by their perverted function, such as difficult deglutition and articulation, spasms of the larynx and pharynx, spasmodic cough, stridulous respiration, &c. "Post-mortem examination discloses considerable cerebral congestion, involving also the cerebellum and medulla oblongata."

*Upon the eye* it produces anæsthesia, amaurosis, visual hallucinations, photophobia, and through the sympathetic, it produces dilatation of the pupil, with brilliant staring eyes, and conjunctival inflammation.

*Upon the throat* it produces excessive dryness; the mucous membrane is of a deep crimson color, with constant inclination to swallow; the secretions are entirely arrested.

The sphincter muscles of the bladder, rectum, and uterus, are completely paralyzed by the Belladonna poison.

*Upon the spinal cord* and its membranes, Brown-Sequard, says: "The two remedies most powerful in diminishing congestion of the spinal cord, are Belladonna and Ergot of Rye. These two remedies are powerful excitants of unstriped muscular fibres in the bloodvessels; in the uterus; in the bowels; in the iris, &c. Both of them dilate the pupil; both are employed with success to produce contractions of the uterus; but each of them has more power in certain parts than the other. Belladonna acts more than Ergot on the bloodvessels of the iris (which is the principal cause of dilatation of the pupils); on the bloodvessels of the breast (which is the principal cause of the cessation of the secretion of milk); on the muscular fibres of the bowels (which is the mode of its action in strangulated hernia); on the sphincter of the bladder, which is one of the causes of its success against nocturnal incontinence of urine. Ergot acts more than Belladonna on the muscular fibres of the uterus, on the bloodvessels of the spinal cord, &c."

*Upon the skin* it has a remarkable and powerful effect; the skin becomes intensely red; painful and hot; parts much swollen, identical with phlegmonous erysipelas, but not with vesicular. The inflammation is more obstinate and deepseated than that which calls for Aconite.

*Upon the generative organs* it produces congestion and spasms.

Marcy and Hunt say: "The specific action of Belladonna is on the cerebral system, which is the central point from which all its symptoms radiate, as from a centre in all diseases. Even the inflammations induced by this remedy always emanate from within outwards, by an incrcased action in the central organ. Thus, in the exanthemata, as soon as the eruption appears, the severe cerebral symptoms, the headaches, and general febrile symptoms (caused by the nervous system irritating the vascular), disappear. When an exanthematous eruption is suppressed, the brain is instantly the seat of a violent attack. Belladonna cures only those diseases of the splanchnic nervous system, or of the abdomen or uterus, in which there is affection of the brain. In all the visceral inflammations cured by Belladonna, we may safely conclude that these diseases were expulsions of inimical agents, which originally threatened to attack the cerebral nervous system. The same remarks apply to all fevers, especially typhus, or the *febris nervosa versatilis.*"

"Belladonna is then the specific remedy for the cerebral nervous system, especially for the fifth pair, and vascular system under the influence of this sphere. An inflammation or fever to which it is applicable, is accompanied by symptoms peculiar to the fifth pair, more or less reddened conjunctiva, the white of the eye is injected, an unsteady or fixed look, distorted features, turgescence of the face, confusion of the head, aching pain in the forehead and eyes."

Speaking of inflammation, Prof. R. Ludlam, says, "Belladonna is centric in its operation. It diminishes the calibre of the bloodvessels, after having just impressed the cerebro-spinal centres. The capillary contraction, occasioned by its primary action, is followed by a relaxation in the fibrous coat of the vessels, which corresponds to

Bennett's second stage of inflammation. This change from contraction to dilatation is more or less marked in degree, and depends upon a diminution in the reflex power of the spinal cord, which Brown-Sequard says, Belladonna and Ergot may occasion. It is due to a disorder in the motor current at its source. The hyperæmia results from a direct derangement in the function of the vaso-motor nerves. In all essential particulars, so far as the local tissue is concerned, the consequences do not differ from those produced by Aconite. But in their mode of action, they are diametrically opposed. And this is the indication to their proper therapeutical employment in the treatment of congestions. Aconite is preferable to Belladonna in the congestive stage of most cases of pleurisy and pericarditis, because the engorgement is due to causes acting *concentrically;* the lesion is idiopathic. The animal nervous centres are not primarily implicated as they are by Belladonna.

"Belladonna reduces the hyperæsthesia of the nervous system, upon which the congestion is consequent. It affords relief by a removal of the cause of the abnormal phenomena. It does not promote diaphoresis, is not critical in its results, has no special relation to the emunctories, but is appropriate to, and exercises a calmative influence over the deranged function of reflex action."

In treating of the action of Belladonna in scarlet fever, P. P. Wells, M.D., says: "The pain, intolerance of light, vertigo, insensibility, sleep, convulsions, &c., which characterize the action of Belladonna on the cerebral apparatus, find their counterpart in the symptoms of acute inflammation, for the most part of the membranes of the brain, or, it may be, of its substance, though this is more rare. In the case before us, the brain is not suffering, as is often thoughtlessly supposed, from inflammation, but from toxication. Not from excessive, but from deficient action. Indeed, in all its characteristics, it discloses a state as nearly the opposite of that produced by the action of Belladonna, as can well be imagined. The drowsiness and coma of Belladonna are accompanied by, if not the result of, active cerebral congestion, and the same is true of the convulsions it produces. Paralysis from the action of Belladonna, is the result of pressure on the brain, either from the accumulation of a continuously increasing congestion of this organ, or of its membranes, or of accumulated serum in its ventricles, and between its membranes, in the effusion of which a previous congestion has terminated. Paralysis, in scarlet fever, is only one of the manifestations of that loss of brain power in general, the sum of which is at once expressed by the term 'Paralysis of the Brain.' The loss of power in distant parts is the result of loss of power in the brain itself."

### *Grand Characteristics.*

The primary perception or starting-point of the affection is in the brain.

"Throbbing headache, with violent throbbing of the carotids."—G.

Furious delirium, with a wild look; wishes to strike, bite, or quarrel; face flushed and eyes red.

"Almost constant moaning; the child remains in a drowsy, sleepy state, with starting and jumping while sleeping, with flushed face and red eyes."—G.

"Child cries out suddenly, and ceases just as suddenly."—G.

"Pains come on suddenly, and leave just as suddenly."—G.

"The symptoms often come on suddenly and disappear with equal suddenness."—G.

"Clutching pains in the abdomen, as if the hand were clawing with the nails."—G.

Involuntary diarrhœa and urination, from paralysis of the sphincter muscles.

"Pressure, as though all the contents of the abdomen would issue through the genital organs; this is particularly felt early in the morning."—G.

"Sensation of heat and dryness in the vagina, with stitches."—G.

"Feeling in the back as if it would break, hindering motion."—G.

Dry, irritating, spasmodic cough.

"The parts have a hot, dry sensation; there is much throbbing; they get worse at three in the afternoon."—G.

Symptoms all worse, 3 P.M.

Adapted to plethoric people, with delicate skin, and disposed to phlegmonous inflammation, and to precocious children with blue eyes and fair hair.

Diseases that affect the right side of the body.

Delirium; sees frightful figures and visions before the eyes.

Desire to escape, with restlessness and nervous anxiety.

"Rage; tears the clothes, bites, kicks, strikes, howls, and shrieks."—LIPPE.

Crying, laughing, dancing, or muttering delirium, with phantasms.

Violent congestion of blood to the head, with loss of consciousness; carotids throb violently; jugulars swollen; face bloated and red.

"Vertigo, with vanishing of sight, stupefaction, and debility."—LIPPE.

When stooping, or rising from a stooping posture, has vertigo, with flickering before the eyes, and a tendency to fall backward or to the left side.

Throbbing headache, with violent congestion of blood to the head, and throbbing of the carotids; worse from motion and touch; light and noise are intolerable.

"Child cries suddenly, then ceases to cry just as suddenly."—G.

"Child is drowsy, with much moaning." —G.

"Sleepiness, but cannot sleep."—G.

"Desires death rather than fears it."—G.

Epilepsy from irritation of the medulla oblongata.

Infantile convulsions, when of an active character, and start from the medulla oblongata.

Neuralgia on the right side of the head and face.

Eyes red, glistening, and sparkling; wild and unsteady.

Congestion of blood to the eyes, with bright redness of the vessels.

Contracted pupils.

Paralysis of the circular fibres of the iris and optic nerve.

Photophobia.

Diplopia.

Distortion, spasms, and convulsions of the eyes.

Things look red; sees sparks of fire.

Neuralgia, particularly affecting the right eye.

Face very red and congested, or great paleness of the face.

Spasmodic distortion of the mouth.

"Thick, swollen upper lip; gums swollen." —H.

Face swollen, bright red, erysipelatous.

Toothache of a drawing, tearing nature, worse at night; from cold air, mental exertion, and from contact.

Inflammation of the inner mouth, with redness, and the mucous membrane swollen.

Tongue hot, dry, red, and cracked; or red on the edges, with brown fur in the centre.

"Sore throat; fauces and pharynx deep red, soft palate and tonsils swollen; swallowing painful, particularly of fluids; speech thick; feels as if there was a lump in the throat, which induces hawking; the throat is swollen outside and sensitive to the touch."—C. HERING, M.D.

Great dryness of the fauces; tonsils bright red and swollen.

Tongue partially paralyzed, right side most affected.

Parotid glands hard, red, and swollen.

Spasms of the throat, cannot swallow.

"Pain, particularly in abdomen and pelvis; comes on suddenly, continues violently, a longer or shorter time, and disappears as suddenly as it came."—C. HERING, M.D.

Spasms of the stomach during a meal.

"Tenderness of the abdomen is aggravated by the least jar, even of the bed or chair upon which she lies or sits. She is obliged when walking to step with great care for fear of a jar."—HERING.

"Colic in hypogastric region, as from clutching and griping with the nails."—G.

Involuntary discharge of the urine, from paralysis of the sphincter vesicæ.

Urine scanty and fiery red.

Involuntary discharge of the fæces, from paralysis of the sphincter ani.

"Piles, with a feeling as if the back would break."—G.

"Piles so sensitive to the slightest touch that the patient has to lie with the nates separated."—RAUE.

"Ovaritis of right side."—G.

"Great pressing in the genital organs, as if everything would protrude."—G.

Spasmodic contraction of the uterus.

Os uteri rigid, hot, and dry.

"Vagina hot and dry."—G.

"Menses too early; blood bright red."—G.

Inflammation of the testicles, with great hardness.

"Breasts feel heavy, are very hard, and redness runs in radii."—G. (Streaks from a centre.)

Indurated mammæ.

Dry, spasmodic cough; worse at night and by motion.

Constriction of the trachea.

"Takes cold from every draft of air, especially when uncovering the head; complaints from cutting the hair."—HERING.

All fevers traceable to an invasion of the functional powers of the brain itself.

"Inflammations come suddenly and leave suddenly."—G.

"Erysipelas, with smooth, shining skin and not much swollen."—RAUE.

"Diseases are usually worse after 3 P.M., and again after midnight."—G.

Eruptions, smooth and scarlet color, with very pale face.

Glands inflamed, swollen and indurated.

## HYOSCYAMUS NIGER.

*Henbane.*

Hyoscyamus acts especially and powerfully upon the cerebro-spinal system. It affects the cerebrum centrically, like Belladonna and Stramonium, but with this difference: "The cerebral condition is equally one of excited and perverted function, *i. e.*, delirium with hallucinations; but there is little or no determination of blood. Hyoscyamus hence takes no place in the treatment of those cerebral hyperæmiæ for which we rank Belladonna so high.

Nor does it reach that height of maniacal disturbance to which Stramonium is applicable. But in delirium of a less violent and inflammatory type, as in many cases of delirium tremens; in the milder forms of mental disorders, especially when occurring in children; and where sleep is restless or too dreamful, from simple cerebral excitement, Hyoscyamus is a most valuable remedy."—HUGHES.

It acts also upon the sympathetic nervous system (slightly); post-mortem examinations have revealed gastro-intestinal inflammation. It affects especially the sphincter muscles, paralyzing their action. Hardly ever produces constipation, mostly always diarrhœa. It very powerfully influences the sexual organs, and from its great value in typhoid fever it must have some hæmatic action.

### *Grand Characteristics.*

Too active condition of the sensorial functions, with great nervous excitability.

"Involuntary loud laughter, with silly actions; convulsive trembling."—G.

"Delirium, with jerking of the limbs, with diarrhœa; red face; wild staring look and throbbing of the carotids."—G.

"Twitching and jerking of every muscle of the body, eyes, eyelids, face and all."—G.

"Lascivious furor, without modesty; she wishes to uncover and expose herself."—G.

"Excited sexual desire, without excitement of the fancy."—G.

"Loud laughter at the approach of the menses, with convulsive trembling."—G.

Involuntary stool.

"Cough always worse as soon as the patient lies down; relieved by sitting up."—G.

Adapted to hysterical subjects; to drunkards, and people with sanguine temperaments.

"Wishes to run away for fear of being hurt."

Severe headache.

"All objects appear red or larger than they really are, or double."—HEMPEL.

"Loss of sight and hearing."—HEMPEL.

"Entire loss of consciousness; sees persons who are not, and have not been present."—G.

"Muttering, with picking at the bed-clothes."—G.

"Giddiness, with stupefaction."—HEMPEL.

"Excessive dilatation of the pupils, with complete loss of sensibility to touch."—HEMPEL.

"Tongue partially paralyzed; red, brown, dry, and cracked."—HEMPEL.

"Violent pain in the stomach, with vomiting and hiccough."—RAUE.

"Violent trembling of the feet and hands during menstruation."—G.

Paralysis of the sphincter ani and vesicæ, with involuntary stool and urine.

"Spasmodic, dry cough, always worse when lying down; relieved by sitting up."—G.

"Hysteric females and young girls, whose bowels are apt to bloat, and who are subject to attacks of diarrhœa, with colicky pains, and frequent urging to stool, or where the sphincters are weak, causing great difficulty in retaining the fæces, and where the least excitement or mental trouble produces the attack."—HEMPEL.

## STRAMONIUM.

*Thorn Apple.*

Acts especially upon the cerebro-spinal system, skin, and sexual organs. The power it possesses of deranging the sensorium and cerebral nerves, is remarkable; it causes more furious delirium than Belladonna, but not so much congestion of blood to the head, but more congestion than Hyoscyamus does. The irritating or neurotic powers of Stramonium seem almost wholly spent on the sensorium. "Functional derangements of the abdominal organs seem to result from a sympathetic irritation, rather than from direct influence of the poison."

Upon the skin it causes "a fiery redness of the whole body, and a petechial rash on the chest and back, and likewise upon the lower extremities." This eruption is caused by irritation of the spinal nerves.

Upon the sexual organs it causes excessive excitement, even to nymphomania.

### *Grand Characteristics.*

"Disposed to talk continually."—G.

"Desires light and company; worse in the dark or in solitude."—G.

"Imagines all sorts of things; that she is double, lying crossways, &c."—G.

"Child is delirious; does not know where it is; calls for papa and mamma, although they may be present trying to console it."—G.

Furious delirium.

"Light of brilliant objects, and contact, renew the spasms."—G.

"Awakens with a shrinking look, as if afraid of the first object seen."—G.

"Young men or women who pray, sing, or talk so devoutly and constantly, as to excite the sympathy of all in the house."—G.

"Wild thoughts when she is awake; frightful sensations, without perspiration."—G.

"Loquacious delirium, with a desire to escape out of bed."—G.

"Pangs of conscience; thinks he is not honest; does not know his friends; raves about his business."—G.

"Mock laughter when looking at the picture of his father; face red; eyes wild, alternating with melancholy."—G.

"Excessive loquacity during the menstrual

period; face bloated with blood; with tears and prayers and earnest supplications."—G.

"All kinds of food taste like straw; in fact she has no taste."—G.

"Nausea with flow of very saltish-tasting saliva."—G.

"Diarrhœa of a cadaverous odor."—G.

"The urine dribbles away very slowly and feebly."—G.

"Vertigo when walking in the dark, day or night; he staggers and falls down every time he attempts to walk. The same when walking in a darkened room in the daytime."—G.

Muttering delirium, with an extreme degree of nervous erethism, trembling convulsions and restlessness.

"Tongue yellowish-brown, and dry on the centre, or swelled and dry."—NEIDHARD.

"Lips sore and cracked, and sordes on the teeth."—NEIDHARD.

"No desire for water, although the mouth is dry."—N.

Pains are unbearable; drive the patient to despair.

Dilatation of the pupils, with staring eyes.

Swelling and redness of the eyes.

Great confusion of sight.

"The face is bloated with blood."—G.

"Troublesome thirst, even with much saliva."—G.

Saliva tastes salty.

"Involuntary discharges of urine; it dribbles away slowly."—G.

"Caries of left hip."—HERING.

"Abscesses, with violent pain, driving one mad."—RAUE.

Puerperal fever and nymphomania.

"Extreme degree of nervous erethism; convulsions, trembling, restlessness, &c."—P. P. WELLS.

## OPIUM.

*Poppy.*

This powerful narcotic expends the most of its action on the cerebro-spinal system. No drug affects the cerebral tissues more profoundly. The cerebral vessels and sinuses are distended with blood of a dark color; blood becomes extravasated into the substance of the brain, and sometimes large clots of coagulated blood have been found in the substance of the brain. This direct action of Opium upon the neurine cells of the brain is directly opposite to the action of Belladonna, for it is a fact that one is a complete antidote to the other. Poisonous effects of Belladonna produce excitement going on to furious delirium. The poisonous effects of Opium are, oppression fast merging into sopor and coma. Now this gives us a clue as to how remedies cure diseases. The remedy must affect the same organ and tissue diseased, and it appears from the action of these remedies that the dynamic power, or spiritual substance (I prefer the latter), of the remedy acts directly opposite to the spiritual substance causing the disease. Now, in diseases calling for the use of Opium we find paralysis, with stupor and deep sleep; these symptoms, we know, are cured every day by Opium; but Opium produces symptoms identical with these. Here we find our great law, *Similia Similibus Curantur*. Two forces that act on the same organ and tissue, producing similar symptoms, when acting together annihilate each other's action.

From the great power Opium has of suspending the secretions of the mucous membrane, increasing the cutaneous secretions, exciting first, and then depressing the circulation, we must conclude that it has a powerful influence upon the ganglionic, as well as the cerebro-spinal system.

Pereira says the action of Opium upon the digestive system is to "diminish secretion and exhalation from the whole canal; dryness of the mouth and throat; excites thirst; lessens hunger; checks the digestive process; in some cases it excites vomiting; diminishes the liquidity of the stools." From the great power it has in lead colic, arresting the spasmodic pains and restoring the action of the mucous exhalants, we must infer that it has a great influence upon the muscular coat of the bowels as well as on the mucous coats.

*Upon the sexual organs* it produces lascivious

fancies, nocturnal emissions, and spasmodic labor-pains in the female.

*Upon the bladder* it paralyzes the muscular fibres of the fundus, rather than the sphincters.

### *Grand Characteristics.*

In all diseases that call for the use of Opium, the central difficulty will be found in the brain.

"Diseases originating in fright, the fear of the fright still remaining."—G.

"Thinks she is not at home; this is continually in her mind."—G.

"Very sleepy, but cannot go to sleep."—G.

Brain oppressed; extreme drowsiness, and coma, with stertorous breathing.

"The face is purplish and swollen, with soporous sleep, stertorous breathing, and vomiting."—G.

"Screaming before or during the spasm.' —G.

Profound coma, patient cannot be aroused from the stupor.

"Constipation; the stools are composed of round, hard, black balls."—G.

"The bed feels so hot she cannot lie on it."—G.

Complete loss of consciousness.

Patient is very sleepy; lies in a soporous state.

Patient is profoundly comatose; pupils intensely contracted or widely dilated, and insensible; face puffed, with dark red or cherry-brown appearance; stertorous breathing; pulse full and labored, or slow and feeble.

Sopor, with delirium; depression of the lower jaw; dilated pupils; and general symptoms of paralysis of the brain.

"Delirious talking; eyes wide open; face red and puffed up."—H.

"Sleepy, but cannot sleep."—G.

"Unrefreshing, soporous sleep, with eyes half open; snoring during inspiration and expiration."—H.

Sleeplessness, with acuteness of hearing; clocks "striking and cocks crowing at a great distance, keep her awake."—B. FINCKE.

"Drunkenness, with stupor as if from smoke in the brain; eyes burning, hot, and dry." —H.

"After a fright with fear, convulsions, or the head hot, and twitching around the mouth." —H.

"After fright; the fear of the fright still remaining."—G.

"Continually thinking she is not at home; face purplish and swollen."—G.

Sleeplessness, preceded by drowsiness.

"Gaping after coughing."—H.

"Nervous and irritable; passes nothing but hard, black balls from the bowels."—H.

Constipation; stools consist of hard, black balls.

"Colic, with great pressure downwards upon the rectum and bladder, without any passing off of fæces, gas, or urine."—RAUE.

Lead colic and hernia.

"Child makes no water with full bladder, and has no stool; from nursing after the nurse had a furious fit of passion."—HERING.

"Paralysis of the muscles of the fundus of the bladder, rather than those of the sphincter." —HUGHES.

"The skin hot and damp, or sweating, even in the morning, and a desire to uncover."—H.

"Twitching, trembling of the head, arms, and hands, now and then; jerks as if the flexors were overacting; body cold; inclination to stupid sopor; motion of the body and uncovering of the head relieves."—B.

Coldness of the limbs; sleepy, but cannot sleep from too much blood in the brain.

"Bed feels so hot cannot lie upon it."—G.

Sudden retrocession of acute eruptions; paralysis of the brain sets in, or convulsions; nervousness; diarrhœa, &c.

Polypus; tincture applied externally.

## ALCOHOL.

*Rectified Spirit.*

Acts especially upon the cerebro-spinal nervous system, great sympathetic nervous system, and the blood.

On the brain, it first produces excitement; jovial, sympathetic, and sometimes indiscreet; confusion of thought; various mental affections, varying with individual character; some become sentimental and affectionate, but the majority become quarrelsome, and some murderous in their ferocity. Some become depressed and sad, and sit quietly by themselves. The imagination and lower impulses predominate. The symptoms are followed by drowsiness and sometimes profound coma. After this state of somnolency, there are vertigo, headache, stupidity, nausea, and vomiting. In some cases the stupor is followed by great cerebral excitement; the face becomes flushed; eyes injected; great restlessness; violent delirium; pulse accelerated, with fever of a typhoid character. In other cases, it develops a tendency to congestive apoplexy; the coma soon becomes profound; face livid, or ghastly pale; pupils contracted, more generally dilated; breathing stertorous, and death takes place in a few hours.

*Pathological Changes.*—The scalp and membranes of the brain are congested; serous effusion occurs under the arachnoid; the substance of the brain is usually white and firm; the ventricles generally empty. "The peculiar firmness of the brain was noticed several times, even when decomposition of the rest of the body had made considerable advance. Typhus fever is the only disease, save induration of the brain, in which a like firmness is often observed." The cerebrum and cerebellum both become indurated, and sometimes softened. The cerebral arteries are in a state of fatty degeneration.

*Nerves of Motion.*—Are especially affected, as seen in the stammering speech; staggering gait; diminished strength, from relaxation of the muscular system; trembling of the hands and arms; trembling motion of the muscles under the skin, and partial paralysis.

*Nerves of Sensation.*—There is hyperæsthesia or anæsthesia; has to move the limbs constantly, from a great feeling of restlessness; formication under the skin, and drawing, piercing pains.

*Great Sympathetic Nervous System.*—The chronic effects of Alcohol upon this part of the nervous system, "are evinced more by the alterations in structure and functions of the various organs of the chest, abdomen, and pelvis, than by any particular sensations;" more rapid digestion; peristaltic action of the bowels increased; increased secretions; fatty degeneration of the heart and liver, which sometimes are much enlarged; the omentum and mesentery become loaded with fat. The stomach becomes congested, and greatly wrinkled, as if a powerful astringent had been taken; in some, the mucous membrane is perfectly white and thickened; in others, it becomes softened and covered with a copious muco-purulent secretion. The appetite is at first increased, but becomes in a short time less and less in proportion as the taste for drink increases. The tongue becomes furrowed from the median line towards the edges, and looks as if varnished. In the morning the throat seems filled with mucus, and gradually it becomes more and more difficult to clear, and the victim has nausea and vomiting every morning, with a long train of dyspeptic symptoms; in some cases the bowels become much irritated, and there is colic, acidity, flatulence, constipation, or alternate constipation and diarrhœa. The kidneys become more or less congested; the pelvis and ureters are generally in a state of chronic slate-gray inflammation.

The skin at first is soft and velvety, but gradually changes and becomes dry, dirty, rigid or yellowish-gray, and there are more or less prurigo, eczema, &c.

The blood becomes fluid and venous, and the proportion of carbon and hydrogen is much increased; contains much albumen and fat, but little fibrin, which accounts for its non-coagulability; blood-globules are diminished.

### *Grand Characteristics.*

Tweedie says: "I. It sometimes happens that when a patient in fever has been going on favorably, the pulse becomes suddenly soft and compressible, the skin cool and damp, accompanied by a feeling of considerable exhaustion; with these symptoms, there need be little hesitation in allowing six or eight ounces of wine in twenty-four hours, at proper intervals.

"II. When the symptoms denoting sensorial disturbance, languor, low muttering, delirium, tremor, or subsultus, progressively increase, if at the same time, the patient lose his strength from day to day, the pulse soft and skin cool.

"III. When the fever assumes the petechial character, more especially if the spots be large and of a dark livid hue.

"IV. In cases of sudden and unexpected collapse."

Coma, with stertorous breathing.

"Melancholy, with inclination to suicide." —P.

"Mania, with inclination to murder."—P.

"Mania, with inclination to incendiarism." —P.

"Maniacal ferocity."—P.

"Mania, with excessive inclination to drink." —P.

Dementia.

Eyes congested (bloodshot).

"Hallucination of sight; sees double, or thinks he sees a variety of objects; men, animals, snakes, good or bad spirits, angels, or demons." This shows that Alcohol profoundly affects that portion of the brain that gives origin to the optic nerve.

"Hallucination of smell; imagines the devil has defiled his bed, and that it smells as the devil is supposed to do."

"Great dryness of the mouth."

Hallucinations of taste.

Throat seems full of mucus, which is hawked up with difficulty.

"Morning nausea and vomiting."

Gagging and vomiting of sour, offensive matter.

Loss of appetite.

Difficult digestion, with colic and flatus.

Constipation, or alternation of constipation and diarrhœa. (See Nux Vomica.)

Adiposis and venosis; fatty state of the heart, and adiposis in general, in gouty and rheumatic subjects.

Dr. Peters thinks it is more or less antagonistic to tuberculosis; in cases where there is great emaciation it may supply the fat; it only aids in developing adipose, never muscular tissue.

Alcohol as a remedy, and as a nutritious substance:—It especially arrests destructive assimilation, "so that for a certain period, during the stay of alcohol in the system, less urea, less phosphates, less water are excreted by the kidneys, less carbonic acid by the lungs, and less digestion goes on in the alimentary canal, showing that the muscles, bones, nerves, &c., are not getting rid of their effete tissue, but retaining it, and making use of it as far as possible."

"But at the same time, they give rise in the body to defensive reaction, which is prominent first, immediately after taking the dose, and then gives place to the special action, and on this ceasing, is again manifested to greater extent."

"So that if a suitable quantity be taken, and both action and reaction are allowed to exhaust themselves before the dose be repeated," there will be a positive gain in vitality; "but if such a large quantity be taken that the reaction is overpowered, or if the manifestation of life is kept down by continuous repetition of the dose, the body is not renewed, because its effete particles are not removed, and the amount of vitality must certainly be reckoned at a loss."

A distinguished politician, who suffered from the effect of habitual intoxication, thus describes it: "In that world of all that is high and noble, the human heart; that consecrated temple of glorious hopes and generous purposes, and godlike aspirations and countless joys, known only to the heart of man, the alcoholic poison breaks up the fountains of the great deep of human passion, and converts the mind into a wild distorted receptacle of passions, lashed into monstrous and phantom forms, by flames, which distil the fountains of human love and charity, and chastity, and kindness, into the red lava of hell's worst hate. And that bright principle of the human intellect, which comprehends the laws that govern the universe and our own mysterious being, instead of being blotted out in darkness, is transformed into the wild architect of a world distorted and ideal, peopled with fiends, such as perverted minds alone can conceive, and fraught with sufferings and agonies, for which breathing nature furnishes no type or parallel."

## CHLOROFORM.

$C_2H, Cl_3$.

This acts upon the cerebro-spinal nervous system, producing anæsthesia, with rapid muscular relaxation and insensibility, and is the best anæsthetic known.

## SULPHURIC ETHER.

$2C, H_5Cl_5O, S_2O_6$.

This also affects especially the cerebro-spinal axis, producing anæsthesia, the insensibility lasting longer than that caused by chloroform. Also produces greater muscular relaxation in the last stage.

## GLONOINE.

*Nitro-Glycerine.*

This powerful remedy acts especially on the cerebral bloodvessels, medulla oblongata, and pneumogastric nerve.

No remedy produces so quickly and so violently such a severe congestive, throbbing, bursting headache, with increased action of the heart and arteries, and sometimes nausea and vomiting. How does it produce this effect? I believe mainly through the ganglionic plexuses of nerves that entwine round the cerebral arteries and control their action. Dr. Hughes differs from this; he says, "I think that the phenomena of both head and heart can be accounted for by supposing that Glonoine acts as a direct sedative upon the *medulla oblongata.* From this centre come off the vagi, to whose depression we have referred the cardiac symptoms of the drug. Through the medulla oblongata also (according to Schiff's observations), the vaso-motor nerves of the brain proper can be excited or paralyzed. The same sedative influence of Glonoine, therefore, upon this nervous centre, would, through the vagi, set the heart off palpitating, and through the vascular nerves, would dilate the cerebral arteries, so as to give us the phenomena I have described." If Schiff's observations are correct, Dr. Hughes is also.

Prof. Hempel says, "Repeated experiments would seem to show that Nitro-glycerine acts upon the medulla oblongata, and that the symptoms of cerebral congestion which it occasions are depending upon a momentary irritation of this great nervous centre. The pneumogastric nerve is involved in its disturbing influence."

### *Grand Characteristics.*

Intense congestion of blood to the head, with a feeling as if the temples and top of the head would burst open.

Violent, throbbing headache.

Vertigo; fainting, with violent throbbing of the temporal arteries.

Congestive, nervous headache, with no gastric or bilious symptoms.

"It has proved the great remedy for sunstroke."—HUGHES.

"It has checked *puerperal convulsions* where cerebral hyperæmia was prominent."—H.

"It is a capital remedy for the disturbance of the intracranial circulation, which obtains in *menopausia*, and for that which often results from menstrual suppression."—HUGHES.

"Nervous palpitation, of emotional origin." —HUGHES.

Has acted well in some cases of neuralgia.

This remedy ought to prove valuable in apoplexy and epilepsy.

Marcy and Hunt say it is homœopathic to

no disease without it has its origin in the nerve-mass.

It produces intense throbbing pains in the epigastrium.

## AGARICUS MUSCARIUS.

*Fly-agaric.*

Especially affects the cerebro-spinal nervous system and the blood. Upon the cerebro-spinal system it produces giddiness and drunkenness, similar to Alcohol; at last, an entire loss of consciousness takes place. The spinal cord is also especially affected; the motor nerves show chorea-like twitchings; "the sensory nerves lose their elasticity and power of resistance; when even feeble pressure is applied to any spot, it pains still a long while after. Neuralgic pains as though sharp ice touched the parts or cold needles ran through the nerves; compare with the Arsenic neuralgia, in which the imaginary needles are red-hot." (Hughes.) The spine is tender to the touch, especially the lumbar portion.

But the most peculiar effect of Agaricus is its septic influence upon the blood, and the power the urine has of producing intoxication. The blood becomes fluid; the brain, lungs, and liver being gorged with this fluid blood. "During life, too, there are many symptoms of septic change; the face is blue; the body swells; the breath, flatus, and stools are fetid."

" A man moderately intoxicated to-day, will, by

the next morning, have slept himself sober; but, as is the custom, by drinking a teacupful of his urine he will be more powerfully intoxicated than he was the preceding day. This intoxicating property of the urine is capable of being propagated; for every one who partakes of this intoxicating urine, has his own urine similarly affected." I have no doubt but a microscopical examination of the urine and blood of one who has been poisoned with the Agaricus, would reveal thousands of fungi in it, capable of reproducing themselves with great rapidity, similar to yeast.

### *Grand Characteristics.*

"Itching, burning, and redness of the toes. with titillation as if frozen."—G.

"Gastric derangement, with itching, burning, and redness of various parts of the body, as if frost-bitten; of the ears, nose, cheeks, fingers, and toes."—G.

"Much hunger, but no appetite."—G.

"Abundance of flatulence."—G.

"Constipation; first part very hard, latter part liquid."—G.

"Menses too profuse, with titillation in the genital organs and desire for an embrace."—G.

"Great selfishness."—G.

Frequent nictitation of the eyelids.

Chilblains itch and burn much, and are very red.

Great chilliness in the open air, striking through the whole body, without thirst.

Worse during the approach of a thunderstorm.

Hysterical subjects, with spasmodic jerkings of different muscles of the body.

It ought to be useful in *delirium tremens*, venous congéstions, and in septic diseases.

## CICUTA VIROSA.

*Water Hemlock.*

Especially affects the brain and spinal cord, producing tetanic spasms, but differing from the tetanus caused by Nux, by the brain being more affected.

Prof. Hempel thinks, "that its irritating action upon the solar plexus is the first cause of these convulsions." The medulla oblongata is also greatly irritated by this poison. It also affects the skin.

### *Grand Characteristics.*

"The letters seem to move about when reading."—G.

"Convulsions, with contortions of the upper part of the body and limbs; with blue face and frequent interruptions of breathing for a few moments."—G.

"The child seems well, and in great spirits, when suddenly it becomes rigid, then relaxation sets in with much prostration."—G.

"Violent shocks through the head, arms, and legs, which cause them to jerk suddenly."—G.

"Violent vertigo, so that the patient falls down."—HEMPEL.

"During the menstrual molimina, has tearing, jerking pains in the os coccygis."—G.

"Spasmodic hiccough in cholera."—HUGHES.

"Thick, whitish scurfs appear on the chin and upper lip; they secrete a dampness; sometimes affects the nose."—G.

## GYMNOCLADUS CANADENSIS.

*American Coffee Tree.*

Acts upon the cerebro-spinal nervous system.

### *Grand Characteristics.*

"One-fourth of all the symptoms are on the left side, and only one-twelfth on the right."—HERING.

"Hard, racking cough, increasing from morning to night."—H.

Useful in typhoid fevers, erysipelas of the face, scarlet fever, hives, &c.

## CAMPHORA.

*Laurus Camphora.*

Acts upon the cerebro-spinal system, ganglionic nervous system, and genito-urinary organs.

*Upon the sensorium* it causes vertigo, confusion of ideas, maniacal delirium, convulsions, frothing at the mouth, and insensibility; when reaction sets in, there is great heat and vascular excitement in the head.

*Upon the ganglionic system*, "the primary action of Camphor seems to be characterized by a depression of vitality; sinking of the pulse; decrease of animal heat; relaxation of the mucous membranes, and diminution of power in those nervous trunks which are specifically affected by Camphor. The coldness and torpor which Camphor causes in the stomach and bowels are characteristic of its primary action upon the mucous coating of those viscera."—HEMPEL.

These primary effects are of very short duration, which are soon followed by organic reaction, with hard bounding pulse; burning heat of the skin; red face; heat in the stomach and bowels; much anxiety and restlessness.

*Upon the genital organs* its primary effect is impotence, with coldness and relaxation of the parts.

It causes inflammation of the urinary organs, and suppression of urine.

Its greatest usefulness appears to be for its primary symptoms, that is, its chill-producing power.

### *Grand Characteristics.*

Sudden and complete prostration of the vital forces, with great coldness of the external surface.

Long-lasting chills.

"Great coldness of the skin, yet the child cannot bear to be covered."—G.

"Extremities cold and blue, with cramps." —G.

"Skin cold as marble, yet the child cannot bear to be covered; rattling in the throat; hot breath."—G.

"Sometimes those cold spells only come on at night and pass off in the morning, with much prostration and diarrhœa."—G.

"Urine emitted slowly, the bladder being nearly paralyzed."—G.

"Red urine, depositing a thick sediment." —G.

"Retention of urine, with constant pressure on the bladder, and desire to urinate."—G.

STRANGURY FROM CANTHARIS POISON.

"Her labor pains have ceased, and her skin is cold and blue."—G.

Especially adapted to choleraic diseases, and to the first stages of catarrhal affections.

"Throbbing pains in the cerebellum, like the pounding of a hammer; synchronous with the beats of the heart."—RAUE.

"Features distorted; eyes sunken; face, hands, and feet, icy cold; great anguish, as though he would suffocate; half stupid and senseless; groans and moans in hoarse, husky voice; burning in the stomach and œsophagus; cramps; touching the stomach causes him to cry out; great faintness and prostration."—RAUE.

"No thirst, no nausea; no vomiting, no diarrhœa, with cramps in the legs."—RAUE.

"Retention of urine, or it is discharged in small quantities; deep red, and depositing a thick sediment."

"Sometimes the urine is green."—G.

Strangury, not relieved by urinating, especially if it is caused by Cantharis.

"Impotence, with coldness, weakness and atrophied condition of the sexual organs, in large doses."—HEMPEL.

Suffocative catarrh, with paralysis of the lungs, from its paralyzing effect upon the pneumogastric nerve; first stage.

Sudden retrocession of eruptions, with cold skin and great prostration.

"Epilepsy, with much congestion of the brain."—MARCY and HUNT.

## ZIZIA AUREA.

*Golden Alexander.*

Acts especially upon the brain, spinal cord, and pneumogastric nerve.

Its characteristics are unknown, but it is a powerful remedy, and will some day be very useful.

It is adapted to many nervous diseases, such as epilepsy, neuralgia, sick headache, hypochondria, &c.

## CUPRUM.

*Copper.*

Affects the cerebro-spinal system, and especially the great sympathetic nervous centres.

Prof. Hempel says: "A careful study of the action of Copper upon the cerebro-spinal axis seems to show that Copper affects the ganglionic centres and the medulla oblongata, but does not act primarily upon the cerebrum in such a manner as to justify its employment in meningitis, hydrocephalus, typhus, and other cerebral diseases, upon homœopathic principles." The cerebral symptoms, although strongly marked, are secondary or sympathetic, from irritation of the abdominal ganglionic nervous centres; this reflex action from the brain may disturb every function in the living organism.

It seems to irritate the pneumogastric nerve in a special manner, so as to produce nausea and vomiting in every case of poisoning.

It produces gastric irritation and inflammation of almost all the abdominal viscera; the stools are more like dysentery than like those of cholera; but in cholera, accompanied with violent cramps in the extremities, it is one of the most reliable remedies we have.

### *Grand Characteristics.*

Spasms, with nausea and violent vomiting of frothy mucus.

"When drinking, the fluid descends with a gurgling noise."—G.

Drinking cold water relieves the vomiting.

"Sensation as if something bitter was in the stomach."—G.

Violent cramps and spasms.

Diseases caused by the suppression of foot-sweat.

Adapted to neurotic diseases and to light-haired people.

Shrieks from fear; anxiety.

Cold face; blue lips; coldness all over.

Face earthy, dirty bluish color.

"Roof of mouth always red."—RAUE.

Nausea and violent vomiting, with cramps in the stomach and extremities, with violent diarrhœa.

Deathly feeling, with pain behind the ensiform cartilage.

"Stools black; copious and painful or bloody, with tenesmus and weakness."—HALE.

Suppression of urine.

Convulsions, with fearful cries.

Cataleptic when coughing.

Opisthotonos.

"Long-continued paroxysms of convulsive coughing, with vomiting of mucus; blue face and lips."—G.

"Sudden attacks of dyspnœa unto suffocation."

Metastasis of the eruption (of scarlatina) to the brain, with vomiting and spasms.

"Paralysis of the brain, when caused by a process of metaschematismus, an irritation of the cerebral substance having been superinduced by the sudden retrocession of some acute eruption, or some other disorder that required Copper at first."—HEMPEL.

## CANNABIS INDICA.

*Indian Hemp.*

The brain is peculiarly affected by this remedy; it also affects the genito-urinary organs.

### *Grand Characteristics.*

Violent burning in the urethra during and after micturition.

Catalepsy.

Adapted to diseases of drunkards, of a neurotic character, and to urinary diseases.

"The characteristics of the intoxication it produces seem to be exaggeration of all perceptions and conceptions; aphrodisia and tendency to catalepsy."—HUGHES.

It is one of our great remedies in gonorrhœa.

## COFFEA CRUDA.

*Arabian Coffee.*

Acts upon the cerebro-spinal system, sexual system, sphincter muscles, vascular system, urinary organs, and lungs.

*Upon the brain* it produces vertigo ; so dizzy that she could not stand ; depression of spirits ; delirium tremens ; headache, as if a nail had been driven into the brain, &c. ; but it is upon the sentient nervous system that Coffea spends most of its action. Stapf says the primary effects of Coffea are "a pathological excitation of all the organic functions. When Coffea acts moderately upon the healthy organism, the irritability of the organs of sense is morbidly increased, the visual power becomes more acute, the hearing more sensitive, the taste is finer, the sensorium is more vivid (hence increased susceptibility to pain), the mobility of the muscles is increased, the sexual desire is more excited ; even the nervous activity of the digestive and secretive organs is increased ; hence a morbid sensation of excessive hunger, increased desire and facility of the alvine evacuations and of the emissions of urine. To what an extent the nervous and animal activity of the organism is increased by Coffea, appears from the sleeplessness which it excites in various shades and degrees ; from the peculiar pathological excitation of the mind and soul ; and from the febrile warmth which it excites to a considerable degree."

Prof. Lehman says, "Coffea increases the activity of the vascular and nervous systems, while at the same time it retards the metamorphosis of plastic constituents."

Prof. Hempel says, "It excites the circulation, stinging and smarting on the skin; increased frequency, although proportionate diminution, in the volume of the pulse. A sort of vascular orgasm, flushes of heat, and transitory flushes in the face." According to Lehman, it "causes violent excitement of the vascular and nervous systems, palpitation of the heart, extraordinary frequency, irregularity, and often intermission of the pulse, oppression of the chest, pains in the head, confusion of the senses, singing in the ears, scintillations before the eyes, sleeplessness, erections, and delirium."

*Upon the Sexual System.*—It first excites *most powerfully* the sexual instinct, producing sexual dreams and nocturnal emissions, followed by great prostration of the whole nervous system. The female sexual organs are also excited in the same manner.

*Upon the Urinary Organs* it generally produces an increased secretion of watery urine. In one case of poisoning it produced an almost entire retention of urine, with continual and painful urging, only passing a few drops of urine at a time; this case was really inflammatory irritation of the bladder.

*Upon the Lungs.*—It causes spasmodic constriction of the lungs and larynx, with dry hacking cough, and sometimes asthmatic breathing.

### *Grand Characteristics.*

The pains are insupportable; feels them most intensely; cannot bear to be touched, the parts are so sensitive.

"She is in a state of ecstasy."—G.

"Inflammation induced by excessive joy." —G.

"Great sensitiveness, with general excitability."—G.

"Ecstasy; full of ideas; quick to act; no sleep on that account."—G.

"The physical system seems exalted and almost transported by the mental exaltation." —G.

"Child cries easily; while crying it suddenly laughs quite heartily, and finally cries again." —G.

Extreme wakefulness.

"Headache, as if a nail were driven into the brain, or as if the brain were torn or dashed to pieces."—G.

"Exceedingly painful colic, so painful as to drive her to desperation."—G.

"Excessive sensitiveness about the vulva, with voluptuous itching; would like to rub and scratch the part, but it is too sensitive."—G.

Adapted to neurotic diseases, in people with a nervous or sanguine temperament, especially if the disease has been caused by excessive joy.

"Headache, as if a nail were driven into the brain; worse in the open air."—HAHNEMANN.

"All the senses are rendered more acute; reads fine print easily; hearing, smell, taste, and touch acute; particularly also an increased perception of slight passive motion."—HERING.

Head feels too small. (Opposite to Nux vomica.—F.)

"Excessive wakefulness."—G.

"Headache, as if the head would fly to pieces; aggravated by noise and light."—G.

"Ice or ice-cold water is the only thing that lessens his violent toothache as long as touching it."—HALE.

"Toothache, especially at night."—TESTE.

"Excessive dryness of the mouth at night."—TESTE.

"Loss of taste."—TESTE.

"Burning, sour eructations."—TESTE.

"Violent, spasmodic eructations, with rising of the ingesta."—TESTE.

"Tension of the epigastric region, with sensitiveness to the touch."—TESTE.

"Colic, so painful as to drive the patient mad."—G.

"Constant alternations of constipation and diarrhœa."—TESTE.

"Spasmodic contraction of the sphincter, with burning and itching in the anus."—TESTE.

The genital organs of both male and female are greatly excited by Coffea.

Nocturnal emissions, followed by great languor and irritability.

Great sensitiveness of the female genital organs; cannot bear to have them touched, they are so sensitive.

"Genital organs itch voluptuously and are very sensitive."—G.

"Aversion to sexual intercourse in women, it is so painful."—TESTE.

"Leucorrhœa of mucus, and sometimes blood."—G.

"Profuse menstruation, with excessive sensitiveness of the organs and voluptuous itching."—G.

"Labor pains insupportable to her feelings; she feels them intensely; weeps and laments fearfully."—G.

"Measly spots on the skin, with dry heat at night; over-excitability and weeping."—HERING.

Continual inclination to cough; feels exhausted after coughing.

"Sensation of rawness in the windpipe."—TESTE.

"Dry hacking, with constant tickling in the larynx."—Teste.

"Spasmodic cough, like whooping-cough, with this difference, that the spasms are principally experienced during the inspirations, not the expirations."—Teste.

"Constriction of the chest; asthma at night."—Teste.

"Tearing pains in the flesh and cellular tissue, rather than in the bones; in the parts between the articulations themselves."—Teste.

"The free use of strong Coffea is a specific for gout and rheumatisms, where there is a disposition to the formation of chalkstones in the joints."—Dr. W. Hamilton.

"Trembling of the hands, with heat in the palms and coldness of the backs of the hands."—Teste.

"Affections after sudden emotions, particularly pleasant surprises."—Hering.

## TABACUM.

*Tobacco.*

Acts especially on the cerebro-spinal centres. More particularly affecting the medulla oblongata and pneumogastric nerve. The motor nerves that preside over the muscular system are perfectly and completely paralyzed; in fact, nicotine, the active principle of Tobacco, produces the most profound and complete relaxation of the muscular system of any poison we possess.

### *Grand Characteristics.*

Adapted to diseases originating in cerebral irritation, followed by prominent gastric symptoms.

Sick headache, that comes on early in the morning, and by noon is intolerable; with deathly nausea and violent vomiting, greatly aggravated by noise and light.

Dreadful faint feeling at the stomach.

Icy coldness; cold sweat and intermittent pulse.

State of collapse, as in cholera.

Strangulated hernia; ileus; complete marasmus; paralysis, and sudden hyperæmia of the brain, with violent nausea; vomiting and great prostratian.

"Violent pain in the small of the back during soft stool, with tenesmus and burning."

## SOLANUM NIGRUM.

*Garden Nightshade.*

This remedy affects the system very similarly to Belladonna, and ought to be valuable in cerebral congestions, scarlatina, cerebro-spinal meningitis, and many spasmodic diseases.

The Solanum lycopersicon, Tomato, is a valuable remedy, used as a poultice for whitlow (felon) and furuncles (boils).

## AETHUSA CYNAPIUM.

*Fool's Parsley.*

Acts upon the cerebro-spinal system and liver. The first action of the poison is directed to that portion of the brain which controls the functions of the liver, giving rise to bilious disorganizations of a most profound nature. It ought to be one of our best remedies in diseases of the liver, with prominent cerebral symptoms.

## LACHNANTES TINCTORIA.

*Spirit Weed.*

Acts upon the cerebro-spinal system.

This narcotic bids fair to be a very useful remedy in many nervous, typhoid, and pneumonic diseases, where the brain is prominently involved.

"Stiff neck; the head is drawn to one side (after diphtheria, scarlet fever)"—(a characteristic).—Lippe.

## AILANTHUS GLANDULOSA.

*Tree of Heaven.*

Acts especially upon the cerebro-spinal axis, pneumogastric nerve, and especially the skin.

This powerful poison ought to prove one of our greatest remedies in scarlet rash, erysipelas, and many cerebral diseases. Its characteristics are unknown, but I will give some of its prominent symptoms.

Severe headache, with dizziness, and hot, red face.

Very drowsy and restless, which soon passes into insensibility, with constant muttering delirium.

Great anxiety.

Intolerance of light.

Inability to sit up, with sudden and violent vomiting.

Covered with a miliary rash, with efflorescence between the points of the rash; all of a dark, almost livid color. The eruption more profuse on the forehead and face than elsewhere.

The pulse small, and so rapid as hardly to be counted.

"The livid color of the skin, when pressed out by the finger, returned very slowly; the whole was a most complete picture of torpor, and seemingly a perfect instance of that manifestation of it which immediately precedes dissolution in these rapidly fatal cases of scarlet fever."—P. P. Wells, M.D.

## GROUP III.

| | |
|---|---|
| Nux vomica, | Conium, |
| Strychnine, | Curare, |
| Ignatia, | Angustura, |
| Cocculus, | Aesculus. |

THIS group constitutes our true spinal remedies. They produce, *primarily*, irritation and congestion of the spinal cord and its membranes; *secondarily*, depression, paralysis, and softening. To this group really belongs Hydrocyanic acid, but I thought it better to place the acids all in one group.

### NUX VOMICA.

*Strychnos Nux Vomica.*

Nux vomica and its alkaloid, Strychnia, act especially upon the spinal cord. The primary effect being first upon the sentient nerves, through which it is carried to the spinal cord, and reflected back upon the motor nervous system.

Also affects the cerebellum, slightly the cerebrum; the medulla oblongata and nervo-muscular tissue of the bowels, and lastly, the sexual organs.

Marshall Hall, M. Brown-Sequard, and M. Bonnefin, have shown, against the opinion of MM. Bernard and Stannius, that Strychnine tetanus results from the primitive augmentation of the excitability of the cord; and we think that the experiments, in which we have directly poisoned the cord, leave no doubt in this regard.

Traumatic tetanus exhibits, usually, the permanent contraction of a certain number of muscles, with exacerbation to general convulsions; the strychnic tetanus exhibits, usually, convulsions, in the intervals of which, all the muscles are in repose, and they enter into contraction again, only after some external excitement has provoked a fresh crisis. It is intelligible, from the peripheric character of traumatic tetanus, that a topical agent, which paralyzes the sensitive extremities of nerves, applied directly on the wound, in the first period of the malady, may cure this, without affording a presumption as to the cure of strychnic tetanus. But even if it should cure both, that would not prove the antagonism asserted between Curare and Nux vomica. We have the similitude of their action, in the facts that they both diminish the excitability of the extremities, and increase that of the cord.

Strychnine, in general, acts upon the cord with more intensity than Curare, and Curare upon the extremities with more intensity than Strychnine. Such is the shade of difference which we arrive at by varying the dose or the mode of administration.

John King, M.D., says: "Nux vomica is an energetic poison, exerting its influence chiefly upon the cerebro-spinal system; it is supposed to affect the spinal cord principally, because the division of this cord does not prevent its poisonous influence; and again when the cord is destroyed by the introduction of a piece of whalebone into the spinal canal, the convulsions immediately cease. In poisonous doses, Nux vomica produces violent tetanic convulsions, without impairing the functions of the brain, with asphyxia and death. When given in doses sufficiently large to influence the system, a sensation of heaviness is experienced, the spirits become depressed, the limbs tremble, and a slight rigidity or stiffness comes on when attempting to move. Frequently the person cannot stand erect; he staggers, and if at this time he be suddenly tapped on the ham, while standing, a slight convulsive attack will often ensue, with an inability to stand. In the most severe paroxysms caused by this medicine, the patient retains his mental faculties, and the slightest noise, or even a breath of wind passing over him, will excite convulsions anew every time these occur; sometimes sudden starts resembling shocks of electricity arise."

It is not necessary that Strychnine should reach the organs through the circulation to produce its effects. "The encephalon and medulla oblongata being exposed, and a solution of Strychnine introduced within the vertebral canal, the animal is soon seized with convulsions, persisting longer in a limb of which the circulation is interrupted, while its nerve communicates with the central system."

Strychnine, like Curare, annuls the action which the excitement of motor nerves normally produces upon the muscles. If a frog be poisoned by a suitable dose of Nux vomica or Strychnine, injected under the skin, after a variable period, and sometimes without there having been the least convulsion, the nerves subjected to the action of electro-magnetism excite no muscular contraction; but if one limb be so prepared that the poison cannot enter it, its nerve will remain alone excitable.

Paralysis of the extremities of the motor nerves is independent of convulsions and of tetanus.

After poisoning by Strychnine, as well as by Curare, galvanism of the pneumogastric does not arrest the beats of the heart. In these cases, the motor nerves have lost their excitability, while the muscles preserve theirs. To the homœopath, this knowledge is of much practical importance.

Prof. Haughton, in the "American Journal of the Medical Sciences," says: "It is generally believed that Strychnine exerts a specific action upon the lower or lumbar portions of the spinal column, exciting the muscular system (at least the voluntary muscles), into a state of tetanic contraction, and ultimately producing death, indirectly, by rendering respiration mechanically impossible, by virtue of the permanent contraction of the pectoral muscles, and not, as was supposed, by its action on the heart."

Prof. Hempel, says: "Nux vomica affects, primarily, the spinal column, motor and sentient nerves; it also affects the brain: we infer this from the injurious action upon the brain, in patients who are attacked with apoplexy, attended with softening of the brain; we infer it from the fact that it has caused stupor, vertigo, buzzing in the ears, sleeplessness, and turgescence of the capillaries of the face."

Upon the alimentary canal, Prof. Hempel, says: "Nux vomica has caused inflammation of the stomach and small intestines; but this sort of inflammation seems to be incidental to a complete disorganization of the nervous life of the organs, rather than the result of a temporary depression of the nervous energy. Inflammations of this kind seem always to be attended with convulsive paroxysms."

Dr. R. Hughes, says: "Nux vomica has little or no influence upon the mucous membranes of the secreting organs, without it is some irritant action upon the respiratory mucous membrane; it acts here, as elsewhere, upon the nerves and muscles."

Dr. C. Dunham, says: "Nux vomica does not diminish the action of the intestine; it rather increases it, but at the same time renders it inharmonious and spasmodic—a hindrance, therefore, and not a help to evacuation. This is the reason why the constipation characteristic of Nux vomica is accompanied by frequent, ineffectual desire for stool—the action of the intestine being irregular and spasmodic, and the constipation is the result of irregularity, and not from inaction."

Upon the sexual organs, both male and female, Nux vomica has a powerful influence. It first excites their action, which is soon followed by depression.

### *Grand Characteristics.*

Especially adapted to people with choleric, sanguine, malicious, irritable temperament, and to those who make great mental exertions.

"The patient cannot sleep after 3 A.M.; ideas crowd upon the mind so as to keep him awake for hours."—G.

"Symptoms always worse in the morning." —G.

"Very irritable, and wishes to be alone." —G.

"The disease seems to be caused by rich living, highly-seasoned food, stimulating drinks, or by a too sedentary life."—G.

"Habitual constipation of large and difficult stools, or small stools with frequent urging to go to stool."—G.

"Frequent calls to go to stool, but not able to defecate."—G.

"Frequent urination; she passes little and often, with much burning."—G.

"Nausea and vomiting every morning, with constipation of large, difficult stools, and great depression of spirits."—G.

"Very dyspeptic; much excited by Coffea, spirituous liquors, or highly-seasoned food." —G.

"Putrid taste, low down in the pharynx when hawking up mucus."—G.

"Food and drink have a fetid smell to her; cannot bear the odor of tobacco."—G.

"Pressure towards the genital organs early in the morning, in bed, or during a walk, with a sensation of contraction of the abdomen." —G.

"Menses irregular, and never at the right time."—G.

Menses too early and too profuse, with very faint spells.

"Every pain during labor produces a desire to defecate or to urinate, particularly the former."—G.

"Much pain in the small of the back, which is made worse by turning in bed."—G.

"Dry cough, with a sense of constriction around the hypochondria."—G.

Patient often troubled with piles.

Hypochondria, with an irritable temper, arising from liver complaint, or in drunkards.

Vertigo, from excessive use of Coffea or liquor.

Headache; feels as if it would split open; with sour vomiting, caused by a sour stomach.

"Sick headache, brought on by wine, coffee, close mental application, sedentary habits; commences in the morning, increases through the day, growing milder in the evening; with dimness of vision; sour, bitter vomiting; constipation; worse from noise, light, in the open air, or after eating."—HERING.

Loses the connection of ideas, and fears she will lose her reason.

"Complaints from the open air; longing to sit or lie down; ill-humored and resisting obstinately the wishes of others."—HERING.

"Very particular, careful, zealous persons, inclined to get angry and excited, or of a spiteful, malicious disposition."—H.

"Over-sensitiveness; every harmless word offends; every little noise frightens; anxious and beside themselves; they cannot bear the least, even suitable, medicine."—H.

"Cannot keep from falling asleep in the evening, while sitting, hours before bedtime."—HERING.

"Hypochondriasis in studious men; sitting too much at home; with abdominal complaints and costiveness."—H.

"Headache in the forehead, as if the eyes would be pressed out, or in the occiput."—RAUE.

"Epilepsy where the spinal centres are prominently involved, as shown by the shocks and jerks so characteristic of Nux."

"Itching and crawling in the face, as though millions of ants were crawling over it."—HEMPEL.

"Objects appear in a bright light."—HEMPEL.

"Taste is sour, musty, bitter, with a sensation of hunger, but the appetite is immediately satisfied, after eating ever so little."—HEMPEL.

"Sensation as if his head were immensely larger than his body; as large as a church." —F.

"Mouth and fauces full of fetid ulcers." —G.

"Mouth dry and sore, with bloody saliva." —G.

No appetite, with loss of energy.

"Food and drink have a fetid smell."—G.

"Nausea and sour, bitter vomiting."—RAUE.

"Rising of sour and bitter fluid from the stomach."—RAUE.

Vomiting of sour mucus in the morning.

"Flatulent distension after eating or drinking."—H.

"Sudden feeling of repletion after swallowing a small quantity of food."—G.

Very dyspeptic, with tongue red and sore and coated yellow at the base.

"Cardialgia, with clawing, constricting, in pit of stomach, extending to the small of the back or anus; brought on by coffee, liquor, nostrums, sedentary habits, mental exertions." —RAUE.

"Pressure over the solar plexus brings on the spasms."—RAUE.

"Colic, with pressure upwards towards the thorax."—RAUE.

Hepatic colic, with sudden severe pain in the right side; spasms of abdominal muscles.

"Hemorrhoidal colic, with horrid tearing, pressing pains in the small of the back and lower bowels; frequent and ineffectual urging to stool; vertigo, headache, &c."—HEMPEL.

"Flatulent colic, as if the bowels, bladder, and rectum were pressed upon with a sharp instrument."—HEMPEL.

"Sensation as if a hernia would form."—F.

Spasmodic recent hernia (Strychnia).

"Constipation, with ineffectual and frequent urging to stool, with a sensation as if the anus was contracted."—G.

"Piles, with shooting shocks in the loins, contractive pains which hinder from rising up, and ineffectual urging to evacuate."—G.

"Wishes to urinate or defecate very often, but little at a time."—G.

Hemorrhage from the anus in hemorrhoids.

Paralytic incontinence of urine from irritation of the lower portion of the spine.

"Bloody urine."—G.

"Nocturnal emissions, from plethora of the sexual organs; or emissions without erections, followed by debility and great relaxation of the parts."—HEMPEL.

Great excitement of the sexual organs of women, with sexual dreams at night.

"Menstruation never at the right time."

Menses too early and too profuse, with weak, faint spells.

"Fetid leucorrhœa, tinging the linen yellow, with pain in the uterus, as if bruised."—G.

"During every labor-pain has a desire for stool, or to urinate."—G.

Dry coryza; worse nights.

"Dry, hard cough, with great soreness of the abdomen."

Spasmodic asthma; muscles of the chest become rigid; great anxiety and suffocation.

"Tetanic convulsions, excited by contact, noise, or any external stimulus."—HEMPEL.

"Affects the cerebro-spinal axis in the same manner as that unseen, immaterial, impalpable cause, which, by its action upon the cerebro-spinal axis, leads to the production of tetanic spasms."—HEMPEL.

"Paralysis, resulting from softening of that portion of the cerebro-spinal axis which sends off nerves to the paralyzed limb; the temperature of the limb is diminished, especially in paralysis of drunkards."—HEMPEL.

"Much pain in the lumbar region."—HEMPEL.

The pains caused by Nux vomica are tingling, hard, aching, sticking pains; aggravated by motion or contact.

"After aromatics in food, or as a medicine, particularly ginger, pepper, &c., and after almost any kind of so-called hot medicine."—GOULLON.

"Will always benefit persons who have been drugged by mixtures, bitters, herbs, vegetable pills, and all kinds of nostrums."—RAUE.

## IGNATIA AMARA.

*St. Ignatius's Bean.*

Acts especially upon the medulla oblongata, producing tetanic convulsions, dyspnœa, asphyxia, and death.

Marcy and Hunt say, "Its specific sphere is the *spine*, from which all the symptoms proceed. It produces nervous diseases, and especially clonic spasms; over-excitement of the spinal nervous system giving rise early to nervous symptoms."

R. Hughes, M.D., says, "Ignatia exalts the impressionability of the incident nerves all over the body. We have, hence, pains and other morbid sensations well-nigh everywhere; increased susceptibility of the special senses; emotional sensitiveness; and probably from reflex excitation, twitchings, constrictions, and spasms. This action of the drug, however, is not deep and lasting. An alternating series of symptoms—numbness, torpor, depression—soon appear, which are themselves as superficial as their predecessors. The febrile symptoms have the same characteristics."

The bean contains triple the amount of Strychnia

that the Nux vomica seeds do, and its action is more energetic.

It debilitates or paralyzes organic or animal life, which is controlled by the spinal marrow, and cerebrum and cerebellum,—as shown by the great depression of the mind, desponding melancholia, low-spirited, with great muscular prostration,—found in many female diseases.

*Grand Characteristics.*

The patient is full of grief; frequent involuntary sighing, with a sensation of goneness or emptiness in the pit of the stomach.

"Strongly inclined to solitude, and to be very secretive and passive."—G.

"Sadness and sighing, with an empty feeling at the pit of the stomach."—G.

"Full of grief; with a weak, empty feeling at the pit of the stomach, which is not relieved by eating."—G.

"Mental symptoms change often from joy to sadness."—G.

"Uterine cramps, with cutting stitches." —G.

"Difficult stool, causing prolapsus ani."—G.

"After stool, a violent stabbing stitch, from the anus upwards into the rectum."—DUNHAM.

"Frequent spasmodic constrictions of the anus after stool."—DUNHAM.

"Piles, attended with pains shooting deep

into the rectum, seemingly up into the abdomen, with a sensation of excoriation or contraction of the anus."—G.

"Child is spasmodic, with sighing."—G.

"The patient is sensitive, peevish, excitable, hysterical, with sanguine nervous temperament; is delicate; falls easily in love; is romantic; bears trials meekly, and readily falls into clonic spasms after mental agitation."—MARCY and HUNT.

Silent grief.

Feeling as if being swung to and fro.

"Great importance about plans and bad feelings, which cannot be described."—G.

Fretfulness of temper, with timidity.

Spasmodic laughter, from grief.

"Disappointed affection, with silent grief constantly preying upon the mind."—MARCY and HUNT.

Silent, concealed grief, combined with mortification; suppressed vexation.

"Fright, followed by sadness or grief."—MARCY and HUNT.

"Sleeplessness, caused by dejection, grief, &c."—MARCY and HUNT.

Excessive convulsive yawning, with stiffness, or pain in the nape of neck.

"Headache, as if a nail were driven out through the side; relieved by lying on it."

"Throbbing pain in the occiput; worse from pressing at stool, from smoking, or the smell of tobacco smoke."—RAUE.

"Nervous headache, when the eyes are involved; more generally one eye, with burning lachrymation; pressure in the eye, from within outwards."—HEMPEL.

Gets sleepy after every coughing spell.

Broods over imaginary trouble.

Spasms and tetanic convulsions in children and hysterical women.

Clonic convulsions in hysterical, fitful women.

"Tetanic convulsions, with frequent inclination to yawn."—MARCY and HUNT.

Chorea; the convulsions are greatest in the mouth, producing much distortion of the face.

"Epilepsy, caused by fright or grief."—RAUE.

Spasms in children from fright.

"In talking or chewing, they bite themselves in the cheek or tongue."—HERING.

"Odontalgia, as if the tooth were crushed or smashed into fragments."—HEMPEL.

"Boring pain in the front teeth, and a soreness in all the teeth; worse after drinking coffee, after smoking, after dinner, in the evening, after lying down, and in the morning."—HERING.

"Feeling of emptiness or goneness in the

stomach, with a sensation as if a number of pins were sticking in it; not relieved by eating."—HEMPEL.

"Excessive flatulence."—HUGHES.

"Gastralgia, with stitching pains, brought on by starvation, care, grief."—HARTMAN.

"Sensation in the stomach, as if one had been fasting too long; as if the stomach were empty, with flat taste and languor in the limbs."—HEMPEL.

"The evacuation of fæces is difficult, because of a seeming inactivity of the rectum; cannot make a violent effort to expel them without danger of eversion and prolapsus of the rectum."—DUNHAM.

"Moderate pressure at stool causes prolapsus ani."—DUNHAM.

"After stool, painful constriction of the anus."—DUNHAM.

"After stool, a stabbing stitch from the anus upwards into the rectum."—DUNHAM.

"Bleeding after and during stool."—DUNHAM.

"Hemorrhoids; the tumors prolapse with every stool, and have to be replaced; they are sore, as if excoriated; both hemorrhage and pain is worse when the stool is loose; dragging pains around the pelvis."—DUNHAM.

Neuralgia of the rectum.

Bowels inclined to be loose.

Pain in the anus, returning regularly every day; worse when walking or standing; relieved by sitting.

"Stitches in the hemorrhoidal tumors during every cough."

"Urine pale and profuse."—G.

"Scanty, dark-colored, and acrid urine."—TESTE.

"Sexual desire, with impotence."—TESTE.

"Menses scanty, black, of a putrid odor."—G.

"Languor, unto fainting, during the menses."—G.

"Uterine cramps, with stitches."—G.

"Chlorosis; the stomach is very delicate; œdema of the lower limbs."—DR. EISENMANN.

"Dry and hollow cough in the morning, on waking."

"Constant hacking cough in the evening, in bed."—TESTE.

"Constrictive sensation above the throat-pit, which compels one to cough."—TESTE.

"Dry, rough, harsh, spasmodic cough, with a sensation of a feather, or the vapor of sulphur in the throat."—JAHR.

"Every time he stands still, during a walk, he coughs."—H.

"Cold hands and feet, up to the knees;

numbness of the feet, legs, and sometimes of the whole lower limbs."—TESTE.

"During the chill, thirsty; external warmth, pleasant; during the fever heat, no thirst; external warmth, very pleasant."

Change of position relieves the pains; aggravated by coffee and tobacco.

"Symptoms occur in the morning and evening, but more particularly in the morning."—TESTE.

"Like Nux, the symptoms are aggravated by contact, motion, open air, and artificial warmth."—TESTE.

"Morning is the best time to give Ignatia."—HAHNEMANN.

## CURARE.

*Indian Arrow-Poison.*

Acts especially upon the spinal cord and motor nervous system, producing paralysis, and doing so from the periphery towards the centre. "Curare acts upon the extremities with more intensity than Strychnine, and Strychnine upon the cord with more intensity than Curare; such is the shade of difference in their action."

"Curare and Strychnine differ in their action only by shades. Curare, like Strychnine, determines convulsions by augmenting the excitability of the spinal cord."—MESSRS. MARTIN, MAGRON, and BUISSON.

Adapted to neurotic, paralytic diseases, to the debility of old people, and exhausting diseases.

## COCCULUS INDICUS.

*Seeds of Anamirta Cocculus.*

Dr. Hughes says: "The testimony of those who have experienced its effects, is that it influences the voluntary muscles, rather than the intellectual powers; with this, Hahnemann's provings entirely agree. I think that the whole range of its curative action becomes intelligible, if we suppose it to influence the motor tract of the cranio-spinal axis, from the corpora striata to the cauda equina.

"The ultimate effect of Cocculus upon the spinal cord, appears to diminish its irritability, so that while convulsions are produced in acute poisoning by the drug, paralytic symptoms abound in the continued experiments of the provers."

Prof. Hempel says: "Cocculus acts upon the spinal system of nerves, causing even paralysis of the motor nerves and tetanic convulsions."

Pereira says: "It acts rather on the voluntary muscles than on the intellectual powers."

It also affects the genito-urinary organs and skin.

In *uterine affections*, one of the most common symptoms is "weakness, so-called by the patient, but better expressed by the words languor, lassitude, inertness, or general sense of prostration, as if it were impossible to make any exertion." This is caused by nervous prostration, or paralysis of the animal life, from irritation of the cerebro-spinal system. No remedy in the materia medica produces this symptom more powerfully than Cocculus, and I would call particular attention to this fact.

### *Grand Characteristics.*

"She feels too weak to talk aloud."—G.

"Always worse for a while after eating, drinking, or talking."—G.

"In the morning or during menstruation she is scarcely able to raise herself in the bed from nausea and inclination to vomit, it makes her so faint."—G.

"Leucorrhœa in place of the menses; she is so weak, is scarcely able to speak."—G.

"Leucorrhœa like serum, mixed with purulent, ichorous liquid."—G.

"Irregular menstruation, with nausea and faintness."—G.

"Painful pressure in the uterus, with cramps in the chest and fainting nausea."—G.

Nausea, even to faintness, with great deprivation of nervous strength, with no disturbance in the vegetative sphere.

Sensation of sharp stones in the abdomen on motion.

"Hard stool every other day; expelled with great difficulty."—G.

"Much paralytic pain in the small of the back, rendering walking very difficult and sometimes impossible."—G.

Adapted to hysterical and spasmodic diseases, that have their origin in "the motor tract of the cranio-spinal axis, from the corpora striata to the cauda equina."—HUGHES.

"Violent headache; unable to lie on the back of the head; is forced to lie on the side; unable to bear the least light; noise excites nausea and vomiting."—HUGHES.

"Head and face hot; feet cold."—G.

"Roaring in the ears, as though there were shells before them."—G.

"Sadness; irascibility; anxiety; tendency to start, especially at night."—TESTE.

"Vertigo increased by sitting up in bed, or by the motion of a carriage."—MARCY and HUNT.

"People who are much injured by sitting up at night, feeling weaker if they only lose one hour's sleep."—MARCY and HUNT.

Trembling of the head; very nervous.

"Paroxysms of vertigo, with nausea."—TESTE.

"Vertigo, as from intoxication."—JAHR.

"Painful concussion in the brain when walking, when moving the head, or when talking."—JAHR.

"The symptoms of the head are all aggravated by talking, laughing, crying, walking, smoking, or drinking coffee."—DOUGLAS.

"Choking constriction in the fauces, with difficulty in breathing and irritable cough." —G.

".Burning in the œsophagus, extending into the fauces, with a taste of sulphur."—G.

"Sea-sickness, where the affection is from cerebral irritation."—TESTE.

"Violent nausea during a ride in a carriage." —TESTE.

"One of the best palliatives for the cerebral form of sick headache, where the vomiting is plainly secondary."—HUGHES.

"Nausea, resembling sea-sickness, as if the stomach heaved up and down; often brought on by looking at a vessel pitching up."—HUGHES.

"Nausea; and on sitting up, the objects around seem to move up and down."—HUGHES.

Flatulent colic at midnight.

"Abdomen distended, and feeling as if full of sharp stones when moving."—G.

Diarrhœa, only in the daytime.

"Hard stool, expelled every other day with great difficulty."—G.

"Menstrual colic; the pains are of a spasmodic, irregular character."—G.

"Dysmenorrhœa, always followed by hemorrhoids."—G.

"Profuse menses, with a sensation of sharp stones in the abdomen on motion."—G.

Severe spasmodic pains in the neck of the uterus.

"Labor pains are of a spasmodic, irregular, paralytic character; has one hard one, then several light ones."—G.

"The condition of the nervous system, set up by menstruation and pregnancy, appears especially favorable to the action of Cocculus." —HUGHES.

Spasms of pregnant women, with great weakness, so much so that she can hardly talk; with much flatulency.

"Irritation and dryness of the larynx, with dry cough."—TESTE.

"Dry, fatiguing cough, owing to the dyspnœa that accompanies it."—TESTE.

The arm and thigh cannot be moved in their joints on account of pain.

Paralysis from functional disorders of the cord on one side of the body.

Much paralytic pain in the small of the back.

Paralysis from diphtheria, in nervous, hysterical subjects.

Especially suited to women and nervous children, of lively turn of mind, troubled with imaginary fears.

Specific for body lice, used topically.

## CONIUM MACULATUM.

*Poison Hemlock.*

Acts upon the cerebro-spinal and ganglionic nervous systems ; also affects the glands, skin, and respiratory organs. Hughes says, "It directly paralyzes the spinal cord from below upwards, killing at last by gradual asphyxia." The feet and legs become first paralyzed, and it gradually passes upwards until it reaches the chest and paralyzes the pectoral muscles, when death ensues.

Prof. Hempel says, "It affects every part of the nervous system, the brain, spinal nerves, and ganglionic system; affects the spinal marrow antagonistically to the action of Strychnine. Conium causes prostration of the nervous power, and subsequently paralysis, whereas Strychnia causes a spasmodic excitement of the spinal marrow, and as a consequence, muscular spasm."

King says, "It is supposed to effect its results by exhausting the nervous energy of the spinal cord and voluntary muscles."

Its action through the vegetative system upon the glands is shown by the wasting away of the mammæ, and eruptions upon the skin.

Upon the respiratory organs by the "dry, hacking, almost continual cough, worse on lying down, and at night."

### *Grand Characteristics.*

"Much troubled with vertigo, particularly when lying down and when turning over in bed."—G.

Much difficulty in voiding urine; it flows and stops again, then flows and stops at each emission.—G.

"Soreness and swelling of the breasts, preceding menstruation."—G.

Induration of the breasts; hard as a stone.

"All cases of indurations from injuries."—G.

"Shrivelling of the mammæ, with increased sexual desire."—G.

"Prolapsus uteri, complicated with induration, ulceration, and profuse leucorrhœa."—G.

"Leucorrhœa of white, acrid mucus, causing a burning or smarting sensation."—G.

During the menses has stinging pains in the neck of the uterus, and vertigo while lying down.

"Violent itching of the vulva, followed by pressing down of the uterus."—G.

"Frequent sour eructations, with hardness and distension of the abdomen."—G.

"Particularly suitable for women with tight, rigid fibres, and easily excited, as well as for those in the opposite condition."—G.

Adapted to the debility of old people; to diseases caused by a blow or fall, and to cancerous and scrofulous people, with tight, rigid fibre.

"Great weakness and trembling after stool." —H. M. N.

"Stools liquid, fecal; mingled with hard lumps; watery; undigested."—J. B. BELL.

Great concern about little things.

Very easily excited.

Easily intoxicated.

"Dreads being alone, but avoids society."—LIPPE.

Vertigo when lying down, particularly when turning over in bed.

Lips and teeth have black crusts on them.

"Vomiting, that looks like black coffee-grounds."—G.

"Terrible nausea and vomiting in women having scirrhosities, during pregnancy."—G.

"Frequent sour eructations, with hardness and distension of the abdomen."—G.

Constipation, with constant and ineffectual urging to stool; with vertigo while lying down.

"Stitches extending from the abdomen to the right side of the chest."—G.

"Frequent stitches in the anus between stools."—G.

"Heat and burning in the rectum during stools."—G.

"The breasts swell, become hard and painful before the menses, when her hysterical symptoms increase greatly; the vertigo, when lying down, becomes very severe."—G.

Indurations of the breasts become very painful at every menstrual period.

Breasts very sore before the menses.

"Induration and enlargement of the ovary."—G.

"Induration of the testicles."

"Dysmenorrhœa, with aching pains about the heart."—H.

"Burning, sore, aching pain in the region of the uterus."—G.

"Rigidity of the os uteri."—G.

Menses wanting.

Stinging pains in the neck of the uterus, with induration and scirrhosities.

"Aching pain in the abdomen during pregnancy; is disturbed between twelve and three o'clock at night, by having to get up to urinate. Has no affection for anybody."—J. C. M.

Eruptions on the vulva, with violent stitches through it.

Acrid, corrosive leucorrhœa.

"Hacking, almost continual, cough; worse at night, when lying down."—Hughes.

"Bruises and shocks of the spine."—Lippe.

Pulse very irregular in fevers.

Cancers produced by a blow, and aggravated during every menstrual period.

Petechia in old people.

## ANGUSTURA VERA.

*Galipœa Officinalis.*

Especially affects the motor portion of the spinal cord.

### *Grand Characteristics.*

"Lock-jaw; the lips are drawn back, showing the teeth."—LIPPE.

"Spasmodic breathing; palpitation of the heart, with anguish."—LIPPE.

Intermittent fever; chill every day at 3 P.M.

Paralytic diseases and tetanus.

## ÆSCULUS HIPPOCASTANUM.

*Horse Chestnut.*

Acts upon the cerebro-spinal, and ganglionic nervous system; more especially affecting the lower portion of the spinal cord, the rectum, and anus. I once thought it powerfully influenced the liver, entirely suspending its secretion, producing white stools; but a better physiology has taught me that white stools are caused by the follicles of the colon not performing their function. "Dr. Inman has shown that the fæces do not become brown until they reach the colon; and that the green stools of infants assume their peculiar color at this point." From this we must conclude that Æsculus acts through the ganglionic system, upon the follicles of the colon, rectum, and anus, entirely suspending their secretion; and this accounts for the white stools, and also for the constipation. But the constipation is also due to paralysis of the motor filaments of the spinal nerves that are distributed to the colon. It probably produces some passive portal congestion.

Dr. E. M. Hall says:

"A careful study of its pathogenesis would lead us to one or two conclusions: (*a*) that it affected the whole *mucous membranes* in a peculiar manner, exciting therein congestion (venous), with irritation, and that this action was the cause of the whole phenomena; or, (*b*) that the starting-point of its action was in the portal system, the circulation of which is deranged in a peculiar and profound manner, and from this cause proceeded the gastric, hepatic, intestinal, and rectal symptoms. It is difficult to hold to one explanation to the exclusion of the other."

The explanation under (*a*) is the nearest to being right.

### *Grand Characteristics.*

"Constriction, protrusion, fulness, aching, dryness, itching, pricking, tenesmus, pains in the rectum and anus."—HALL.

"Dry, uncomfortable feeling in the rectum, which feels as if it was filled with small sticks." —HUGHES.

"Excessive dryness of the rectum, with a feeling of heat."—HALL.

Hemorrhoids; "there is little tendency to

hemorrhage, but much severe fulness and bearing down, with constipation."—HUGHES.

"Dreadful pain in the anus; could not sit, stand, or lie down. The pain was like a knife sawing backwards and forwards; almost a martyrdom for agony."—HUGHES.

"Large hemorrhoids, which quite block up the rectum, without much hemorrhage."—HUGHES.

The hemorrhoidal tumors protrude from the rectum; are of a blue-purple color, with sharp, shooting, cutting pains in them, running up into the sacrum.

"An intolerable burning, itching pain, with a feeling of fulness of the anus."—T. C. DUNCAN.

"Aching, swelling, and rigid hardness of the rectum, with constipation."—T. C. DUNCAN.

"A painful weakness of the loins, with dull aching pain."—DR. W. M. CUTHBERT.

"Soreness in the rectum, with increased secretion of mucus, or as if the folds of the mucous membrane obstructed the passage, and as if, were the effort continued, the rectum would protrude."—BOYCE.

Dull aching pains in the small of the back; much aggravated by walking.

"Severe aching pains in the lumbar and

sacral regions, with stiffness of the back; almost impossible to walk."—G.

Exhausts the nervous power of the spinal cord, so that its functions cannot be performed.

Severe lumbar and sacral pains.

Capillary congestion of the mucous membrane of the bowels.

White, soft, papescent stools.

Prolapsus ani, with constipation.

Lumbar and sacral pains from hemorrhoids or female diseases.

"Lameness in the small of the back, worse on walking."—F.

*Constant backache, affecting* the *sacrum and hips*, aggravated by walking or stooping.

# GROUP IV.

Sulphur,
Calcarea carb.,
Lycopodium,
Silicea,
Hepar sulph.,
Phosphorus,
Cistus can.,
Sarsaparilla,
Sanguinaria,
Kali carb.,
Kali bichromicum,
Kali hyd.,
Electricity,
Causticum,
Rumex crispus,
Carbo veg.,
Carbo an.,
Alumina,
Stannum,
Graphites,
Juglans cinerea,
Thuja,
Magnesia,
Dulcamara,
Corallia rub.,
Psorin.

THIS group represents our true antipsoric remedies, and may be called our vegetative, or organic group, their grand sphere of action being on the ganglionic, or great sympathetic nervous system. In all diseases, acute or chronic, where there is more or less structural change, such as is found in inflammation, ulceration, &c., either active or passive, involving the arterial or venous circulation, there is, essentially and really, a disorder of the ganglionic, or great sympathetic nervous system of organic life.

This great nerve of organic life, under whose direction are performed all the functions of the body which are entirely out of the reach of the will, "arises from a series of ganglia, extending along each side of the vertebral column, from the head to the coccyx. These two gangliated cords lie parallel with one another as far as the sacrum, on which bone they converge, communicating together through a single ganglion (*ganglion impar*), placed in front of the coccyx. Some anatomists claim that the two cords are joined at their cephalic extremity, through a small ganglion (*ganglion of Ribes*), situated on the anterior, communicating artery." From these ganglia nerves are distributed to all the viscera of the body.

"The ganglionic system, as the primary and fundamental seat of life, must contain all the hereditary elements of health and disease, which latter may be considered as latent, till they begin to be transmitted to some of the organizations which this system supplies. But as the ganglionic system supplies to each of the involuntary vital organs all that is involved in their nutrition, structural, and functional life, it must at the same time impart to them the germs of its own constitutional dyscrasia. Then that, which for the briefest space only may be supposed to have been absolutely latent in the solar plexus, may be apparently latent in the vital organs for a longer or shorter season, or passing harmlessly through them, be ultimated in the skin. And many forms of organic disease, which, from an accompanying tenderness of some corresponding spinous processes, have commonly been attributed to 'spinal irritation,' are thus seen to be the direct result of the psoric miasm flowing into these organs with the vital currents from the ganglionic system. And it is believed that the germs of hereditary dyscrasia, latent in the sympathetic ganglia, may be discovered in the form of minute tubercles in the voluntary organs, in the spinal marrow, and in the brain. Will it be possible for microscopic pathology to discover such germs in the ganglionic centre of life itself?"—PROF. J. H. P. FROST.

Remedies of this class are more especially adapted to chronic, rather than acute, scrofulous diseases, of a psoric origin. For a full exposition of psora, or semi-vital miasm, the common mother of most chronic diseases, vide Chronic Diseases, written by the greatest physician that ever lived, SAMUEL HAHNEMANN.

## SULPHUR.

*Flowers of Sulphur.*

This king of remedies, around which centres the whole materia medica, acts especially upon the vegetative or ganglionic nervous system, and through it, upon the venous capillary vessels throughout the body; upon the mucous membranes; the skin; the portal system; the genito-urinary organs, and lastly, upon the cerebro-spinal axis.

Prof. Hempel says: "That it is the venous capillary system which receives the primary shock of this mighty agent, together with that portion of the ganglionic system of nerves which is immediately connected, or interwoven with the capillary tissue. If you remember that under the depressing action of Sulphur, the venous capillaries become congested, the stagnant blood resisting the arterial current, which seeks to drive it onward, you cannot have any difficulty in understanding the various drawing, tearing, cramping, boring, laming, stitching, and other pains, which Sulphur is capable of exciting."

When it is remembered that venous capillary vessels are to be found in every organ and tissue in the body, and that Sulphur produces through the ganglionic system, which forms plexuses or retinæ around the capillary vessels, paralysis of their walls, we can readily understand the consequences of paralysis and stagnation in the venous capillaries, such as "chronic congestion, exudation, and suppuration of internal organs, and the various eruptions, vesicles, pustules, boils, ulcers, &c., with which Sulphur is in so eminent a degree in curative adaptation." This explains why Sulphur has such a vast and wide range of usefulness.

*Upon the mucous membranes*, especially those of the eyes, bronchi, urethra, vagina, and rectum, it produces burning, acrid, mucous discharges, with much itching.

*Upon the skin*, it causes an eruption so much resembling the itch, that one of the provers feared it might be this disease. It also causes vesicles, pimples, blotches, boils, various forms of herpes, erythema, tinea capitis, ulceration of the nails, intertrigo, and various other forms of ulceration.

*Upon the portal system*, it has a great influence, producing venous engorgement, with a long train of symptoms, especially in the lower portion of the digestive organs.

*Upon the sexual organs*, especially of women, it has a powerful influence, producing swelling of the external parts, acrid leucorrhœa, and the menses become profuse, the blood is black, clotted and gluey.

*Upon the cerebro-spinal system*, it produces many prominent symptoms, but whether through the animal nervous system, or the venous system, it is hard to determine, probably through both.

Sulphur is the first remedy, as a rule, to be thought of in treating all chronic diseases; but it is very frequently indicated in acute diseases, where well-chosen remedies do not have the desired effect. A close examination of the patient will reveal the *psora* element well represented in the case; here Sulphur is the remedy *par excellence:* give a dose of Sulphur, and *do not be in a hurry* to repeat the remedy. A delay of six, twelve, or twenty-four hours, or even longer, may be required to realize the best results. And the rule is *imperative* here, to repeat *no dose*, and give *no* additional remedy while improvement is progressing, from that already given. And in these cases the high dilutions *must be chosen* in order to get the full benefit of the remedy.

### *Grand Characteristics.*

"Constant heat in the top of the head."—G.

"Flashes of heat, which pass off with moisture and debility."—G.

"With single doses of Sulphur 55 m., I have

cured numerous cases of incipient phthisis,—indicated by the usual symptoms."—F.

"She comes out of her spasms very happy, and everything seems beautiful to her; at the termination of each spasm she discharges large quantities of colorless urine."—G.

"She is very happy, and imagines she is in possession of beautiful things; awakes at night singing, she is so happy; dreams very happy dreams."—G.

"She feels very weak and faint from eleven to twelve, A.M.; she must have her dinner."—G.

"Child has great voracity; wishes to put into its mouth everything it sees; watches eagerly for everything."—G.

Stools of children are very excoriating; the child jumps, starts, and screams fearfully.

"The first effort to stool is often very painful, compelling the patient to desist."—G.

"Tenesmus for an hour after stool; on attempting to sit down at stool the pain in the anus prevents her from doing so."—G.

"The discharging of stool and the flow of urine are painful to the parts over which they pass."—G.

Constipation from abdominal plethora; stools hard, knotty, and insufficient, especially if accompanied with hemorrhoids.

"Itching and burning of the anus."—HUGHES.

Excoriations around the anus in little children.

Ascarides and lumbrici.

"Diarrhœa in the morning, driving the patient out of bed; has hardly time to keep herself from being soiled."—G.

"Menses thick and black, and so acrid as to make the thighs sore."—G.

"Menses too early, too profuse, and last too long, with flushes of heat, and weak, faint spells."—G.

"Chronic hemorrhage; she seems to get almost well, when it occurs again and again, day after day, for weeks; she is weak, and has weak, faint spells."—G.

"Offensive, corrosive, ichorous leucorrhœa; it burns like salt, making the vulva sore."—G.

"Weak, faint spells, occurring frequently through the day."—G.

Feeling as if a lump of ice in the right chest.

"Very sore feeling, and disposition of the parts to excoriate; the skin is full of pimples and eruptions."—G.

"The child has a tendency to excoriate, especially about the anus, and wherever the skin is folded upon itself."—G.

"Pimply eruptions filled with pus."—G.

Vesicular eruptions, that burn much at night when going to bed.

"Feels suffocated; wants the doors and windows open."—G.

"Dry, suppressed, choking cough."—G.

"Much rattling of mucus in the chest."—G.

Burning in the soles of the feet, especially at night; has to keep them uncovered.

"Especially suitable for lean persons who walk stooping."—LIPPE.

"Diseases caused by suppressed itch, and by suppression of hemorrhoidal discharge, especially 'bilious colic.'"—FROST.

*Sensorium.*—"Has happy dreams; wakens singing; is very happy."—G.

Despondent; out of humor; weeps much.

Talks much in sleep; awakens with a start.

"Irresistible drowsiness in the daytime, and wakefulness the whole night."—H.

"Short naps of sleep all night, or a dead, heavy sleep, which produces exhaustion."—G.

*Head.*—Burning hot distress on the top of the head; constant symptom.

Chronic vertigo.

"Rush of blood to the head, with roaring

in the ears, and burning creeping in the face." —HEMPEL.

Throbbing headache at night.

Small vesicles on the head, filled with limpid fluid; itch a great deal, and form dry, yellow or brown crusts.

Tinea capitis, dry form.

*Ears.*—"Deafness, with roaring, itching, and dampness of the ear."—HEMPEL.

*Eyes.*—"Dimness of vision; gas or lamp-lights appear to be surrounded with a halo." —HEMPEL.

"Scrofulous ophthalmia, with chronic inflammation and hypertrophy of the lids, with itching, and smarting, and purulent exudations."—MARCY and HUNT.

*Face.*—Vivid redness of the face.

Liver spots on the face.

"Chronic swelling and inflammation of the nose, face, and lips."—HUGHES.

"Comedones; black pores of the skin, particularly in the face."—H.

*Mouth and Tongue.*—"Child is voracious; wishes to put into his mouth everything it sees."—G.

Sour, clammy taste.

Tongue coated whitish or yellow.

*Organs of Digestion.*—Abdominal plethora.

"Chronic constipation; the stools are hard, dark, and dry, and are expelled with great straining, even to such an extent that blood is discharged; with itching and burning of the anus, and frequently accompanied with piles. In such a case give Sulphur for one or two weeks, when another remedy must be chosen; if continued it will spoil the case."—HUGHES. (Better wait for the Sulphur to do all it can.)

Chronic hemorrhages from the bowels.

"Piles, either blind or flowing, with discharges of dark venous blood, and violent bearing-down pains in the small of the back, towards the anus."—RAUE.

"Suppression of piles, with hemorrhoidal colic, congestions, palpitation of the heart, pulmonary congestion, rigidity of the small of the back, as if it had been bruised."

"Diarrhœa in the morning, driving the patient out of bed; has hardly time to keep from soiling himself."—G.

"Tenesmus for an hour after stool."—G.

"Pulsation in the anus, after stool, which continues all day."—RAUE.

Sour diarrhœa.

"Fetid, watery diarrhœa of scrofulous children."—RAUE.

"Alternate diarrhœa and constipation, from enlargement of the mesenteric glands."

"Chronic diarrhœa of mucous and fecal matter."—RAUE.

"Itching, soreness, and discharge of acrid fluid from the anus."

Cutting pains before and after stool, in the anus.

"Chronic diarrhœa in phthisical patients. Give one dose very high."—F.

"Soreness, excoriations, exudations, and itching of the anus."—RAUE.

"Stool so acrid that the child becomes excoriated."—G.

Lancinating pains all night in the anus.

*Urinary Organs.*—Incontinence of urine; urinates very often, with feeling of obstruction in the sphincters, and great pressure on the bladder.

Cloudy urine, with penetrating odor.

Weak and slow stream of urine.

Chronic gonorrhœa, with shooting, burning pains, or without pain, with discharge of white mucus.

*Generative Organs of Women.*—"Menses thick, black, and so acrid as to make the vulva and thighs sore."—G.

Has a cough in the evening before menstruation.

"Pain in abdomen during the menses, as if

the intestines were strung up in knots by threads; has to take a sitting posture for relief."—G.

"Menses too early, too profuse, and last too long."—G.

"Chronic hemorrhages; she seems to get almost well, when it occurs again and again for weeks, with weak faint spells."—G.

"Acrid leucorrhœa, making the vulva sore."—G.

"Burning in the vagina, so violently she can scarcely keep still."—G.

"Voluptuous itching; scratching relieves; after it burning; sometimes little vesicles."—H.

"After nursing, the nipple chaps and bleeds, with much smarting and burning."—G.

"Profuse suppuration of the mammæ, with chilliness in the fore part of the day, and heat in the after part."—G.

*Chest.*—"Suppressed, choking cough."—G.

"Much rattling of mucus in the lungs; the cough worse in the morning."—G.

Catarrhal symptoms become worse and worse.

"She feels suffocated; wants the doors and windows open."—G.

"Does not walk erect; stoops or bends over forwards in walking or sitting."—H.

"Morning sweat setting in after walking." —H.

Acute, plastic form of pleurisy. It will disperse rapidly; use the tincture.

Weakness in the chest in the evening.

"Chills and fever; no reaction; stupid; constantly sinking."—G. H. W.

An excellent remedy in chronic cases of ague, take all the constitutional symptoms.

"Comes out of her spasms happy; at the end of each spasm, voids large quantities of colorless urine."—G.

Dry, husky, scaly skin; no sweat from beginning; pulse frequent; skin, especially of the feet, very hot; no change from day to day, in cases of continued fever.

"In all such cases Sulphur 3 m. in water every two hours, until sweat, which occurs always in about twelve hours, and is followed by convalescence."—D. R. GARDINER.

Chronic rheumatism, Sulphur is almost always the first remedy to be given.

*Skin.*—"After violent scratching; aching numbness of the skin; swelling of the skin, even ulceration."—B.

In itch, Sulphur is the specific. The eruption is vesicular or pustular; much worse at night; warmth of bed greatly aggravates the itching.

In boils, nettle-rash, and nearly all kinds of skin diseases, this is the first remedy to be thought of.

Scrofulous people, that are frequently troubled with boils and every little scratch has a tendency to fester.

"Varicose ulcers, which bleed easily, secrete a fetid pus, and burn and itch much."

Rachitis, with the general constitutional symptoms.

"Finds himself in the night lying on his back."—H.

"Rhagades after washing."—LIPPE.

"Hang-nails."—LIPPE.

*Extremities.*—"Unsteady gait; tremor of the hands."—H.

"Standing is the most disagreeable position:"—H.

"Cramps in the calves and soles, particularly at night."—H.

Heat in the soles of the feet, or cold feet with burning soles; wishes to find a cool place for them, or puts them out of bed.

Most of the pains are in the left side.

"On going to sleep, one leg is suddenly drawn up and shot out again, particularly when rousing him."—RAUE.

"Child dislikes to be washed and bathed." —H.

"Hot flushes, with spells of faintness, or passing off with a little moisture, and fainting with debility."—G.

In most chronic diseases a few doses of Sulphur at first will be found of great benefit.

Adapted to lymphatic temperaments, venous constitutions, disposed to hemorrhoids, with constipation, or morning diarrhœa; to scrofulous diseases which seem to get almost well, when they return again and again, and especially to diseases caused by suppressed itch.

"During the action of Sulphur, all excretory organs are brought to increased activity, discharging carbon and nitrogen from the body." —H. M. M.

## CALCAREA CARBONICA.

*Impure Carbonate of Lime.*

Acts especially upon the ganglionic vegetative nervous system, affecting particularly the osseous system, producing imperfect ossification, difficult and slow dentition, rachitis, &c. Also affects the mucous, serous, fibrous, and cutaneous tissues, and lymphatics. It especially affects the reproductive organs of women.

Marcy and Hunt say: "In constitutions in which we see defect in the reproductive system; obstructions, deposits, intumescence in the lymphatic and glandular systems; dyscrasial affections of the membranous structures, of all the white structures which have but little vitality or blood, and are nourished chiefly by lymph. Obstructions in cartilages, tendons, serous membranes, where development is arrested; obstructions in the lymphatics. In early infancy these structures predominate, and in them, Calc. carb. is specific where there is any arrest of the development of the organs; imperfect formation of the blood, as in scrofulosis. The only cases of hemicrania curable by it, are those caused by disease in the reproductive system, or in whom scrofula was visible in early life. Characteristics: large head; bloated abdomen; narrow chest; flabby, poorly developed muscles; bones containing but little phosphate of lime."

R. Hughes says: "It is in the large class of diseases due to disorder of the secondary assimilation, that Calc. carb. finds its curative place; where the assimilation of the digested food to blood and tissue does not proceed as it should do, there are few agents more powerful than Calcarea for restoring healthy functions. The three great forms of assimilative derangement are scrofula, tuberculosis, and rachitis; in all these it is a principal remedy. It is the constitutional tendency that it controls, rather than the local manifestations."

It has a special and profound influence over the generative organs of women; in fact, this is Calcarea's greatest sphere of usefulness.

### *Grand Characteristics.*

Especially adapted to the constitutional diseases of scrofulous women and children, of leuco-phlegmatic temperaments, prone to affections of the mucous membranes.

"The assimilation of the digested food to tissue, does not proceed as it should do."—HUGHES.

"Children, with dry and flabby skin; large, open fontanelles; much perspiration in drops,—of the head,—which wets the pillow far around where the child is sleeping."—G.

"Pale and fair children; their muscles soft and flabby; their hair dry, and looking like tow."—G.

"She is very weakly in general; walking produces great fatigue; in going up stairs, is out of breath; has to sit down."—G.

"Very sensitive to the least cold air, which seems to go through and through her."—G.

"Swelling over the pit of the stomach, like a saucer turned bottom up."—G.

"Menses are too soon, too profuse, and last too long; difficult to stop menstruating."—G.

"Leucorrhœa like milk."—G.

"Constant aching in the vagina."—G.

"Her feet feel as if she had on cold, damp, stockings, continually; they are cold in bed."—G.

Vertigo, on running up stairs.

"Fear of going crazy, or that people will observe her, and suppose her to be crazy."—H.

"Anxiousness, shuddering, and awe, as soon as the evening comes near."—H.

"Despairing; hopeless of everything, with fear of death; tormenting all around him day and night."—H.

"As often as the patient falls asleep, the same disagreeable feelings rouse him."

"Head too large; the fontanelles not closing."—H.

"The head and upper part of the body sweat profusely."—G.

"Headache, with an unusual accumulation of dandruff on the top."—G.

"Excessive mischievousness."—G.

"Cannot sleep after 3, A. M."—G.

"Vertigo, on ascending a height."—LIPPE.

"Itching of the scalp; children scratch when their sleep is disturbed, or they are awakened." —H.

"Chronic headache, depending on brain fag; the pain is dull; worse in the morning; the head is often cold."—HUGHES.

Much dandruff on the scalp.

"Excessive secretion of mucus in the eyes." —MARCY and HUNT.

"Troubled about an absent son; imagined he saw him at the bottom of the river; could not rest, but constantly walked about."

"Painful and difficult urination; the urine

being clear, and having a peculiar strong, pungent, fetid, odor."—J. B. Bell.

"All objects look as if seen through a mist."

"Long-lasting super-orbital neuralgia."

"Pupils inclined to dilate."—Marcy and Hunt.

"The tongue is sore on the tip, sides, or dorsum, so that she can scarcely eat."—G.

"Sour taste in the mouth, or of the food; sour vomiting, especially with children during dentition; also sour diarrhœa."—H.

"Longing for eggs; particularly with children, in sickness, or during convalescence."—H.

"Vomiting of ingesta, which taste sour."—Lippe.

"Cannot bear tight clothing around the hypochondria."—G.

"Stools whitish and watery."—Raue.

"Diarrhœa worse towards evening."

"Diarrhœa, of sour smell; putrid; during dentition; generally painless."—Lippe.

"Chronic diarrhœa; clay-like stools."—Hughes.

"Much crawling and itching in the anus."—G.

"White, chalk-like stools."—G.

"Feeling of coldness in the abdomen and thighs."—G.

"Involuntary emissions of urine on walking."—G.

Urine has a brown, bloody, or white sediment.

"The history of the case shows that the menses have been too profuse, and return too often, and too soon."—G.

"The least excitement causes the menses to return."—G.

"Leucorrhœa like milk."—G.

"Much moisture between the labia and thighs, with biting pain."—G.

"Inflammation, redness, and swelling of the vulva, with purulent discharge."—G.

"Finds it difficult to stand on account of a pressing down, as if the internal organs would press out."—G.

"Albuminous leucorrhœa, from the cervical canal, with great lassitude, debility, sinking, and trembling at the stomach, and burning pains in cervical canal."—Marcy and Hunt.

"Breasts are distended; milk scanty; she is cold, and there seems to be a want of vitality to bring the milk forward."—G.

"Cough, with rattling of mucus in the bronchi; the cough is worse in the morning."—G.

Chronic hoarseness.

Glands of the neck swollen.

The skin is dry and flabby.

" Eruptions, white, hard, and elevated."—G.

In fever, horrid visions when closing the eyes.

" Headache, ameliorated by closing the eyes." —H.

Lifting the child up, produces pains.

" Difficult dentition with children."—H.

" Children self-willed; inclined to grow fat." —H.

" Growing too fat and thick with young people."—H.

" Hard hearing after abuse of Quinine."—H.

" Feet constantly cold and damp, as though she had on damp stockings."—G.

Offensive sweat on the feet, making the soles of the feet raw.

" Cramps in the toes and soles of the feet." —G.

The pains are aggravated by the slightest touch, as from a current of air, cold or warm, noise, excitement, &c.

## LYCOPODIUM CLAVATUM.

*Club-Moss.*

Acts especially on the great sympathetic nervous system, and is truly a vegetative remedy.

Hughes says: " It is a purely vegetative remedy, affecting the three great tracts of mucous membranes, with their cutaneous continuation. The digestive canal and liver is the most important seat of its action."

The kidneys and lungs are especially affected. I think the greatest centre for the action of Lycopodium is upon the kidneys.

### *Grand Characteristics.*

*Red sand in the urine.*

"I find it the very best medicine where the patient is suffering from an excess of lithic acid gravel, and look upon the copious sediments of this nature as one of the most unerring indications for its choice in dyspepsia." —HUGHES.

"Terrific pain in the back previous to every urination, with relief as soon as the urine begins to flow."—G.

"She has a constant sensation of satiety; takes no food, and if asked 'Why?' replies, 'She wants nothing, because she is so full, and that the least morsel causes a sensation of fulness up to the throat.'"—G.

"Much borborygmus, particularly in the left hypochondria."—G.

"Cutting pain across the hypogastrium, from right to left."—G.

"Constant sense of fermentation in the abdomen, like a pot of yeast working."—G.

"Constipation; almost impossible to evacuate the stools."—G.

"Fan-like motion of the alæ nasi in respiratory diseases of young people and children." —D. WILSON, M.D.

Diseases of the throat, that commence on the right side and spread to the left.—LIPPE.

"Aggravation of the disease at 4, P.M.; better after eight or nine in the evening." —G.

Adapted to subacute and gradually advancing chronic diseases, and to people with sallow complexion and cold extremities.

Lycopodium is of the greatest importance in many of the worst cases of TYPHOID fever.—Incarcerated flatulence, borborygmus, and tympanitis, will draw attention to this remedy in such cases; and many other symptoms will be found to correspond, especially those of the skin, stool, urine, and the great prostration. Such, apparently hopeless cases, I have seen recover under Lycopodium high.

"Give the *two hundredth* in very rare or single doses (as milder and safer in its action) in preference to the still higher potencies,—which latter I have seen act with dangerous violence."—FROST.

"Great fear of being left alone."—G.

"Observing dispositions."—RAUE.

"Mental, nervous, and bodily weakness."

"Dry porrigo of children."—G.

Grayish-yellow color of the face.

"Pain in the temples, as if they were being screwed towards each other."—G.

"Constant sense of satiety."—G.

Sour vomiting.

Great accumulation of flatulence in the small intestines.

"Slow and depraved digestion."—G.

"Acidity and heartburn, with unconquerable sleep after dinner."—RAUE.

"Great fermentation in the abdomen, and discharge of much flatulence. She says her abdomen is like a yeast-pot, so great a fermentation goes on there."—G.

"Obstinate constipation, especially in children; caused by heavy, farinaceous, and fermentable food."—G.

"Enteritis in children, caused by flatulent, indigestible food."—RAUE.

Old hepatic congestions.—POPE.

"Children always cry before urinating."—G.

"Much red sand in the urine."—G.

"Red sand in the child's diaper."—G.

Renal colic, right side.

"Profuse leucorrhœa, with cutting pains across the right side to the left."—G.

"Chronic dryness of the vagina."—G.

"Discharge of wind from the vagina."—G.

"Sharp pains run round each labia."—G.

"Menses too soon and too profuse."—G.

"Nipples bleed much and are very sore."—G.

Passive catarrh of the air-passages.

"Expectoration of large quantities of pus; cough day and night; hectic fever; circumscribed redness of the cheeks."—Raue.

Dr. Pope says: "Few medicines are so valuable in pulmonary phthisis as this, when persistently used. The cough, gastric irritation, exhaustion, and intercurrent attacks of pleurisy, are wonderfully mitigated by it."

Persistent catarrh, with much general weakness; aptness to take cold.

Chronic inflammatory diseases of the skin.

Slow degeneration of the skin.

"Plica polonica."—Hughes.

"Great emaciation of the upper part of the body, while the lower portion is enormously distended."—Raue.

One foot cold, the other hot.

"The babe cries all day and sleeps all night."—G.

"Inflammation of the ends of bones."—Lippe.

"Night sweats; perspiration cold, clammy,

sour, fetid, bloody, smelling like onions."—LIPPE.

Disease always worse about 4, P.M., and better in the evening.

## SILICEA.

*Silicic Acid.*

This remedy so influences the vegetative system, as to produce a depressing and disorganizing action upon the osseous, lymphatic, and mucous systems.

Dr. Hughes says: "Silicea influences the nutrition, rather than the functional activity of the tissues, which come within its sphere of action; it is hence suited to organic changes rather than to functional disorders. Its deep and slow action, moreover, makes it appropriate to chronic rather than acute diseases. Silicea has an extraordinary control over the *suppurative process*, seeming to mature abscesses when desired, and certainly reducing excessive suppuration to moderate limits. Its main sphere is in the diseases of the vegetative tissues and organs. I regard it as a remedy even more important than Calcarea for *rachitis* in children. Like most of the vegetative medicines, it acts powerfully upon the *lymphatic glands;* promoting, when they are enlarged, either their maturation or their dispersion. It has probably some power over the nutrition of the *nervous centres*, and has proved curative in some forms of paralysis, and perhaps also of epilepsy."

Silicea has a special influence on the venous capillary vessels.

*Grand Characteristics.*

"Constipation before, and during menstruation, of hard lumps, which remain long in the rectum, as if it had no power to expel them." —G.

"Hungry, but she cannot get down food, it is so nauseous."—G.

Paroxysms of icy coldness over the whole body, at the appearance of the menses, and icy cold feet during the menses.

Much perspiration in children about the head.

"Terribly offensive sweating of the feet." —G.

She is occupied with pins, counts them, hunts for them, and is always worse during the increase of the moon.

Adapted to chronic scrofulous suppurative diseases, especially to rachitic children, where the nutrition of an organ is assailed, rather than the function.

Sanguine lymphatic temperament, and to children with large bellies, weak ankles, much perspiration about the head, and disposition to uncover.

"Lymphatic swellings, with suppuration,

inflammation, swelling of bones, caries, suppurating ulcers in membranous parts, ulcers of all kinds."—LIPPE.

"The head is wet from sweating, particularly at night; likes wrapping up."—H.

"Vertigo, falling forward after stooping, riding, or looking up; rises from the neck into the head with nausea."—H.

"Yielding mind, faint-hearted, anxious mood."—H.

Open fontanelles.

"Water tastes badly; vomits after drinking."—H.

"Scrofulous children during dentition keep grasping at their gums continually."—G.

"Taste of blood in the morning."—G.

"Hungry, but cannot get down the food."—G.

"Particularly indicated where there are spinal affections, and constipation of difficult stools, as if the rectum had not power to expel them; the stool recedes after having been partially expelled."—G.

"Always great costiveness immediately before and during the catamenia."—H.

"Increased menses, with repeated paroxysms of icy coldness over the whole body."—H.

"Discharge of white water from the uterus instead of the menses."—G.

"Pure blood is caused to flow from the uterus every time the babe nurses."—G.

"Nipples ulcerate easily."—G.

"Fistulous ulcers of the mammæ; the substance of the mammæ seems to be discharged in the pus; one lobe after another seems to ulcerate and discharge into one common ulcer, often with great pain, or there may be several orifices, one for each lobe."—G.

"Silicea has an extraordinary control over the suppurative process, seeming to mature abscesses when desired, and certainly reducing excessive suppuration to moderate limits."—HUGHES.

Chronic suppuration of joints.

"Induration and suppuration of the lymphatic or glandular system in any part of the body."—HUGHES.

"Spongy, readily bleeding ulcers, with torpid callous edges."—FRANKLIN.

"Fistulous ulcers, secreting a thin, ichorous, fetid, yellow fluid."—FRANKLIN.

"Caries of bones, with fistulous openings, and discharge of thin pus and bony fragments." —FRANKLIN.

"Fistula lachrymalis."—RAUE.

"Diseases brought on by exposing the back to any slight draft of air."

"Want of vital warmth, even when taking exercise."—H.

"Foot-sweat with rawness between the toes, or a bad odor; also complaints after checking it."—H.

"Ailments following vaccination, abscess, &c., even convulsions."—H.

"Small foreign bodies under the skin or in the larynx."—H.

Worse every new moon.

Specific for whitlow.

Debilitating night sweats.

Profuse night sweats, 6000th.—HOLCOMBE.

## HEPAR SULPHUR.

*Calcium Sulphuratum.*

Especially affects the mucous membrane of the respiratory organs, and skin; also affects the glandular system and joints.

### *Grand Characteristics.*

In diseases where suppuration is inevitable.

"The child seems croupy, decidedly so, and the phlegm is loose and choking."—G.

"Rattling, choking cough, worse after midnight."—G.

Hoarseness with aphonia.

"Child smells sour."—G.

The slightest injury causes ulceration.

"Ulcers have a bloody suppuration, smelling like old cheese."—G.

Especially after the abuse of mercury, or metallic preparations.

Adapted to scrofulous diseases, where there is more or less suppuration, and to diseases of the larynx and trachea.

Falling out of the hair.

Headache at the root of the nose.

Nightly pain in the skull-bones.

Pustules on the scalp, that secrete a quantity of humor, with glandular swellings.

"Hasty speech and hasty drinking."—H.

"Rising in the œsophagus, as if she had eaten sour things."—G.

"Sensation as if there was a fish-bone in the throat."—H.

"Swollen tonsils and hard glandular swellings of the neck."—G.

"Stomach inclined to be out of order; longing for sour or strong-tasting things."—H.

"Green, slimy diarrhœa, of a sour smell." —H.

"Fetid diarrhœa, the child smelling sour." —G.

"Laryngo-tracheal catarrh, either acute or chronic, with much hoarseness."—H.

"Croup after dry cold wind, with a swelling

below the larynx; with great sensitiveness to cold air or water."—H.

"Cough, with hoarseness all the time; worse before midnight or toward morning."—H.

"Croup, with loose rattling cough; worse in the morning."—G.

Cough excited when any part of the body gets cold.

"Chronic bronchitis, with tickling in the terminal ramifications of the air-passages; violent cough, with sensation as if hot water were trickling through the bronchia; expectorates bloody, frothy, tuberculous masses."

"Sweats day and night, without relief."—H.

"Cannot bear to be uncovered; coughs when any part of the body is uncovered."—H.

"Ailments from west or northwest wind, or soon after it, improved by warmth."—H.

"Strumous suppuration of joints."—Hempel.

"Strumous enlargement of glands, especially where these can only be cured through suppuration, especially the tonsils."—Hughes.

"Stomatitis, where suppuration seems inevitable, with no other symptoms."—G.

Scrofulous ophthalmia, when disorganization and ulceration of the cornea is present.

"Stinging, burning of edges of ulcers, smelling of old cheese; little pimples on smooth ulcers surround the painful ulceration."—H.

"Suppuration of long-inflamed boils on the body, or on the limbs, commencing with blisters; every cut or hurt suppurates."—H.

A slight injury causes suppuration.

Rhagades of the hands and feet.

"Eruptions on the bends of the elbows and popliteal spaces."

"Fainting, with pains."—H.

"Anxious feeling about the heart, with palpitation, in cases of hypertrophy."—R. KOCH.

## PHOSPHORUS.

This powerful remedy acts especially upon the ganglionic nervous system, destroying its nerve-force or life; through it producing congestion, inflammation, and disorganization of the stomach, small intestines, liver, spinal cord, sexual organs, kidneys, muscles, brain, and especially the lungs, blood, maxillary bones, and teeth.

*Upon the stomach* and intestines Phosphorus produces a low grade of gastro-enteritis.

*Upon the liver* it has a specific and powerful influence, producing congestion, inflammation, fatty degeneration, jaundice; or the skin becomes remarkably semi-transparent or waxy in appearance.

*On the spinal cord* it produces degeneration, deliquescence, and paralysis. And through it the sexual organs are first greatly excited, which is soon followed by complete paralysis and impotence.

*Upon the kidneys* it produces irritation, congestion, and inflammation, resulting in a profuse secretion of albumen and exudation-cells in the urine.

*Upon the brain* it has a special influence. Prof. Hempel says: "Phosphorus seems to be in relation with the element or principle in the brain which regulates the renovation of the nervous tissue. As Iron plays an important part in diseases of the blood, so does Phosphorus in affections of the nervous system. If the reproduction or supply of nervous tissue is deficient, or abnormally altered by some cause or other, Phosphorus is, under certain circumstances, the great power which enables us to repair the damage."

It does this through its action on the ganglionic nervous system and blood.

*Upon the lungs*, no remedy has a more powerful and profound action, and well has it shown the beauties of specific medication in pneumonic diseases, especially in the second stage, typhoid form, with gray hepatization and purulent infiltration.

*Upon the blood*, it completely extinguishes and destroys its vitality, producing blood-metamorphoses, which result in hemorrhages, either by ecchymosis into the tissues, or by exudation into the cavities.

*Upon the maxillary bones*, Phosphorus spends a large share of its action; attacking first the periosteum, producing first periostosis, which soon passes on to the bone, causing complete caries and necrosis.

*Grand Characteristics.*

Tall, slender people, with fair skin, sanguine nervous temperament, sensitive disposition, quick and lively perceptions.

It is especially suited to fevers, where death seems inevitable, in consequence of the deep-seated injury inflicted upon the vital forces; and to acute, and subacute, and chronic diseases of the brain, jaws, teeth, lungs, stomach, intestines, liver, kidneys, sexual organs, and blood.

"Sensation of weakness and emptiness in the abdomen; this distresses and aggravates all the other symptoms."—G.

"Belching up large quantities of wind after eating."—G.

"Very sleepy after meals, especially after dinner."—G.

"Sharp, cutting pains in the bowels, sometimes with sour vomiting."—G.

"Stools are long, narrow, hard, and very difficult to expel."—G.

"Profuse, watery diarrhœa, pouring away as if from a hydrant."—Raue.

"Sexual desire almost irresistibly strong." —G.

Tightness across the chest, with a dry, tight cough; in pneumonia, rusty sputa.

Cold feet and legs.

Occasional attacks of profuse hemorrhage.

"Fearfulness, as if something were creeping out of every corner."—G.

"Anxiety during thunder-storms."—DOUGLASS.

"Great depression at twilight."—G.

Clairvoyance; laughing against the will; very sleepy during menstruation and after eating.

"Loss of hearing, with cold extremities."—G.

"Deprivation of sight, with great dilatation of the pupils, and darting pains in the eyeballs."

Attacks of sudden blindness; objects appear veiled.

"Small bald spot over the ear."—DOUGLASS.

"Hemicrania; the forehead or occiput is swollen; touching the swollen part causes the most excruciating pain."

"Face semi-transparent, like polished ivory."—HEMPEL.

"Tongue parched, dry, cracked, and covered black, or glazed."—HILL and HUNT.

"Thirst and dryness of the mouth, with great tympanitis of the stomach, and mucous enteritis, with complete prostration of the ganglionic system, with typhoid condition, dry heat of skin, sallow complexion, cold extremities," &c.

"Constipation; the fæces being slender, long, narrow, dry, tough, and hard, like a dog's; voided with difficulty."—H.

"Chronic, painless diarrhœa of undigested food, with much thirst for water during the night."—R.

"Green and bloody passages; the anus remaining constantly open."—HOLCOMBE.

Watery diarrhœa in the morning; grains like tallow in the rice-water evacuations.

Mucous stools; the anus remaining open.

Thick, turbid, and scanty urine.

"Albumen and exudation-cells in the urine."—HEMPEL.

Irresistible desire for sexual intercourse.

"Impotence from sexual abuse."—HEMPEL.

Nocturnal emissions without dreams.

Discharge of prostatic juice, during hard stools.

"Profuse menstruation, with sexual excitement."—G.

Fistulous openings and abcesses of the breast.

Profuse, smarting, corrosive leucorrhœa.

"Leucorrhœa, acrid, drawing blisters."—LIPPE.

Fatty degeneration of the liver, with malignant jaundice, and a weak, gone sensation in the abdomen.

"Cannot talk on account of pain in larynx." —H.

Green mucus in the nose.

"Dry, tickling cough in the evening, with tightness across the chest; expectoration in the morning."—H.

"Cough worse coming from the warm room into the cold air."—H.

"Pain in chest, with coughing; relieved by external pressure."—H.

Hoarseness, with loss of voice; worse in evening.

Dry, tickling cough; worse evenings.

Capillary bronchitis; severe and exhaustive cough.

Tearing, irritating cough, with expectoration of mucus, pus, and blood.

Pneumonia, with sanguineous infiltration of the parenchyma, and red hepatization; face, livid; brickdust expectoration.

"Trembling of the whole body while coughing."

"Great emaciation."—LIPPE.

"Profuse hemorrhages; pouring out freely, then ceasing for some time."—RAUE.

Degeneration and liquefaction of the brain

and spinal cord, producing complete paralysis of motion and sensation.

"Hemiplegia from apoplexy, with formication in the paralyzed limb."—HEMPEL.

Sexual abuse, producing dorsal consumption, trembling, imbecility, mania, epileptic fits, and impaired digestion.

Typhus, with paralysis impending.

Fistulous ulcers, with callous edges, secreting a thin, foul pus, and of a blue appearance.

Slight wounds bleed much.—HAHNEMANN.

Dr. Sauer uses Phosphor oil, in the worst forms of croup, to the throat.

## CISTUS CANADENSIS.

*Rock Rose.*

Acts especially upon the lymphatic and glandular system; also upon the throat, nose, eyes, and ears.

### *Grand Characteristics.*

Adapted to scrofulous subjects, with swelling and suppuration of glands, especially of the throat; with great sensitiveness to cold air.

"Diarrhœa after eating fruit; after drinking coffee; thin, hot, yellow; worse from midnight till noon."—LIPPE.

"Coldness, of the tongue,—in the throat,—in the stomach,—in the chest, and in the abdomen. Cold feet."—F.

## SARSAPARILLA.

*Smilax.*

Acts through the ganglionic system, upon the kidneys and lymphatic system.

### *Grand Characteristics.*

"Urine either too often, copious and pale, or scanty, slimy, flaky, clayey, sandy."—B.

"Much pain at the conclusion of passing urine, almost unbearable with women, also with men."—G.

"He has to get up two or three times in the night to urinate."—HERING.

Frequent discharge of pale copious urine.

Obstinate constipation, with urging to urinate.

Feeling as if the bowels would be pressed out during stool.

"Pain of tips of fingers on pressure, as if ulcerated, or as if salt were put into the wound." —H.

"Great emaciation; the skin becomes shrivelled, or it lies in folds."—LIPPE.

## SANGUINARIA CANADENSIS.

*Blood Root.*

Acts especially upon the mucous membrane of the lungs; also affects powerfully the stomach and liver; slightly the motor and sentient nervous system.

### *Grand Characteristics.*

Tough, rusty-colored sputa, in the second and third stage of pneumonia.

"Troublesome, harassing cough, with marked inflammatory action, where you are uncertain whether you are dealing with a chronic bronchitis or an incipient tuberculosis."—HOLCOMBE.

"Breath and sputa smell bad, even to the patient."

Excessive dyspnœa.

"Circumscribed redness of the cheeks in the afternoon; patient lies on his back; the pulse is small and quick."—H.

"Roundish or oval, whitish, and raised patches on the mucous membrane of the nose, mouth, prepuce, and anus."

"Sick headache. Pain commences in the back of the head, rises and spreads over the head, and settles down over the right eye, with nausea and vomiting; has to be in the dark and perfectly still."—H.

Annoying flushings at the climacteric age.

## KALI CARBONICUM.

*Carbonate of Potash.*

Acts upon the mucous membranes, especially affecting the mucous membrane of the respiratory organs; also affects the genito-urinary organs.

### *Grand Characteristics.*

Distressing, darting, stitching, shooting, cutting pains.

"Stitching pains in the right side, commencing in the back and going through the chest, which are worse at night, when lying down or rising."—H. N. MARTIN, M.D.

"Stitches in the liver; worse in the cold air."—MARTIN.

"Dry, hard cough, especially aggravated about 3 A.M."—MARTIN.

Dry cough, night sweats, hectic fever; sometimes expectorates bloody pus.

"Great heavy aching weight in the small of the back, especially during menstruation."

Menses bad pungent odor, and very acrid, excoriating the thighs, with great backache and sticking pains in the abdomen.

"Feels very badly a week before menstruation."—G.

"Yellow leucorrhœa, with much burning and itching."—G.

"Constipation, with distress one or two hours before stool, with colicky stitching pains."—G.

"Intense thirst, morning, noon, and night."—G.

"He talks of pigeons flying in the room, which he tries to catch with his hands."—RAUE.

"Great aversion to being alone."—G.

"Great dryness of the hair."—G.

Herpes, becoming moist on scratching.

"A blowing noise and a louder second tick of the pulmonary artery is heard."—KAFKA.

"When touched ever so slightly on his feet, he jerks them up much frightened."—RAUE.

"Dropsical affections, and paralysis of old people."—LIPPE.

"Dry, hard cough, at 4 A.M., with sticking pains in the left side."—H. M. M.

"Swelling over the upper eyelid, in the morning looking like a little bag."—J. B. BELL.

"Stinging pains in joints and inner parts."—LIPPE.

All the symptoms get regularly worse about three in the morning.

Adapted to aged people inclined to be fleshy.

Colic in lying-in women, characterized by stitching pains.—F.

"STITCHES are the most characteristic symptoms."—F.

## KALI BICHROMICUM.

*Bichromate of Potash.*

Acts through the ganglionic system upon the mucous membranes, the glandular system (liver and kidneys), fibrous tissue, and skin.

This remedy has a powerful and peculiar effect upon the mucous membranes, affecting more especially those portions which are covered with columnar, ciliated epithelium; these are found in the nares (excepting that portion to which is distributed the olfactory), larynx, trachea, body of the uterus, and Fallopian tubes. It so changes the functions of the mucous follicles, as to cause them to secrete a *tough, viscid, ropy mucus*, capable of being drawn out into fine threads, two or three feet long.

Hughes says, "The action of Kali bichromicum on the *mucous membranes* should be compared with that of Arsenic, of Mercury, and of Tartar emetic. It causes a marked increase in the quantity of mucus formed, which mucus is sometimes tough and stringy, and sometimes degenerates into pus. Higher grades of the inflammatory process are seen in the respiratory mucous membrane, and (when the poison has been swallowed) along the alimentary tract. In the former region, false membranes have been formed; in the latter, the tendency is towards ulceration. The portions of the mucous membranes chiefly affected, are the mouth, throat, cardiac portion of the stomach, duodenum, jejunum, and rectum; the whole respiratory membrane, including the conjunctiva, and the ureters."

*Upon the liver* and *kidneys* it produces congestion, going on to the stage of softening; and exudation of plastic lymph.

*Upon the fibrous tissue*, about the joints and the periosteum, it has a marked and powerful influence. It also affects the *cartilages*, especially that of the nose, which it has entirely destroyed.

*Upon the skin* it causes papules, pustules, and ulcers.

### *Grand Characteristics.*

Especially adapted to fat, light-haired people, and to scrofulous, catarrhal, and syphilitic diseases.

Discharges from the nose, mouth, throat, stomach, vagina, or any of the mucous membranes, of a tough, stringy mucus, which sticks to the parts, and can be drawn out into strings three feet long.

Cough, with expectoration of tough, stringy mucus, which sticks to the throat, mouth, and lips; the cough is choking and croupy; worse in the morning.

True membranous croup.

Chronic hoarseness.

Especially in chronic bronchitis, with tough, stringy expectoration, and burning pain in the trachea and bronchi.

Fetid discharge from the nose.

Caries of the bones of the nose.

"Profuse mucous discharge from the nose; at first it is clear water; lastly, thick, tough mucus; finally, the nostrils become filled with hard, elastic plugs."—HUGHES. (Clinkers.)

Perfect loss of smell.

"For chronic cold in the head, there is no medicine like it."—HUGHES.

Catarrhal and strumous ophthalmia.

Tongue coated with a thick, yellow felt.

Chronic inflammation and ulceration of the pharynx, especially if of a syphilitic origin.

"Pseudo-membranous lesions of a diphtheritic nature, affecting the respiratory mucous surfaces, the nares, superior portion of the pharynx, larynx, trachea, and bronchial tubes; the deposits are firm in texture, apt to be developed into casts, which are cartilaginous, or pearly in appearance, elastic, fibrinous, and more securely attached to the subjacent integument."—LUDLAM.

Gastric catarrh, with vomiting.

Ulceration of the stomach and duodenum.

"In chronic intestinal ulceration, it vies with mercury."—HUGHES.

"Dull pains in the right hypochondrium, especially when limited to a small spot, with whitish stools."—HUGHES.

Bloody stools, or mucus and blood.

Deep red urine; complete suppression of urine, with dull pains in the small of the back.

"Prolapsus uteri, seemingly caused by hot weather."—G.

"Menses too soon."—G.

Yellow, ropy leucorrhœa, that can be drawn out into long strings.

In pustular diseases of the skin, it will be found of great value.

"Chronic rheumatism of a cold variety."—HUGHES.

"Periosteal and syphilitic rheumatism."—HUGHES.

Large ulcers, with dark centre, and overhanging edges.

Solid eruption, like measles, over the whole body.

## KALI HYDRIODICUM.

*Iodide of Potassium.*

Through the vegetative nervous system, it especially affects the mucous membranes, acting more powerfully upon that of the respiratory tract and kidneys; it also has a profound influence upon the glandular and lymphatic systems. And lastly, the blood is more or less affected by this remedy.

### *Grand Characteristics.*

Especially adapted to scrofulous people, who

have been thoroughly saturated with mercury; to secondary and tertiary syphilis, and to chronic rheumatism.

Has disease of the mucous membrane of the mouth, respiratory organs, or kidneys.

Congestion of the brain, from suppression and habitual catarrhal discharge from the nose.

"Complete blindness, from effusion of water on the brain, with dilated pupils, staring watery eyes, frequent crying out, and vomiting."—Frank.

Œdema of the eyelids.

Chronic angina faucium, with ulceration of the velum, in scrofulous subjects.

Heat in the whole mouth, with swelling.

"Violent ptyalism, with irregular superficial ulcerations of mucous lining of the mouth; the surface looks white, as if covered with milk."—Hempel.

Fetid odor from the mouth.

Gums recede from the teeth, which are loose.

"Impossible to open the mouth."—Hempel.

"Impressions of the teeth are left on the swollen tongue."—Hempel.

"Degeneration of the mucous membrane of the stomach, with vomiting, heartburn, emaciation, and diarrhœa."—Hempel.

Enuresis at night, in scrofulous children.

Profuse flow of urine.

"Gonorrhœa of long standing, with discharge of green, thick mucus, without pain, or constant urging to urinate; very sensitive and irritable urethra."—HEMPEL.

Mucous discharge from the urethra in both sexes.

"Red, swollen nose, with constant discharge of a watery, acrid, colorless liquid."—HEMPEL.

"Watery nasal discharge, that feels cool, and causes no excoriation."—HUGHES.

"Painful sneezing, profuse lachrymation, injected conjunctiva, and throbbing distress in the frontal sinus."—HEMPEL.

Chronic catarrh of the frontal sinus, in scrofulous people.

"Dry, hacking cough, afterwards followed by copious green expectoration."—HEMPEL.

"Mucous phthisis, with purulent expectoration, exhausting night sweats, and loose stools." —H.

The best-known antidote for all the bad effects of mercury.

"Drinking cold milk aggravates all her symptoms."—G.

## ELECTRICITY.

*Electric Fluid.*

Affects both the ganglionic and cerebro-spinal nervous systems; especially affecting the nerves of motion and sensation. There are two currents of

Electricity; one that flows out is called *positive*, and the point of the substance or body with which it is connected is called the positive pole. The current that flows inward is called *negative*, and its point of connection with the positive pole is called the negative pole. The positive, or outgoing current, produces *heat*, *relaxation*, and *expansion;* the muscles become relaxed and expanded, and the nervous system prostrated.

The inward, or negative pole's action, is directly opposite to that of the positive; it produces *tonicity*, *contraction*, and *excitement;* the muscular and nervous systems become greatly stimulated by its action.

I have seen such wonderful cures of old skin diseases and ulcers, by Electricity, I cannot but believe it does this by its action on the vegetative or ganglionic nervous system; but some claim that these cures are made through its chemical action, "by which it is supposed to decompose and resolve into more simple components, unhealthy formations and secretions; either changing them into healthful secretions, which are absorbed or excreted, or entirely dissipating them. It is to this action of galvanism that the speedy and wonderful cures of tumors, boils, cataracts, felons, warts, etc., is attributed."

I must dissent from this. These cures are not chemical, but dynamic, similar to those made by Thuja, Nitric acid, &c.

"In health, each nerve is a perfect magnet, possessing the positive and negative forces properly balanced, the brain and spinal cord being the nervous centre. The brain, in health, is in a positive condition, and the current flows from it; that is, from the centre to the surface. In disease, the electrical equilibrium of the system is more or less disturbed. In certain diseases the condition of the nervous system, throughout a portion or the whole of the body, is *too highly exalted*, and needs to be depressed, soothed, calmed. In certain other diseases there is a depressed state of the nerves, requiring stimulating, exciting, elevating, to bring them into proper action.

Now, we can, by sending artificial Electricity in certain directions, according to the indications, cure these diseased conditions.

*General Treatment.*—If there is much excitement of the nervous system and congestion of blood to the head, the *positive* electrode should be gently passed over the upper surface of the body, commencing at the head, while the *negative* electrode, in a wet sponge, is applied at the coccyx; or the negative electrode may be placed in a vessel of warm water, in with the feet. If there is a prostrated condition of the nervous system, the electrodes should be reversed, using the positive at the base of the spine or feet, and the negative to the head and upper surface of the body.

For the use of Electricity in specific diseases, the reader is referred to larger works on this subject.*

* Garratt's is the largest, and also the best.

In surgery, Electricity is being used as a *galvano-caustic*, with wonderful utility. A fine platinum wire is made instantly white hot, by means of a current of Electricity sent through it from a battery of sufficient power. This fine wire can be thrown around small tumors in the larynx, nasal passages, and places difficult of access, and with a little traction, the tumor is removed without hemorrhage, and but little pain. For the removal of hemorrhoids and polypi, it is the remedy *par excellence.* In hemorrhages, where the bleeding vessels cannot be ligated, the galvano-caustic will be found just the remedy.

## CAUSTICUM.

*Kali Causticum.*

Acts upon the vegetative nervous system, especially affecting the respiratory and urinary organs; also, slightly affects the motor nervous system and skin.

### *Grand Characteristics.*

"Cannot keep the upper eyelids up; they are nearly paralyzed, and will fall down over the eyes."—G.

"Sudden and frequent loss of sight, with a sensation of a film before the eyes."—G.

"Great melancholy; looks at everything on the dark side, especially during menstruation."

"Excessive sympathy for others."—G.

Very yellow complexion.

"Burning, itching in the face, discharging an acrid fluid, which forms crusts when drying."—RAUE.

"Neuralgia, right side, cheek-bone to mastoid process; worse at night."—RAUE.

Facial paralysis.

"Constant sensation, as if lime was being burned in the stomach, with flatulence, water-brash."—RAUE.

"Pressure and fulness in the abdomen, as if it would burst; nourishment greatly increases the pain."—G.

"Pains in the abdomen, causing her to bend double; greatly aggravated by the least nourishment, or tightening her clothes."—G.

"Obstinate constipation, with varices in the anus."—G.

Very apt to have hemorrhoids, which are made intolerable by walking.

"Painful pustules near the anus, discharging pus, blood, and serum."—RAUE.

"Spasms of the rectum; preventing walking."—G.

Involuntary urination when coughing and at night.

"Urine loaded with lithic acid and lithates, with great debility."—HUGHES.

"Difficult, frequent, and painful urination."—HUGHES.

"Menses too early and too abundant; after its cessation, a little blood is passed from time to time for many days, which smells badly." —G.

"It is the best medicine I know of for catarrhal aphonia."—HUGHES.

Chronic, morning hoarseness, with dry cough.

"Weakness of voice from over-exertion."—HUGHES.

Phlegm in the throat that cannot be hawked up, which produces nausea.

Cough, with involuntary emissions of urine.

Sour perspiration.

Chronic eczema.

Said to be very useful in small-pox.

Glandular indurations.

Caries of bones.

Secondary and tertiary syphilis.

Adapted to weak, scrofulous people, with yellow complexions, and to diseases of the respiratory organs and kidneys.

## RUMEX CRISPUS.

*Yellow Dock.*

Acts through the vegetative nervous system, upon the respiratory mucous membrane, more especially affecting that of the larynx; also affects the alimentary mucous membrane, skin, and lymphatics.

*Grand Characteristics.*

"Great exaltation of the mucous membrane of the larynx and trachea."—DUNHAM.

"Violent, incessant, dry, fatiguing cough, with little expectoration; aggravated by pressure, talking, and especially by inspiring, cool air, and at night."—DUNHAM.

"Sense of excoriation behind the sternum."

"The left chest is more often affected than the right."—DUNHAM.

"Brown, watery, morning diarrhœa."—SMALL.

## CARBO VEGETABILIS.

*Vegetable Charcoal.*

Through the vegetative nervous system, it affects the mucous membranes, blood, and skin.

*Grand Characteristics.*

Great foulness of the secretions.

Especially adapted to adynamic diseases, with much putridity.

"Patient wants more air; wants to be fanned all the time."—G.

Great prostration, with Hippocratic face, cold breath, and cold knees in bed.

Gums bleed readily, and are spongy.

Sensation as if the œsophagus was contracted.

"The most innocent food disagrees."—G.

"Frequent eructations, which afford only temporary relief."—G.

"When eating or drinking, sensation as if the stomach or abdomen would burst."—G.

"Much belching of sour, rancid food."—G.

Desire for acids.

"She eructates involuntarily a mass of tough, glairy mucus, which runs continually from her mouth."—DR. GOULLON.

"Profuse and constant salivation of stringy saliva."—J. B. BELL.

Burning distress in the stomach.

"Cardialgia in nursing-women."—G.

"Stomach and bowels greatly distended with flatulence; the gas is generated by the walls of the viscera, rather than from fermentation of the ingesta."—HUGHES.

"Slimy, fecal diarrhœa in scrofulous people."—G.

Tendency to diarrhœa, rather than to constipation.

Stools of foul blood and mucus.

"Stool tough, scanty; not properly cohering; breaks off; afterwards difficult of expulsion."—G.

"Unceasing emissions of flatulence by the rectum."—G.

Especially liable to hemorrhoids; they are large and blue.

"Morning leucorrhœa; discharges very acrid, excoriating the parts."—G.

"Aphthæ of the vulva, with much itching, heat, and redness."—G.

"Extraordinary rush of voluptuous thoughts." —G.

Frequent emissions; onanism during sleep.

"Great and long-lasting hoarseness."

"Greenish, fetid expectoration."—JAHR.

Ulcers, secreting a foul, ichorous pus, emitting an offensive odor.

"Icy coldness of the parts; they have a livid, purple look. (Gangræna senilis.)"

Inveterate herpes.

"Lymphatic swellings, with suppuration and burning pains."—LIPPE.

## STANNUM.

### *Tin.*

Through the vegetative nervous system, it acts upon the digestive, sexual, and respiratory organs. It also has a powerful prostrating action upon the cerebro-spinal system. In diseases where Stannum is indicated, one of the most marked symptoms will be found to be great prostration of the animal nervous system.

### *Grand Characteristics.*

"The pains commence lightly, increase gradually to a very high degree, and decrease again as slowly."—Hahnemann.

"Neuralgia of the head; begins lightly and increases gradually to its highest point, and then gradually declines."—Hahnemann.

"Goes up stairs well, but becomes very faint on coming down."—G.

Insatiable hunger.

Vomiting of blood.

"Pressure in the abdomen relieves the pains when the child is crying with colic; relief is at once obtained by carrying it with its abdomen resting upon the point of the nurse's shoulder."—G.

Children are frequently afflicted with worms.

Symptoms not relieved by stool.

Excited sexual desire.

"Scratching the arm produces an intolerable sensation of pleasure in the genital organs, which extends to the uterus, and produces a real emission."—Teste.

"Her distress of mind ceases as soon as the menses begin to flow."—G.

"During menstruation has hard pain in the malar bone."—G.

"Leucorrhœa, with marked loss of strength; the weakness seeming to proceed from the chest."—G.

"Labor-pains produce great exhaustion, from weakness in the chest; is all out of breath; cannot answer questions, feels so weak."—G.

"Reading aloud or talking produces great exhaustion."—G.

"If she has a cough, with expectoration, the expectoration causes a weakness in the chest."—G.

Expectoration of a sweetish taste.—F.

"Profuse, greenish expectoration."—DOUGLAS.

Chronic bronchitis, with profuse, greenish, expectoration, and great weakness.

"Feels so weak she can hardly sit down; she must drop down suddenly, but can get up very well."—G.

Great weakness of the legs; they are not able to support the body.

The great prostration of the cerebro-spinal nervous system is remarkable, compared to the slight disturbance of the vegetative sphere.

## CARBO ANIMALIS.

*Animal Charcoal.*

Acts, through the vegetative nervous system, upon the glandular system, digestive organs, and skin; also produces great prostration of the animal nervous system.

### *Grand Characteristics.*

"Low-spirited and desponding."—G.

Earthy-colored face.

"Copper-colored eruptions on the face and body."—G.

"Saltish water rises from the stomach."—G.

"Weak, sore, empty feeling at the pit of the stomach."—G.

Teeth very sensitive to the least cold air; looseness of the teeth, with bleeding gums; bending, tearing pains in the teeth from salt food.

"The menstrual function seems to exhaust her remarkably, so that she is hardly able to speak."—G.

"Violent pressing in the loins, the small of the back, and the thighs, during the menses." —G.

"Menses too soon; last too long; but not profuse: feels so greatly exhausted during its continuance, she is hardly able to speak."—G.

"Watery, acrid, burning leucorrhœa, particularly when walking; turns the linen yellow."—G.

"Lochia too long continued; acrid; excoriating the parts, and very offensive."—G.

Uterus swollen and hard.

"Malignant ulcerations of the neck of the womb, with foul discharges."—G.

"Great numbness and languor in the thighs, particularly during the menses."—G.

Glands become indurated with burning and tearing pains.

Glandular diseases of a scirrhous nature.

## ALUMINA.

*Aluminum.*

Acts through the vegetative system upon the sexual organs, mucous membranes, and probably upon the spinal cord, producing paralysis of the motor nervous system. It produces a great dryness of the mucous membranes, especially that of the rectum. During menstruation, the animal system is greatly prostrated.

### *Grand Characteristics.*

"Thinks his mind is some one else's."—G.

"Groans at night, and says it is not him, and wants them to stop."—G.

"As soon as she sees blood, or a knife, wants to kill herself."—DOUGLAS.

"Stupid; thinks he is falling forward."—DOUGLAS.

"Excessive dryness of the scalp; it goes to sleep; feels light, and the hair falls out."—J. S. DOUGLAS.

"Disposition to colds in the head."—DOUGLAS.

"Constriction of the œsophagus, when swallowing; food is felt until it enters the stomach."—D.

Great dryness of the throat.

Specific for painter's colic.

Constipation, from great dryness of the mucous folicles of the rectum.

"Great inactivity of the rectum; even a soft stool can only be passed by great pressing and straining."—G.

"Diarrhœa, from acidity of the primæ viæ; in children, the stools are green."—HEMPEL.

"She cannot pass her urine without straining at stool; she has to strain at stool to pass her urine."—G.

Hardness of the testicles.

"Profuse, transparent, acrid leucorrhœa, running down to the heels in large quantities."—G.

Leucorrhœa worse from walking.

"Abundant discharge of mucus before the

menses, which are delayed, scanty, and pale." —G.

"During the menses, corroding urine is frequently passed day and night."—G.

"After the menses, she is so weak in body and mind, that a little exercise prostrates her." —G.

"Stitches in the left side of the vulva, extending up as far as the chest, with throbbing pains in the vagina."—G.

"Bearing-down pains, as if everything would fall through the vagina."—DOUGLAS.

Copious mucous expectoration; tastes salty.

"Tearing cough; every turn of cough being accompanied by involuntary emission of urine, which reduced the patient to despair."

"Pain in the back, as if a hot iron were thrust through the lower vertebræ."—LIPPE.

"Rheumatic and traumatic paralysis in gouty subjects."—DR. LOBETHAL.

"Always awaking with palpitation of the heart."—G.

"Chronic diseases which occur in dry, thin subjects, and old people."—HUGHES.

## GRAPHITES.

*Plumbago.*

Acts upon the skin, lymphatics, sexual organs, and digestive organs. It especially affects the skin and sexual organs.

Prof. J. S. Douglas says: "It acts more powerfully on the female genital organs, than either Pulsatilla or Silicea."

### *Grand Characteristics.*

"Burning, round spot on the top of the head."—G.

"Congestion of the head, with roaring in the ears in young people."—G.

"Phlegmonous erysipelas of the head and face, with burning, tingling pains."—DOUGLAS.

Burning of the eyes.

Black sweat-pores on the face and nose.

Breath smells like urine.

Cachectic, earthy color of the face.

"Constipation; large, difficult, knotty stools."—G.

"Especially adapted to females inclined to obesity, and whose history reveals a disposition to delaying menstruation."—G.

"Menses too late, pale, and scanty."—G.

"Very profuse leucorrhœa; the discharge occurs in gushes, day or night, and is often excoriating."—G.

"She feels so weak, that it is with difficulty she can persuade herself to perform her accustomed duties."—G.

"She is drowsy during the day, and does not sleep well at night."—G.

"Morning sickness during menstruation."—G.

"During the menses, severe pain in the epigastrium, as if everything would be torn to pieces."—G.

"The ovaries are very apt to be affected."—HUGHES.

Deep cracks in the nipples.

Vesicles upon the nipples.

"Mastitis, in all cases where there are many old cicatrices, from former ulcerations, that the milk can scarcely flow: this remedy high, will now cause the milk to flow easily, and ward off the impending abscess; although many times tried, has never failed me in a single case."—G.

"Hoarseness and cough during the menses, through the day; no cough at night."—G.

"Rhagades, excoriations, and ulcers on the skin."—HUGHES.

"Eruptions, oozing out a sticky fluid."—G.

"Burning and swelling of the feet."—G.

"Rawness in bends of limbs, groins, neck, behind the ears, especially in children."—L.

"Unhealthy skin; every injury suppurates."—L.

The great characteristic in skin diseases is, the eruption discharges a sticky, glutinous fluid.

## JUGLANS CINEREA.

*Butternut.*

Acts especially upon the skin and mucous membranes.

Excellent in many skin diseases.

## THUJA OCCIDENTALIS.

*Arbor Vitæ.*

Through the vegetative nervous system, it especially affects the genito-urinary organs, the rectum, anus, and skin.

Dr. Wolf, says: 1. "It produces irritation of the mucous membrane of the genital organs, extending itself over all organs.

"2. Changing of the naturally mild secretion into one of an acrid, corroding, infectious quality.

"3. Over-irritation of the nerves, with tendency to centripetal paralysis.

"4. Disturbance of the digestion and sanguification; tendency to destruction; dissolution of the fluids, and of the whole organism."

It produces inflammation of the prepuce and glans, warts, tubercles, ulcers; in the female, leucorrhœa; retarded menstruation; fig-warts, condylomata, &c., and is the great representative of the *sycotic poison* (a combination of psora and syphilis). This sycotic poison renders all diseases more obstinate and pernicious, and arouses into action any and every disease man is predisposed to.

*Grand Characteristics.*

The great antidote to disease of a sycotic origin, which generally shows itself in the shape of warts, condylomata, cauliflower excrescences, on or about the genital organs and hairy parts of the body, especially if they are also syphilitic.

"The vagina is filled with warty excrescences, with great burning and smarting pains." —G.

"She is so sensitive in the vagina that she cannot possibly bear an embrace."—G.

"Profuse mucous leucorrhœa, with thin long warts, or fig-warts, on the face or genitals."—G.

"Sycosic ulceration of the womb."—G.

"Retarded menstruation."—HUGHES.

"Fig-warts and condylomata all over the genital organs of both sexes."—G.

"Ulcers on the internal surface of the vulva, with cramp-like pain in the vulva and perineum, when rising from a seat, extending up into the abdomen."—G.

"A terrible distressing pain occurs in the left iliac region, when walking or riding; she must lie down to get relief; the same pain occurs during her menstrual periods, and extends into the left groin."—G.

Red, smooth excrescences on the glans penis.

"Round, flat, unclean ulcers, on the corona glandis; painful and burning; surrounded with redness."—RAUE.

Chronic gonorrhœa, with sycosis, with burning during and between urination.

"Copious and frequent urination, with burning in the urethra."—HUGHES.

"Violent contraction in the anus and rectum, followed by tearing pains, as if in the bowels."—G.

"Violent burning and pricking in the anus."—G.

"During an attempt at stool, the pain in the rectum and anus is so great that she has to desist, she cannot pass the stool; the suffering and pain in the anus is greatly increased during motion."—G.

"Feeling in the rectum as if boiling lead was passing through it."—RAUE.

"Extremely scrupulous about the least thing."

"The patient often feels as though she could not exist any longer."—G.

"Sensation as if the whole body were very thin and delicate, and could not resist the least attack; as if the continuity of the body would be dissolved."—G.

"Cannot sleep after 3 P.M. and at night."—G.

"Headache on the left side, as if a convex button were being pressed on the part."—G.

Induration of the eyelids.

Sycosic erosions of the fauces.

Polypus of the nose and uterus.

Dry, teasing cough.

"Nævus maternus."—HUGHES.

For warts, and condylomata, apply the tincture externally, and a high dilution internally.

Teste says, "It is particularly suited to persons of a lymphatico-sanguine, or of a sanguine temperament. People with dark complexion, black hair, dry fibre, and not very fat."

## MAGNESIA.

*Epsom Salt.*

We use the muriate and carbonate more than any other form.

They affect especially the epithelial cells of the alimentary canal and generative organs. The muriate is about the best remedy for constipation in the materia medica, at the 200th dilution.

## MURIATE OF MAGNESIA.

***Grand Characteristics.***

"Constipation of large difficult stools, crumbling as they pass the verge of the anus."—G.

"Hysterical complaints and spasmodic turns;

many spasms day and night, with great sleeplessness; fainting fits."—G.

"Uterine spasms, extending to the thighs."—G.

"Leucorrhœa after every stool."—G.

"Much excited at every menstrual crisis."—G.

"Much weakness of the limbs."—G.

"Continual rising of white froth into the mouth."—G.

"Slow dentition, with large distended abdomen."—G.

"Dreams of robbers in the house; on awaking will not believe to the contrary until search is made."—G.

"Aptness to take cold."—LIPPE.

"Swelling of glands; blood boils."—LIPPE.

## CARBONATE OF MAGNESIA.

### *Grand Characteristics.*

"Green, sour-smelling diarrhœa, lasting a long time; many stools day and night."—G.

"Green, slimy stools, resembling the scum of a frog-pond."—G.

"Watery, sour stools."—G.

"Much colic, relieved by a green, liquid stool."—G.

"Sour vomiting."—G.

"All her symptoms are aggravated every third week."—G.

"Has a sore throat during every menstruation."—G.

"Menses dark, acrid, and thick; washed out with great difficulty."—G.

"Menses flow only in the absence of pain, and at night."—G.

"Much pain in the head and right shoulder; she can hardly raise the arm."—G.

"Insupportable pains during repose; she must get up and walk about."—G.

"Sad and disconsolate."—G.

"The knees are painful when walking."—G.

"Œdema of the feet up to the calves."—G.

"Disposition to furuncles, and headache; the tongue coated dirty yellow."—G.

Face dirty, dark yellow.

"Scirrhous indurations of the womb, discharging black clots of blood."—G.

## DULCAMARA.

*Bitter Sweet.*

Acts especially upon the mucous membranes, producing catarrhal inflammations, similar to those produced in damp, rainy weather, and if used as a prophylactic after exposure to damp, rainy weather, it will ward off all bad effects; also affects the skin, medulla oblongata, and pneumogastric nerve. It paralyzes the action of the pneumogastric nerve-filaments of the lungs. It also produces in the kidneys and system, a state closely resembling the first stage of Bright's disease.

### *Grand Characteristics.*

Especially adapted to catarrhal and rheumatic diseases in damp, cold weather.

"The patient's symptoms are aggravated when the weather suddenly becomes colder, especially if the weather is damp."—G.

"Increased secretion of the mucous membranes and glands; those of the skin being suppressed."—LIPPE.

"Every time she takes cold has urticaria, or some other cutaneous affection."—G.

"The skin is delicate and sensitive to cold, and liable to eruption from being exposed to the cold."—G.

"The child gets worse at every cold change in the weather, or from exposure to cold air." —G.

"Retrocession of the eruption from exposure to damp cold air."—G.

"All her symptoms are aggravated by a cold change in the weather; even the sexual desire is greatly increased."—G.

"Dropsical affections, after suppression of sweat, by damp, cold air."—H.

"From taking cold; the neck stiff; the back painful; the loins lame."—H.

"Dysentery caused by cold and damp, and becomes worse as the weather grows colder." —G.

"Diarrhœa in cold, damp weather; stools mucous, green, watery and whitish; may be caused from repelled eruptions, chills, or teething."—G.

"On awaking in the morning giddy and dizzy; dark before the eyes; trembling and weakness."—H.

"Inclination to scold without being angry." —H.

"Cannot find the right word for a thing." —H.

"Inarticulated speaking, from a swollen tongue, but talks incessantly."—H.

"If cold air chills him, his tongue gets lame, and even the jaws".—H.

"After the disappearance of tetters in the face, face-ache and violent asthma."—H.

"Always as a forerunner of the catamenia a rash appears on the skin."—Gosewich.

Suppression of the menses in damp, cold weather.

"Lochia suppressed by cold or dampness; and the quantity of milk much diminished." —G.

"They have to cough a long time to expel phlegm, especially in infants and old people, from threatened paralysis of the vagi."—HUGHES.

"Oppression of the chest from mucus."—LIPPE.

"Tetters, oozing watery fluid; bleed after scratching."—H.

"Thick, brown herpetic crusts on the face, forehead, temples, and chin, with reddish borders, bleeding when scratched."—G.

"Small furuncles on places formerly hurt by concussion."—JEANES.

"Nettle-rash, with much itching; after scratching, it burns, increases in warmth, disappears in cold, with gastric fever."—H.

"Exostosis on the upper part of the right tibia, with bluish-red spots, suppurating lumps."—H.

## CORALLIUM RUBRUM.

*Red Coral.*

Affects especially the respiratory ganglion of the medulla oblongata and the pneumogastric nerve, in its distribution, producing spasmodic convulsive cough.

### *Grand Characteristics.*

Violent, spasmodic cough, so violent that

children lose their breath, and grow purple and black in the face.

"Pertussis in children that take very little food or drink."—G.

"Nervous, hysterical cough."—HUGHES.

"Trickling of mucus from the posterior nares into the fauces."

"Laryngismus stridulus, and chronic convulsive cough."—TESTE.

## PSORIN.

### *Grand Characteristics.*

"Profuse perspiration from the least exertion, and at night, with great debility."—J. B. BELL.

"Its great field is debility, independent of any organic disease."—J. B. BELL.

"Very offensive, dark brown, thin fluid stools."—P. P. WELLS.

"When well chosen remedies do not act, and the patient shows a psoric taint, give Psorin."
—H.

"Great weakness; debility, from loss of fluids, or remaining after severe acute diseases."—LIPPE.

"The patient is hopeless, and despairing of recovery."—LIPPE.

"Vertigo, with headache."—LIPPE.

"Headache, as from a heavy blow on the forehead, waking him at night."—LIPPE.

"Dry, or moist, fetid, loathsome eruptions on the head."—LIPPE.

Pimples and ulcers on the face.

Corners of the mouth sore.

"Inveterate cases of itch; repeated outbreaks of single pustules, after the main eruption seems gone."—H.

"Dry, tetter-like eruptions in the hollow of the knees."—RAUE.

"Urticaria, after suppressed itch, comes after every exertion."—RAUE.

"Moist, itching, condylomata."—G.

Stools liquid, mucous, or bloody.

Dry coughs, with shortness of breath.

"Profuse colliquative sweats."—LIPPE.

Better when lying quietly.

"Used in cutaneous affections, diarrhœa, and complications of typhoid fever."—FROST.

In diseases where sulphur is indicated, but fails to act.

"Sitting aggravates the dyspnœa (asthma) and pain in the heart."—LIPPE.*

---

* A full rendering of this important, and truly valuable, but much neglected remedy, may be found in this author's "Text-Book" of Materia Medica.

## GROUP V.

Mercurius, and its various preparations,
Iodine, and its compounds,
Chlorine, and its compounds,
Bromine, and its compounds,
Ammonium,
Podophyllum,
Iris versicolor,
Phytolacca,
Arsenicum,
Sepsin,
Leptandria,
Stillingia,
Aloes,
Argentum,
Spongia,
Baryta carb.,
Croton tig.,
Aurum,
Potassium, in its various forms.

REMEDIES of this group have for their starting-point of action, the glandular and lymphatic systems, and may be called the glandular group. They also affect, powerfully, the mucous membranes, and, in fact, about the whole organism. They also constitute the great forces we have to wield against that malignant and filthy miasm, syphilis, and consequently are our anti-syphilitic glandular group.

### MERCURIUS.

*Quicksilver.*

The effects of Mercurius corrosivus, Mercurius vivus, Mercurius solubilis, and Mercurius dulcis, resemble each other so closely that I shall include them all under the above heading.

Mercury, through the vegetative nervous system, affects, more or less, every tissue in the body, but has for its grand starting-point of action, the epithelial cells of the lymphatic glands; bile-cells, and the whole of the epithelial cells of the digestive apparatus, increasing and disordering their functions.

It also especially affects the glandular system; the mucous membranes; the serous membranes; the fibrous tissue; the dermoid tissue; the nervous tissue; the osseous tissue, and the blood.

*Upon the glandular system*, especially the salivary glands and liver, through the peripheral ramifications of the nerves that preside over secretion. Small doses of Mercury so irritate these peripheral nerves, as to cause constantly increased secretion of saliva or bile. Very large doses carry the irritation beyond the secreting-point, and then we have acute congestion, diminished secretion, icterus, inflammation, and organic changes, such as profuse salivation. "The tongue sometimes projects from the mouth, in consequence of its greatly augmented bulk, and is covered with a thick, soft, yellow-white fur, extremely offensive to the smell; the parotid and submaxillary glands become much enlarged, and painful; the patient cannot open his jaws; swallows with great difficulty and pain, and is wholly unable to articulate; the head requires to be supported on a pillow, and the saliva runs in streams from the mouth; the odor of the breath is insupportably fetid, and sometimes scents the whole apartment; ulceration of the gums, cheeks, and tongue takes place, with occasionally copious and exhausting hemorrhage; the teeth loosen and fall out; even gangrene of the soft parts and necrosis of the alveolar processes sometimes occur; and in not a few instances, death has taken place, or recovery has been attended with revolting or very inconvenient deformity. One of the greatest dangers is from hemorrhage, though a fatal result may also be owing to the joint effect of gangrene and a depraved state of the blood. Not only is the salivary secretion increased, sometimes enormously, but there is, perhaps, not one of the secretory functions which is not liable to be similarly affected, though rarely in an equal degree; the hepatic secretion is often energetically stimulated; a true cholera morbus, with copious vomiting and purging of bile."—WOOD.

It also affects the pancreas in a manner analogous to its action on the salivary glands. The increased secretion of bile, and of the epithelial cells of the digestive apparatus, cause watery and bilious stools. But if the dose is a large one, the stools, instead of being watery, are mucus and blood, or pure blood, with violent tormina.

*Upon the mucous membranes*, it produces destructive ulceration, especially of the mouth and fauces; small doses greatly augment the secretion of mucus. It seems to affect the colon and rectum more than the small intestines.

*Upon the skin*, it produces eruptions of the vesicular and pustular type; the parts are much swollen and raw. Sometimes it produces profuse perspiration.

*Upon the nervous system*, it especially affects the ganglionic nervous system, destroying its nutritive force to its very foundations. Also affects the motor nerves, producing tremors.

*Upon the osseous tissue*, it especially affects the periosteum, producing periostitis, and caries of the bones.

*Upon the serous membranes*, it especially affects the peritoneum, producing inflammation, and effusion of serum into its sac. It also slightly affects the arachnoid membrane.

*Upon the blood:* Dr. Headland says: "By some inscrutable, chemical power, whose agency we know nothing of, it is able to decompose the blood; by some destructive agency, it deprives it of one-third of its fibrin, one-seventh of its albumen, one-third or more of its globules, and at the same time, loads it with a fetid, fatty matter, the product of decomposition."

"Hence we have, as a result of the diminished fibrin, ecchymoses and hemorrhages; as the sign of the absent corpuscles, the anæmia of which we have read in our Watson, and the peculiar fetor of the secretions."—HUGHES.

Mercury is the great antidote for the syphilitic miasm, or poison, and has cured millions of cases, both primary and secondary in form. Its action upon the genito-urinary organs very closely resembles that of syphilis.

### *Grand Characteristics.*

All the symptoms are worse at night, and in damp, rainy weather.

Much perspiration accompanies most complaints, but does not relieve.

"Cold, clammy sweats on the thighs and legs at night."—G.

"The parts are much swollen, with a raw, sore feeling; worse at night."—G.

Glandular swellings.

Hepatic diseases, with much jaundice.

Very fetid breath.

"The gums bleed, and are inclined to ulcerate about the teeth."—G.

Teeth sore and loose; some of them are too long.

Odontalgia; worse at night, with periosteal inflammation and ulceration.

Teeth all feel on edge.

Profuse flow of saliva.

Saltish, metallic taste.

Red tongue, with much burning and intense thirst.

"Moist tongue, with great thirst."—G.

"Swelling of the tongue, which is covered with a whitish, thick, tenacious coat, that is detached in shape of little skins."—HAHNEMANN.

"Grayish ulcers on the inner surface of the lips, cheeks, gums, tongue, palate."—HAHNEMANN.

"Ulceration of the tonsils."—HAHNEMANN.

"False membranes; grayish, thick, with shred-like borders, adherent or free, but of a marked consistence when they are attached." —HAHNEMANN.

Salivary glands greatly swollen, with excessive secretion of saliva, and breath extremely fetid.

"Very sensitive about the pit of the stomach and abdomen."—G.

Inflammation of the liver, with great tenderness of the liver, and much jaundice.

"Much colic; relieved by a bloody stool, with tenesmus."—G.

"Faint, sickish pain in the abdomen, entirely relieved by a muco-sanguinolent stool, with severe and prolonged tenesmus."—G.

"Mucous or muco-sanguinolent stools, with severe and prolonged tenesmus."—G.

"Yellow, or mucous, and bloody or dark-green stools, with tenesmus."—G.

For mucous and serous diarrhœas in children, Mercurius dulcis is the specific.

Urine scanty and red, with strong smell.

Urine highly albuminous.

Suppression of urine.

"Prolapsus of the vagina, with sensation of great rawness; worse at night."—G.

"Itching, burning, smarting, corroding leucorrhœa, with sensation of rawness in the vagina; discharges of flocks of pus and mucus, large as hazelnuts; worse at night."—G.

"Pain in the mammæ, as if they would ulcerate at every menstrual period."—G.

"Ascarides creep out of the anus, and can be seen on the perineum and buttocks, even at night in bed."—G.

"Lumbricoides escape easily and freely, and the abdomen is hard and distended."—G.

"Watery vesicles and blotches; turn yellow and maturate."—G.

Ulcerations and eruptions are swollen, and have a raw appearance.

Adapted to bilious fevers and hepatic diseases, in lymphatic or scrofulous temperaments, and especially to syphilitic diseases.

Merc. cor. is especially adapted to the diseases of men, and Merc. vivus, sol., and dulcis, to those of women and children.

## MERCURIUS PROTO-JODATUS.

*Iodide of Mercury.*

Affects especially the lymphatic and glandular system, particularly of the throat, including its mucous membrane. Its action upon the system is somewhat similar to Mercury and Iodine, but not exactly similar to either. It affects more or less the whole organism.

Wood and Bache say: "It should never be given at the same time with Iodide of Potassium, which converts it immediately into Biniodide and Metallic Mercury."

### *Grand Characteristics.*

Its grand sphere of usefulness is in scrofulous diseases of the glandular and lymphatic system; in diphtheritic affections and secondary syphilis.

"It is the only form of Mercury that ought to be used in induration of the parotid and cervical glands and tonsils, when these conditions attend scarlatina and measles."—DR. FRELEIGH.

"Diseases of the glands, acute or chronic; conglobate or conglomerate; swelling of the parotids and tonsils during scarlatina."—DR. G. W. COOK.

"Enlargement, engorgement, or torpor of the liver or spleen during fevers, particularly those of a typhoid type."

"Enlargement of the inguinal glands and testicles during gonorrhœa or lues."—COOK.

"Tabes mesenterica; ganglionitis."—COOK.

"Excessively tired feeling of the whole body, especially of the limbs; indisposition to do anything, and desire to lie down, with dull, aching pains in forehead and bones of the face."

"Always worse during rest; better when exercising actively."

"Worse in a warm room; better in the open air."

"Symptoms disappear during care and anxiety; soon as relieved, symptoms appear more violently."

Dizziness while riding and when rising from a chair.

Dull headache, affecting the whole head.

"Neuralgia of the left side of the head."—BLAKELY.

"Sharp, throbbing, boring pains, from within outwards, deep in the left ear."

Soreness of the bones of the face, with headache.

"The headache is always on the top of the head or right side."

Great soreness and stiffness of the neck.

"Great deal of mucus in the nose; much of it descends through the posterior nares into the throat."

"Polypus of the nose."—HEMPEL.

"Thick, yellow coating at the base of the tongue; the tip and edges bright-red."—BLAKELY.

Tongue coated with a thick, yellow, dirty coating.

Teeth feel too long; very painful when closing the jaws.

"The functions of the mucous follicles of the entire cavity, including those at the root of the epiglottis, are so disordered as to cause them to yield an opaque, viscid, and tough substance, which is sometimes expectorated with great difficulty."—COOK.

"The surface of the mucous membrane is raw, the epithelium being entirely destroyed."—G. W. COOK.

"Pseudo-membranes located upon the tonsils, tongue, uvula, velum palati, pharynx, or some portion of the alimentary tract."—LUDLAM.

"The deposit should be of limited extent, of feeble organization, transparent, pellicular, albuminous, and easily detached."—R. LUDLAM.

"To those cases in which there is but a feeble effort at a reorganization of false membrane, when it has been removed or dropped off spontaneously."—LUDLAM.

It especially affects mucous membranes covered with squamous epithelium.

"The buccal, submaxillary glands, and tonsils, are enlarged, inflamed, painful, throbbing, with abundant flow of tough saliva."—COOK.

Great thirst for water in the evening.

Pain in the liver, with dizziness all day; the pain proceeds from the right to the left, producing dizziness and nausea.

Colic, followed by soft, yellowish-brown stools.

Copious, very thin, brown stools, accompanied by froth and wind; preceded by cutting pains in the abdomen.

Stools in the daytime are copious, soft, and of a dark or light-brown color; the stools at night are scanty, hard, and black.

Stools every evening about 10 P.M.

Urine dark, red, and copious.

Sharp pains in the chest.

Very troublesome itching over the whole body.

Deep bone-pains, especially at night.

## ARUM TRIPHYLLUM.

*Indian Turnip.*

Affects the mucous membrane of the digestive apparatus, especially that of the tongue, buccal cavity, and fauces. The fresh plant is an acrid poison, causing violent inflammation of the buccal mucous membrane, tongue, and fauces; rapid tumefaction of the tissues takes place, with a feeling as if a thousand little needles were being run into the tongue and lips, superficial ulceration, acute stomatitis, salivation, œdema of the glottis, vomiting, diarrhœa, and convulsions. It also slightly affects the respiratory organs and kidneys.

### *Grand Characteristics.*

"Discharge of burning ichorous fluid from the nose, excoriating the nostrils and upper lip."—LIPPE.

"Nose stopped up; can only breathe with open mouth."—LIPPE.

"The corners of the mouth, buccal cavity, and even the throat, become raw and sore, emitting blood; so sore, in fact, that the patient refuses all food and drink, in consequence of the suffering occasioned by mastication or swallowing."—G.

"Throat sore; feels as if excoriated; cannot swallow."—LIPPE.

"Excessive salivation, saliva acrid."—LIPPE.

"Raw condition of the mouth and throat; putrid odor emanating from the mouth, and if it be a case of fever, the fever is very intense. The thirtieth potency, or higher, in water, will speedily produce a gratifying change, and the patient will advance rapidly to recovery."—G.

"Swelling of the submaxillary glands."—LIPPE.

"Tongue sore, red, papillæ elevated."—LIPPE.

"Frequent discharge of abundant, pale urine."—LIPPE.

"Hoarseness; voice uncertain, and changing continually."—LIPPE.

"An excellent remedy in clergyman's sore-throat."—LIPPE.

"Accumulation of mucus in the trachea."—LIPPE.

"Exanthema like scarlet rash; the skin peels off afterwards."—LIPPE.

In the higher dilutions it is especially valuable in scarlet rash.

Dr. Lippe says, "It should not be given in low potency or repeated often, as bad effects often follow."

"After a long paroxysm of cough, he raises mucus, traversed with yellow threads."—J. S. DOUGLAS, M.D.

## IODIUM.

*Iodine.*

Acts through the ganglionic vegetative system upon the glandular system, especially affecting the thyroid and mesenteric glands, lacteal vessels, liver, pancreas, mammæ, ovaries, and testicles. It also affects the mucous and serous membranes, skin, respiratory organs, heart, head, the glandular or secreting portion of the uterus, stomach, blood, and the motor and sentient nervous system.

*Upon the glandular system*, Dr. Hughes says, "Its true action is one of a depressant character, exerted upon the lacteal vessels and mesenteric glands. Giving a sluggish taking up of the fatty elements of the food by the lacteals, and an insufficient elaboration of their contents by the mesenteric glands, and we have at once a most important channel of nutrition choked up and rendered useless. The fatty aliments being those taken up by the lacteals, the emaciation becomes more rapidly apparent than if it had been the albuminous constituents of the diet whose supply was cut off. The action on the glands, of which the emaciation of Iodine is thus a prominent instance, displays itself also in the salivary glands, the liver, the glands of the generative system, and the thyroid. Salivation is produced by Iodine more frequently than by any other drug save Mercury.

"*Upon the glands of the generative system* it exerts a depressing and atonizing influence. The mammæ and testes have more than once wasted and disappeared under its use ; and a diminution of the functional energy of the ovaries makes it probable that these are similarly affected. It has caused barrenness in young females previously prolific, and in full iodism the menses are commonly suppressed, less often becoming profuse and watery."

No remedy has a greater action upon the thyroid gland.

It affects the whole of the *mucous membranes*, but acts more especially upon that of the respiratory tract.

*Upon the skin* it produces pustules and an erythematous eruption.

*The blood* it causes to become thin and watery.

*Upon the motor system* it causes trembling of the extremities. In the sentient, we have illusions of the sense of touch, partial loss of vision, and deafness. It has a great influence over the action and nutrition of the heart.

### *Grand Characteristics.*

Scrofulous people, with a low, cachectic state of the system.

"Scrofulous women, with dwindling and falling away of the mammæ."—G.

"Mammæ hang down heavily, and lose their fatness."—G.

"Acute pain of the mammæ, developed by the inflammation of the uterus; they are very sore."—G.

"There is a remarkable and unaccountable sense of weakness and loss of breath in going up stairs."—G.

"Great weakness during the menses, particularly when going up stairs."—G.

"Long-lasting uterine hemorrhages."—G.

"Uterine hemorrhage after every stool, with cutting pains in the abdomen, loins, and back."—G.

"Premature and too copious menses, with

goitre, dwindling away of the breasts, and great weakness when going up stairs."—G.

"Leucorrhœa, corrosive even of the thighs and linen; worse during the menses."—G.

"Continual empty eructations, from morning till evening, as if every particle of food was turned into air."—G.

"Continual taste of salt in the mouth."—G.

"Tabes mesenterica, with rapid emaciation, night sweats, slow fever, dry laryngeal cough, diarrhœa, &c."—HUGHES.

"Phthisis pulmonalis, with constant tickling and inclination to cough, in the windpipe, and under the sternum; expectoration of transparent mucus, streaked with blood; morning sweats; emaciation; wasting fever; rapid pulse; diarrhœa; and in females, amenorrhœa."—HUGHES.

"It appears capable of doing everything, but checking the deposition of fresh tubercle." —HUGHES.

"Extension of a sore throat along the Eustachian tube, causing catarrhal deafness."—HUGHES.

Membranous croup in healthy subjects.

"Chronic congestive headaches and vertigo, especially in old people."—HUGHES.

Bronchocele from chronic irritation, causing

hypertrophy of the gland. It is the best remedy for this disease we have.

"Emaciation with good appetite."—LIPPE.

"Chronic rheumatism in joints without swelling; worse at night."—LIPPE.

Bad effects of mercury.

Induration and swelling of the uterus, especially affecting cervix uteri.

Face, dark-brown color, or paleness alternating with redness.

## CHLORINE.

Characteristics not known. It is useful in diseases of the respiratory organs, and putrid, septic diseases.

## BROMINE.

*Brominum.*

Acts especially upon the respiratory organs, skin, glands, and bowels. Affects mostly the left side. Most important in croup.

### *Grand Characteristics.*

All the symptoms are worse from evening to midnight, and during rest; better during motion.

Spasms of the larynx.

Suffocating cough, with hoarse, whistling, croupy sound.

Impaired respiration, with rattling, wheezing, and gasping, with false membrane in the trachea.

Much rattling of mucus in the larynx; when coughing, heat of the face.

Extensive hepatization of the lower lobes of the lungs.

"Colic as if the abdomen would burst."—G.

"Loud emissions of wind from the vagina." —G.

"Membranous dysmenorrhœa."—G.

Malignant erysipelas, and boils.

"Swelling and induration of glands."—LIPPE.

"Adapted to juvenile subjects, with light hair, blue eyes, and fair skin."—G.

## KALI BROMIDUM.

*Bromide of Potassium.*

It especially affects the throat and generative organs, lower portion of the spinal cord, and glandular system. It also affects the cerebro-spinal system, ganglionic system, and respiratory organs.

### *Grand Characteristics.*

Anæsthesia of the whole surface, and loss of power of the lower extremities.

"Complete anæsthesia of the throat, so that the finger may be carried to the base of the tongue, touch the amygdala or posterior nares, and even tickle the uvula, without inducing any effort at vomiting or deglutition." This may facilitate the use of the laryngoscope in operating on the throat.

"Blind, intensely painful varices, with black stools."—HALE.

Spermatorrhœa from irritation of the spinal cord, with paralytic symptoms. It is one of my best remedies for this disease. No remedy controls the nightly emissions better than this.

Induration of the womb.

Epileptic fits from sexual irritation.

In spasmodic cough.

In long-lasting scrofulous ulcerations, given in the crude form, it is of great value.

## AMMONIUM CARBONICUM.

*Carbonate of Ammonia.*

Acts upon the spinal and ganglionic nervous systems; through these nearly every organ in the body has its functions increased for a short time; more especially affecting the lungs, heart, muscular system, secretions of the mucous membranes and skin. It also has the power of liquefying the blood.

### *Grand Characteristics.*

The moment he falls asleep he is aroused again for want of breath.

Face pale.

Nose obstructed.

Vast hemorrhages from the bowels.

Tendency to gangrenous ulceration.

Urine acrid, excoriating the parts.

"Violent and acrid leucorrhœa."—G.

Menses composed of black clots, premature and abundant.

"At every menstrual period discharges blood from the bowels."—G.

Dyspnœa from retrocession of an eruption.

"Incessant cough, excited by a sensation as of down in the larynx."—HUGHES.

"Adapted to scurvy and spanæmic diseases."—HUGHES.

Affects the right side of the body more than the left.

## PODOPHYLLUM PELTATUM.

*Mandrake.*

Acts through the ganglionic system, especially upon the glandular system of the intestinal canal, and its mucous membrane. Also affects the muscles of the bowels. The rectum, small intestines, and stomach are violently inflamed by its action, accompanied with vomiting, purging, violent colic, dysentery, tenesmus, and prolapsus ani. The hepatic secretion is greatly augmented, urine dark color, &c. Sometimes it has produced salivation.

### *Grand Characteristics.*

Morning diarrhœa; stools watery and green; or, they may be natural, but exhaustive.

Prolapsus ani from debility.

"Hemorrhoids, with prolapsus ani and morning diarrhœa."—G.

Severe colic every morning, with stools of blood and green mucus.

"Green, sour stools in the morning."—G.

"Flatulence during dentition, with green, sour stools in the morning."—G.

"Black stools, only in the morning."—HALE.

"Severe straining during stool, with emissions of much flatulence; mucous stools, with spots and streaks of blood; thirst, but no appetite."—DR. E. P. ANGEL.

"Dysenteric diarrhœa, depending upon inflammatory irritation of the rectum."—HUGHES.

"Food turns sour, with belching of hot flatus, which is very sour."—RAUE.

Vomiting, with severe spasms of the stomach; vomits bilious matter, mixed with blood.

"The patient is constantly rubbing and shaking, with his hands, the hypochondriac region."

Has an extensive reputation for the expulsion of gall-stones.

"Biliousness, with nausea and giddiness; bitter taste, and risings; tendency to bilious vomiting and purging, with dark urine."—HUGHES.

"Prolapsus uteri; particularly following parturition; with prolapsus ani, accompanied with exhausting, frequent, but natural stools; more in the morning."—RAUE.

## IRIS VERSICOLOR.

*Blue Flag.*

Through the ganglionic system it especially affects the glandular system, and upper portion of the alimentary canal, but affects all parts of the digestive apparatus. It causes increased secretion of the salivary glands, pancreas, liver, and epithelial cells of the alimentary canal; accompanied with vomiting, and profuse watery diarrhœa, little inclined to run into inflammation. No remedy has a more specific action upon the pancreas than Iris. I believe that to be its starting-point of action in the system. No remedy produces such burning agony in this gland, as does this one. All the animals I poisoned with it, had genuine inflammation of this gland. It also has a profound action upon the lymphatics and skin.

### *Grand Characteristics.*

The pains caused by Iris are of a sharp, cutting character, of short duration, and change often.

Headache in the forehead and eyes; more on the right side; with distressing vomiting of sweetish mucus or bilious matter; aggravated by rest.

For gastric sick-headache it has no equal.

Neuralgia of the head, eyes, and temples; pains, cutting in nature, of short duration, with vomiting of sweetish water or bilious matter.

Salivation, with profuse flow of saliva.

"Gums and tongue feel as though covered with a greasy substance."—LIPPE.

Great burning distress in the epigastrium; at the same time the mucous membrane of the mouth burns like fire.

Burning distress in the stomach, with vomiting, watery diarrhœa, and great prostration.

Violent pains in the bowels before vomiting or diarrhœa.

Watery diarrhœa; worse at night, with great debility.

Severe burning in the anus, with watery diarrhœa.

In colic, or, as Dr. Kitchen has it, "Grumbling bellyache," it is very useful.

Cholera morbus, with vomiting; grumbling pains in the bowels, and watery diarrhœa.

Urine very high-colored and scanty.

Seminal emissions, with amorous dreams.

Influenza; constant sneezing; sharp, bearing pains in the centre of temples; light, mushy, painless diarrhœa.—C. H. W.

In pustular skin diseases, especially if on

the scalp, it is one of our most useful remedies.

Use it internally and externally.

## PHYTOLACCA DECANDRA.

*Poke Root.*

Through the ganglionic system it especially affects the glandular system; especially affecting the glands of the throat and mammæ, the periosteal and fibrous tissues, muscular system, skin, and upper portion of the alimentary canal (mucous membranes), kidneys, and slightly the motor nervous system.

A few years since I recommended this remedy to the profession, as the best known remedy for diphtheria, where the pseudo-membrane did not extend into the respiratory organs. Since then I have used it constantly whenever called to attend those cases, and I wish no remedy to give better satisfaction. I can now repeat, that it is still *the best known remedy* for diphtheria, when the air-passages are not involved, its action on the system being identical with that of diphtheria. The tincture prepared from the green root is the only preparation that should be used.

### *Grand Characteristics.*

The patient is of a rheumatic diathesis, and is frequently afflicted with rheumatism of the periosteal and fibrous tissues, or is suffering from the bad effects of syphilis.

Eyelids reddish-blue and swollen.

Granular inflammation of the lids; aggravated in the morning, more especially in the left eye, in rheumatic subjects.

"Irresistible inclination to bite the teeth together."—DR. MERRELL.

Roughness in the pharynx, with great dryness of the throat.

Sensation as if there was a lump in the throat, that causes constant efforts to swallow.

Congestion and inflammation of the back part of the mouth and fauces.

Diphtheritic inflammation and ulceration of the throat.

Fauces, tonsils, and pharynx covered with dark-colored pseudo-membrane.

Excessive fetor of the breath.

Chronic inflammation and ulceration of the tonsils.

Induration of the tonsils.

Feeling as if a ball of red-hot iron had lodged in the fauces.

Salivation, with metallic taste.

Pain at root of tongue on swallowing.

Great roughness and rawness of the throat.

Easy vomiting, without much nausea.

Vomiting of the ingesta, bile, and blood, with a great accumulation of flatus in the stomach and bowels.

Albuminous urine.

Dark-red urine, leaving a deep-red stain in the vessel.

Menses too often, too profuse, with increase of tears, saliva, bile, and urine.

Painful menstruation in barren females.

Mastitis, where the hardness is very apparent from the first, with much sensitiveness (*vide* Graphitis).

Chronic rheumatism, where the periosteum is involved; worse in damp weather.

Syphilitic rheumatism.

## ARSENICUM.

*Arsenious Acid.*

This greatest of remedies acts upon almost every organ and tissue in the body, but affects more especially the ganglionic nervous system. Its action upon the cerebro-spinal system is powerful, but not so great as it is on the ganglionic system. Through the ganglionic system it especially affects the alimentary canal,—whose organic functions are stricken down and destroyed from the inmost recesses of vitality. Its action somewhat resembles that which Aconite has upon the infinitesimal ramifications of the great sympathetic, throughout all the arterial capillary vessels. Arsenic affects these same capillary vessels, but more powerfully, and its action is more lasting.

The mucous membrane is affected throughout

its whole length, but more especially the mouth, throat, stomach, duodenum, and rectum.

Its action upon *the intestinal tract* is so similar to that of cholera, that in an epidemic of cholera, no man could tell the difference. The innumerable follicles of the immense intestinal tract are completely paralyzed, and the watery elements of the blood exude through the relaxed tissues, in immense quantities. But, if the poison taken is large enough, this paralysis goes on to inflammation and destructive ulceration of the most malignant kind; the mucous membrane becomes dry, or exudes a thin, ichorous discharge, with violent vomiting, diarrhœa, dysentery, ulceration of the stomach and intestines, gangrene of the anus, aphthæ of the buccal mucous membrane, violent thirst, with low, prostrating fever.

*Upon the serous membranes* it produces subacute inflammation, with speedy and copious serous effusions, affecting most frequently the pleura, but not so powerfully the peritoneum and arachnoid.

*Upon the skin* it has a profound action, producing almost every form of cutaneous irritation, from simple erythema to malignant erysipelas, pustular inflammation, and gangrene. But the most common form is the squamous and vesicular.

It has also a powerful action upon the kidneys, liver, and salivary glands.

Through the ganglionic system it has a powerful hæmatic action. "The poison acts directly on the red corpuscles, diminishing their power of taking up the oxygen supplied to them in the lungs; and the carbonaceous compounds thus unconsumed, deposit themselves in the form of fat. If this direct action on the corpuscles be granted, many of the phenomena of arsenical poisoning become explicable. No wonder that the blood is black and non-coagulable, resembling that of malignant fever and cholera; that petechial effusions frequently occur, and the chronic poisoning takes the form of a profound cachexia."—HUGHES.

Its action upon the animal or cerebro-spinal system is not so powerful as it is upon the organic system; nevertheless it has a profound influence upon this system, as shown by the convulsions, paralysis, anæsthesia, neuralgia, melancholy, anxiety, anguish, irritability, great restlessness, and even softening of the brain, which it occasions.

It also has an irritant action upon the muscular system, heart, and lungs.

### *Grand Characteristics.*

Rapid and great prostration, with sinking of the vital forces.

Burning pains; the parts burn like fire.

Pains worse during rest; relieved by motion.

"All the symptoms are worse at night, particularly after midnight."—G.

Great anguish, extreme restlessness, and fear of death.

"Great thirst for cold water; drinks very often, but little at a time."—G.

Cold perspiration, with great prostration.

Great loss of flesh.

"Wants to be in a warm room."—G.

"Constantly licking the dry, cracked lips, with great burning heat of the whole body."—G.

White, waxy, pale face, with great debility.

Cadaverous face, nose pointed, eyes sunken.

"Tongue dry, brown, or black."—RAUE.

"Voice hoarse."—RAUE.

Violent burning pains in the stomach.

"Skin wrinkled, dry, cold, and blue; or cold, sticky perspiration."—RAUE.

"Cannot lie down for fear of suffocation; highest degree of dyspnœa."—G.

"The stomach does not seem to assimilate cold water; it is wanted, but cannot drink it."—RAUE.

"Stomach disordered after eating fruit or ice-cream."—H.

Nightly vomiting.

"Violent vomiting of ingesta, serous liquids, with flakes, also brown and black substances, with violent burning pains in the stomach, and watery diarrhœa, accompanied with cramps of the abdominal muscles and extremities."—RAUE.

Sensation as if a stone was in the stomach.

"Diarrhœa of a cadaverous smell, scenting the whole atmosphere of the room."—RAUE.

"Diarrhœa is renewed after eating or drinking."—G.

"Great enervation after stool; the anus burns like fire."—HEMPEL.

"Varices burn like fire, particularly at night."—G.

"Acrid, burning, corroding discharges, often extremely offensive."—G.

Painful lienteria.

"Leucorrhœa, thick, yellow, corroding the parts which are touched."—G.

Thin, corrosive leucorrhœa.

General anasarca, with white, waxy paleness of the face, and great debility.

Feeble cachectic condition, with aphthæ.

"Eruptions disappear suddenly, with rapid prostration."—G.

"Burning, internal or external, in eruptions, &c., relieved by heat."—H.

"Sensation as if warm air was streaming up the spine into the head."—G.

"Neuralgia; the pains are burning, with agony and great restlessness; often intermittent; worse during rest; relieved by exercise."—G.

Chronic inflammations of serous membranes, with copious, serous effusions.

Phagedenic ulcerations, constantly extending in breadth.

Chronic, organic, valvular disease of the heart, with intermittent pulse, dyspnœa, anasarca, hypertrophy, palpitation, &c.; worse towards evening and at night, on going up stairs, from deep inspirations, or anger.

"Bran-like, dry, scaly eruptions, with itching and burning; the latter increased by scratching, and followed by bleeding."—H.

"Poisoning from decayed or morbid animal matter, by inoculation, inhalation, or swallowing."—H.

"Bad effects from China or Iodine."—LIPPE.

"Gangrene, better from heat."—LIPPE.

"Complaints caused by chewing tobacco." —H.

Adapted to lymphatic nervous temperaments, sad and irritable; to dropsical and choleraic diseases, malarial fevers, especially if they have been abused by Quinine.

## SULPHATE OF SEPSIN.

*The Poison generated in Putrefaction.*

"Drs. Bergman and Schmiedeberg have communicated to the Centralblatt (German), an account of the isolation of a crystalline substance, which they believe is the proper poison generated in putrefactive fermentation. This poison, the terror of the dissecting-room, has hitherto been known only by its effects. The substance which these chemists have succeeded in isolating, they call the Sulphate of Sepsin. The London Lancet gives the following details of its preparation. It is obtained by diffusion through parchment-paper, precipitation with corrosive sublimate, removal of the mercury by silver, of the silver by sulphuretted hydrogen; evaporation and purification of the residue. Large, well-defined, acicular needles are thus obtained, which are deliquescent in the air, and melt and carbonize when exposed to heat. They possess a powerfully poisonous action. A solution, containing scarcely more than one-hundredth of a gramme, was injected into the veins of two dogs. Vomiting was immediately induced, and after a short time diarrhœa, which in the course of an hour became bloody. After nine hours the animals were killed, and on examination their stomachs and large intestines were found ecchymosed, and the small intestines congested. Frogs could be killed in the same manner." I have copied this article entire from the Scientific American, believing that it will prove a remedy equal to Arsenicum in usefulness, which it so closely resembles in action. Providence permitting, I for one, will do my duty in developing its therapeutic powers. From the many cases of poisoning we have, in the dissecting-room and elsewhere, of this poison, a good proving can now be collected.

## LEPTANDRIA VIRGINICA.

*Black Root.*

Acts through the ganglionic system, especially upon the liver, intestinal glandular system, and mucous membrane of the colon and rectum.

### *Grand Characteristics.*

"Black, profuse, papescent, tar-like, very fetid stools, generally in the afternoon or evening."—HALE.

Congestion of the portal system, with constant distress in the lower part of the epigastrium, and upper portion of the umbilical region, with frequent sharp pains in the same region.

Congestion of the liver, with an icterode condition, yellow coated tongue and brown urine.

Aching pains in the liver.

Chronic diarrhœa, with inflammation of the mucous membrane of the colon, and hepatic derangement very prominent.

Stools, mucus, blood, and black fecal matter.

Stools of pure mucus, with much abdominal pain.

This is one of the best known remedies for chronic diarrhœa, especially when the stools are worse in the afternoon and evening.

## STILLINGIA SYLVATICA.

*Queen's Root.*

Acts upon the glandular and lymphatic system, lungs, and skin.

Its characteristics are unknown, but has been used very successfully in many chronic scrofulous affections, in venereal and skin diseases, and in chronic rheumatism.

## ALOES.

*Socotrine Aloes.*

Acts through the ganglionic system upon the liver, muscular portion of the large intestines, especially the rectum, and the generative organs and skin. It produces great congestion of the portal circulation.

### *Grand Characteristics.*

Violent tenesmus, with stools of bloody water, great faintness during and after each stool.

Sharp pains in the bowels, with large quantities of flatus with the stools.

"Stools in consistence like jelly-cakes; a quantity of clear jelly-like substance, which may be green or white, adheres like congealed mucus."

"Sense of insecurity in the bowels, as if diarrhœa might occur at any time."—HUGHES.

"Diarrhœa, with want of confidence in the sphincter ani. The rectum seems full of fluid, which feels heavy, as if it would fall out."—H. N. M.

"Fistula in ano; it never has disappointed me."—DR. BOYD.

"Yellow, fecal, bloody, jelly-like mucus; worse when walking or standing, after eating, or passing urine."—J. B. BELL, M.D.

"Diarrhœa at 10 P.M. and 10 A.M."—H. N. M.

"Diarrhœa, pain, soreness and burning in the rectum; stools copious and watery, with much flatus; great exhaustion and faintness after stool, at 2 or 3 A.M.; every morning is driven out of bed for stool."

Hemorrhoidal congestions; the hemorrhoids bleed often and profusely.

Dysentery, with prolonged and severe tenesmus; the rectum is much affected; much pain and faintness during stool.

"A peculiar, heavy, dull, pressing pain in the forehead, of no great severity, but which indisposes to or even incapacitates for all exertion, especially for intellectual labor."—DR. P. P. WELLS.

Dull heavy headache, with dull pains in the liver.

"Falling out of the hair in adults."—TESTE.

Eberle says, "Experience has shown that this drug is among the most efficient agents for exciting the uterine vessels, and directing the afflux of blood to them, and deserves to be accounted the best remedy we possess against those protracted, exhausting, and obstinate hemorrhages from the uterus, which occur in females of nervous, relaxed, and phlegmatic habits, about the critical period of life."

## ARGENTUM.

*Silver.*

Acts especially on the cerebro-spinal system, the bones, articulations, cartilages of the ears, Eustachian tube, tympanum, cartilages of the nose, false ribs, tarsal cartilages, muscles, tendons, ligaments, particularly those in the neighborhood of joints, heart, testicles, salivary glands, and skin.

### *Grand Characteristics.*

"Time seems to pass very slowly, everything done seems done so slowly. She has, for instance, been flowing for an hour, and to her it seems hours; we work rapidly for her safety, and she thinks we are so very slow."—G.

"Moral and nervous disturbances come on in quite regular paroxysms every night, in the morning, or at noon, more particularly after dinner."

"Dizzy, and much confusion in the head."—G.

Headache not severe, but dull and constant.

"The spasms are violent, and are preceded by a sensation of expansion of the whole body, especially of the face and head."—G.

"The stomach seems as if it would burst with wind, accompanied with great desire to belch, which is accomplished with difficulty, when the air rushes out with great violence." —G.

"Diarrhœa of green fetid mucus, passing off with much flatulence."—G.

"After taking any fluid, it appears as though it were running straight through the intestinal canal without stopping."—G.

"Dysenteric stools, consisting of masses of epithelial substance, connected by muco-lymph, and colored red or green, shreddy, frequently passed with severe bearing down in the hypogastrium. On rising, sense of weight in the back. Advanced stages of dysentery, with suspected ulceration of the bowels."—J. C. M.

"Sandy stools."—G.

Sugar in urine.

Ragged ulcers on the prepuce.

"The urethra feels swollen inside."—G.

Genital organs shrivelled; sexual desire gone.

"Uterine hemorrhage, with much trouble in the head, greatly aggravated by motion."—G.

"Bleeding ulcers of the womb."—G.

"She has a presentiment of the approaching

spasm; she is in constant motion from the time she comes out of one spasm till she goes into another."—G.

Great debility, particularly in the lower extremities, with much chilliness.

"Paraplegia from debilitating causes."—RAUE.

Pain in the joints, aggravated by motion.

Dry cough only in the daytime.

Ophthalmia neonatorum, specific.

## SPONGIA.

*Spongia Marina Tosta.*

Acts especially through the ganglionic system on the larynx and trachea, thyroïd gland, ovaries, and testicles.

### *Grand Characteristics.*

"Cough dry and sibilant, sounding like a saw driven through a pine board, each cough corresponding to a thrust of the saw."—G.

"Chronic hoarseness and cough; the voice frequently giving out when talking or singing."—G.

Great dryness of the larynx, with hoarse, hollow, wheezing cough.—G.

"Menses too early and too profuse, preceded by colic, soreness in the sacrum, and craving in the stomach."—G.

Violent drawing in the upper and lower extremities during the menses.—G.

"Smooth swelling and induration of the testicles."—HEMPEL.

"Awakes often in a fright, and feels as if she was suffocating."

"Is inconsolable, and wishes to die at once."

"Keeps the head high up in bed."

"Every day several attacks of heat, with anxiousness, pain in the region of the heart, and weeping."

"Thinking of it renews the one-sided heat of face."

Goitre in persons who live in villages.

## BARYTA CARBONICA.

*Carbonate of Baryta.*

Acts upon the cerebro-spinal system, but especially through the ganglia on the glandular system, more especially the glands of the throat, and the sexual organs.

### *Grand Characteristics.*

Especially suited to dwarfish women, with scanty menstruation, and troublesome weight about the pubes in any position.—G.

To scrofulous children, that do not grow.—G.

Submaxillary and parotid glands are swollen and tender.

Chronic induration of tonsils.—F.

Tonsils enlarged, and suppurate often.

"It is our best remedy in tonsillitis to prevent suppuration."—HUGHES.

"The throat looks pale, is sore, with putrid breath."

Impotence.

Especially adapted to diseases of old men.

"When convalescing from pneumonia, sensation as if the lungs were full of smoke; she smells pine smoke."

## CROTON TIGLIUM.

*Croton Oil.*

Acts on the cerebro-spinal and ganglionic nervous systems; from the ganglionic irritation a transudation of the watery part of the blood is thrown out into the intestinal canal, causing copious watery stools in less than an hour, from one or two drops placed on the tongue. Also acts upon the lymphatic system and skin.

### *Grand Characteristics.*

"Neuralgic pains, from pupil of left eye to the back part of the head."—G.

Watery stools, that escape suddenly from the bowels, with great prostration.

"Colic and diarrhœa immediately after nursing."—G.

"Diarrhœa, worse after drinking."—G.

"Pain extends from the nipple through to the shoulder-blade; every time the child draws at the breast the suffering is excruciating."—G.

Most intense itching and burning of the skin. No drug causes such intolerable itching and violent burning of the skin as Croton tiglium.

Vesicles on the skin, which are red, and burn like fire.

Urticaria of the skin of the abdomen.

Intense redness of the skin, with a yellow, plastic exudation; burns like fire.

Bad effects from suppression of the characteristic eruption.

## AURUM.

*Gold.*

Acts upon the brain and osseous system; especially the nasal and palatine bones. Also affects the glandular system and periosteum.

The grand KEY-NOTES for Aurum, are:

Great melancholy.

The mind constantly tends towards self-destruction.—G.

No medicine produces such great loathing of life.

Sensation of internal weakness.

Otorrhœa; the bones come from the ears.

Ozæna, with fetid discharge from the nose.

Swelling of the skull-bones.

Caries of the nasal, palatine, mastoid, and ossicular bones.—RAUE.

Falling out of the hair.

Nightly bone-pains.

Swelling of the periosteum of the forearms and shin-bones.

Exostosis, especially of the skull and shin-bones.

Craves nothing but sour things.

Nightly diarrhœa.

Induration of the os uteri.

"Great nervous weakness, with utter despair."—RAUE.

"Feeling as though the heart ceased beating for a while, and then at once a hard thump is felt."

The scrofulous element may be often extinguished by gold.

Especially adapted to syphilitico-mercurial affections. In these affections the Muriate of Gold will be most useful.

"Caries of bones, paining worse at night." —LIPPE.

"Hysterical spasms, with alternate laughing and crying."—LIPPE.

## GROUP VI.

| | |
|---|---|
| Ipecacuanha, | Euphorbia, |
| Antimonium crud., | Bismuth, |
| Lobelia inflata, | Robenia. |

THIS group constitutes our emetic remedies. All affect prominently the pneumogastric nerve in its various ramifications. Nausea and vomiting is the great characteristic pathogenetic symptom of this group. Tartar emetic, and Veratrum viride, might be classed with this group, but their more appropriate place is in the Aconite, or inflammatory group.

### IPECACUANHA.

*Cephaelis Ipecacuanha.*

This remedy acts especially as an irritant to the peripheral extremities of the pneumogastric nerve, producing spasmodic asthma in the respiratory organs, and in the stomach violent nausea and vomiting. Its action upon the respiratory organs and stomach seems to be about half neurotic and half phlogistic in character. In the diseases to which it is homœopathic, there is both the spasmodic and the inflammatory element.

*Upon the mucous membranes*, it excites an increased secretion of mucus.

*Upon the skin*, it acts as a diaphoretic.

### *Grand Characteristics.*

Violent and continual nausea, with vomiting of large quantities of tenacious, white, glairy mucus.

Constant and continual nausea.

"Stooping causes him to vomit."—H.

"Nausea, with distension of the abdomen and dryness in the throat; after vomiting, inclination to sleep."—H.

"Vomiting, thirst, sweat, and bad breath." —H.

Nausea and vomiting of blood.

Feeling of qualmishness, emptiness, and flabbiness about the stomach, with profuse flow of watery saliva.

Flat taste, with white, thickly-coated tongue.

"Stools as if fermented, as green as grass, with nausea and colic."—H.

Green, watery, or fermented stools; worse in the evening, with nausea.

Stools of blood and mucus, with continual nausea.

Diseases from eating unripe, sour fruit.

"Continual discharge of bright-red blood from the womb."—G.

"During hemorrhages from the womb, they commence breathing heavily."—H.

"Much distress about the navel, but it runs off to the uterus, the seat of the disease."—G.

The chest seems full of phlegm, but does not yield to coughing.

"Phlegm rattling on chest; sometimes vomited up by young children."—H.

Incessant and most violent cough with every breath, in delicate children, with great paleness of the face.

"Headache, as if the brain was bruised through all the bones of the head, and down into the root of the tongue."—H.

"Loses breath with the cough; turns pale in the face, and stiffens."—H.

"Suffocation threatens from constriction in the throat and chest; worse from the least motion."—H.

Ipecac is frequently indicated in "the sneezing of hay-fever, the violent expulsive cough of pertussis, the spasmodic forms of croup, and cases of half bronchitis and half asthma."—HUGHES.

"Backache, short chill, long fever; mostly heat, with thirst, headache, nausea, cough, and sweat, last."—H.

Intermittents, where the gastric symptoms predominate.

"With every movement, a cutting pain almost constantly running from left to right."—G.

"One hand cold, the other hot."—H.

Adapted to gastric and lung diseases.

Especially suited to the incessant, dry cough, which sometimes attacks children of delicate constitution, suffering with measles.—F.

## ANTIMONIUM CRUDUM.

*Antimony.*

Especially affects the mucous membranes, skin, and pneumogastric nerve. Its action upon the mucous membranes hardly ever goes on to inflammation, but the mucous membranes become loaded with mucus, producing slow digestion, fermentation, &c.

### *Grand Characteristics.*

Thick, milky-white coating on the tongue.

"The mucous membranes are loaded with mucus, with slow digestion, fermentation of food, with nausea and vomiting."—Hughes.

"Sore, cracked, and crusty nostrils, and corners of the mouth."—H.

"Decayed teeth ache worse at night; cannot bear to be touched by the tongue."—H.

"Stomach out of order; belching, with the taste of food, nausea, and hard stool."—H.

"Stools often liquid, containing portions of solid matter."—H.

"Sensation as if a copious stool was going to take place, when only flatus comes forth; finally a hard stool is voided."—G.

Diarrhœa at night, with great thirst for cold water.

"Tenderness over the ovarian region, with nausea, vomiting, and white tongue."—H.

"Distinct pressure in the womb, as if something would come out, with hemorrhage."—G.

"Sentimental mood in the moonlight; particularly ecstatic love."—H.

"The greatest sadness and woful mood, with intermittent fever."—H.

"Child cannot bear to be touched or looked at."—H.

"Crushed finger-nails grow in splits, and like warts, and with horny spots."—H.

"Corns or callosities in the soles of the feet." —H.

"Complaints after bathing, particularly in cold water."—H.

"Cannot bear to be looked at."—BELL.

"In aged people, malformations of the skin, corns, horny excrescences, fistulous ulcers, fungus articularis, obesity, excessive hemorrhages, and dropsical effusions."—LIPPE.

## LOBELIA INFLATA.

*Indian Tobacco.*

Its main sphere of action is especially upon the pneumogastric nerves. "About opposite the pharynx, as the starting-point, it passes in both directions, involving the phrenic, solar, and cardiac plexuses, and finally the cerebro-spinal system."—HALE.

*Nerves of Sensation.*—Lobelia first affects the nerves of sensation. "The pneumogastric being made up of both sensory and motor filaments, the impression passes down the extremities of that nerve, and the brain sends a motor current to eject the drug. While this is being done, the sensation has gone on to the great sympathetic, and finally it is felt at the finger-ends and toes. The sensation is felt most severely in the solar plexus; the depression upon this and the other plexuses of the sympathetic system is such, that the patient imagines that death is about to ensue."—HALE.

"*Nerves of Motion.*—This system is brought most powerfully under the action of this drug. The inferior laryngeal seems to be the first one called into action, which causes a constricted feeling at the larynx; passing on the œsophagus, contracts its whole length; then the stomach contracts from below upwards, and emesis follows. In the meantime the bronchi and chest contract, and the patient feels as if suffocation was impending. Now the voluntary muscles are called into action, and if the drug is carried far enough, convulsions and death ensue.

"*Muscular System.*—This system suffers severely, the whole nervous energies being brought so completely under the control of this drug. The involuntary muscular fibres are the ones first involved, as we observe by the vermicular motion of the muscular fibres of the œsophagus, the contractions of the stomach and bronchi, and the lateral action of the heart. The voluntary muscles do not seem to be affected until the involuntary are completely under its influence.

"In the reductions of luxations, the Eclectics use it much as we do Chloroform, to relax the muscular fibres, until the patient is as 'limber as a rag.' This is why it is of service in rigidity of the os uteri, perineum, intussusceptions, and herniæ."—HALE.

### *Grand Characteristics.*

Spasmodic asthma; worse from exertion; disordered stomach, and especially a feeling of weakness in the pit of the stomach.

Hawking up copious quantities of mucus.

Burning pricking in the air-passages.

Dyspnœa, with a sense of a lump in the pit of the stomach rising into the mouth.

"Increased flow of saliva with most ailments."—LIPPE.

Dyspnœa in emphysema.

Violent nausea and vomiting, with great loss of strength.

Chronic vomiting, in paroxysms, with nausea, profuse perspiration, prostration of strength, with good appetite; lateritious urine.—DR. JEANES.

Sick headache, with vertigo; dull headache,

violent nausea, vomiting, and great prostration.

"Eruption between the fingers, on the dorsa of the hands, and on the forearm, consisting of small vesicles, accompanied by tingling and itching, resembling itch-pustules exactly."

## EUPHORBIA COROLLATA.

*Large Flowering Spurge.*

Acts especially upon the pnemogastric nerve, alimentary canal, and skin.

Its characteristics are unknown, but it is adapted to diseases of the digestive organs, resembling those of Ipecac.

## BISMUTHUM.

*Subnitrate of Bismuth.*

Acts upon the cerebro-spinal axis, the pneumogastric nerve, and digestive apparatus; especially affecting the stomach.

### *Grand Characteristics.*

"Solitude is unbearable."—LIPPE.

Dull, heavy headache.

Craves cold drinks in the evening.

Nausea after every meal.

Feeling of pressure in the stomach after every meal.

Burning in the stomach, with vomiting.

"Desire for stool in the evening, but cannot evacuate anything."—G.

"Flashes of heat, especially upon the head and chest."—LIPPE.

Adapted to dyspepsia, and diseases of the stomach.

## ROBINIA PSEUDO-ACACIA.

*Black Locust.*

Affects especially the pneumogastric nerve, intestinal canal, glandular system, and also acts upon the cerebro-spinal system.

Through its action upon the pneumogastrics and medulla oblongata, it produces the most acid state of the stomach of any remedy in the materia medica. This was noted when I first introduced the remedy to the profession, and all who have used it testify to this fact.

### *Grand Characteristics.*

Excessive acidity of the stomach.

Vomiting of intensely sour fluid, setting the teeth on edge.

Frequent eructations of sour fluid.

Great distension of the stomach and bowels, with flatulency; the intestines distended almost to the point of rupturing, with severe colic.

Dull, heavy, squeezing pains in the stomach, especially after every meal.

"Water taken before eating at night, returned in the morning, green and sour."

Sour regurgitations of infants.

Sour stools of infants; the whole child smells sour.

Desire for stool, but only flatulence passes off; finally, constipated stools.

Dull, frontal headache, much aggravated by motion, with neuralgic pains in the temples.

Low-spirited, with great irritability.

Especially adapted to gastric diseases, and sick headache.

# GROUP VII.

| | |
|---|---|
| Ferrum met., | Helonias dioica, |
| Manganese, | Hypophosphites, |
| Zinc, | Calcarea. |

THIS group constitutes our anæmic remedies, all of them acting through that part of the vegetative ganglionic system that presides over the blood, produce a decrease of the albumen, and an increase of water in the serum sanguinis, and at the same time, diminish the red blood-corpuscles. In health, each blood-corpuscle lives a certain period of time, and after that it dissolves and disappears, and a new one forms in its place. Thus a constant rotation between life and death goes on in these minute bodies, in order to sustain the life of the whole body. Now this group of remedies, especially Iron and Manganese, destroy this equilibrium through the ganglionic nervous system, and more red corpuscles die than are newly generated; causing great weakness of the muscular system, nervousness, palpitation, and a bellows-sound of the heart and large arteries, murmur in the jugular veins, hydræmia, chlorosis, anæmia, and oligocythæmia, with their long train of symptoms. Other remedies affect the plasma of the blood in a similar manner, but none so profoundly as the above group. Calcarea will be found in the Sulphur group.

## FERRUM.

*Iron.*

Acts upon the spleen, producing atrophy, rendering it unable to perform its functional support of the process of sanguification, causing anæmia, or hydræmia; especially affects the blood-plasma, decreasing the albumen and red-corpuscles, increasing the water in the serum sanguinis, producing chlorosis and oligocythæmia. Also affects the digestive and urinary organs, and lastly, the sexual organs.

### *Grand Characteristics.*

"Weakly persons, with fiery-red face."—G.

"Least emotion or exertion produces a red, flushed face."—G.

"Ashy pale or greenish face; with pains or other symptoms, the face becomes bright red."—Raue.

Anæmia, with pale face and lips, with great debility.

"Cannot keep the head quiet; at intervals the face looks earthy and pale."—G.

"Great paleness of the mucous membranes, especially that of the cavity of the mouth."—Raue.

"Face becomes suddenly fiery-red, with vertigo; ringing in the ears; great palpitation of the heart and dyspnœa."—G.

Bellows-sound of the heart, and anæmic murmur of the arteries and veins.

Muscles are feeble, and easily exhausted from slight exertion.

"The bowels feel sore on touching them, as if they had been bruised, or weakened by cathartics."—RAUE.

"Vomiting at midnight."—G.

"Everything vomited tastes sour and acrid; vomiting of food, with fiery-red face; renewed vomiting after eating."—G.

"Vomiting of the ingesta after every cough." —G.

Lienteria, with stools of undigested food without pain.

"Frequent diarrhœic stools, corroding the anus; the face being fiery-red."—G.

"Obstinate diarrhœa, composed of slime and undigested food; the stools are painless, excoriating, and exhausting."

"Diarrhœa worse mornings; bad sleep before midnight."—J. C. M.

"Leucorrhœa like watery milk, smarting and corroding the parts when first appearing." —G.

"Previous to the menses, she has stinging headache, ringing in the ears, and discharges of long pieces of mucus from the uterus."—G.

"Menorrhagia in weakly persons, with fiery-red face. It occurs too frequent, is too profuse, and lasts too long."—G.

"The menses intermit two or three days, and then return, the blood being very pale." —G.

"Much itching of the vulva, in delicate, weakly females, with fiery-red face."—G.

"Spitting blood, with flying pains in the chest."—G.

"Hæmoptysis; better when walking slowly."

"Rheumatism of the deltoid muscle, of a tearing, laming nature; worse in bed."

"Remitting pains; worse at night, driving him out of bed; motion diminishes the pain."

"Œdematous swelling of the body; cool skin; constant chilliness, and evening fever, simulating hectic fever."—HEMPEL.

"Always better from walking slowly about, notwithstanding weakness obliges the patient to lie down."—G.

"General hemorrhagic tendency."—LIPPE.

Especially adapted to cachectic and leucophlegmatic individuals, and to diseases where the vegetative system is involved.

## MANGANUM.

*Manganese.*

Acts especially upon the plasma of the blood, destroying its vitality; on the bones, especially the periosteum; skin, alimentary canal, respiratory organs, and the motor nervous system.

*Grand Characteristics.*

Bones very sensitive to the touch, with intolerable digging pains at night.

Chronic suppurations of the skin, especially about the joints.

"Rheumatic affections of joints, with red, shiny swellings."—LIPPE.

"Rhagades in bends of joints."—LIPPE.

"Skin does not heal readily."—LIPPE.

"Pain, after eating food, in weakly females." —G.

Paralysis of the nerves of motion.

Symptoms are worse at night.

This is a close analogue of Iron, and will be found adapted to similar diseases.

## ZINCUM.

*Zinc.*

Affects the cerebro-spinal system, especially irritating the peripheral sentient nerves and nerves of motion. It also has a powerful influence over the ganglionic nervous system, as shown by the great depression of nutrition. Its action upon the blood is slight compared to that of Iron. Zinc corresponds to diseases of the nervous system, the same as Iron does to diseases of the blood. It is, in fact, the greatest tonic to the nervous system we have.

### *Grand Characteristics.*

"Incessant and powerful fidgety feeling in the feet or lower extremities; must move them constantly."—G.

"The flow of the menses always relieves all her sufferings, but they return again soon after the cessation of the menses."—G.

"During the menses, heaviness of the limbs, with violent drawing around the knees, as if they would be twisted off."—G.

"A constant, distressing boring pain in the left ovarian region, only partially relieved by pressure or during menstruation, but returns again soon after the flow."—G.

"Menses too early, too profuse; lumps of coagulated blood pass away, mostly when walking."—G.

"Sexual desire several times through the night; irresistible desire for onanism."—G.

"Uterine ulcers, have a bloody acrid discharge, but is of itself rather destitute of feeling; an excessively violent and obstinate pain in the brain sometimes accompanies this ulcer. This pain may even assume the form of an intermittent."—G.

"Sudden oppression of the stomach; she has to loosen her dress."—G.

"Great greediness when eating; cannot eat fast enough from canine hunger."—G.

"Terrible heartburn after taking sweet things; much nausea, vomiting, and fidgety feet."—G.

Taste of blood in the mouth, and sweetish risings from the stomach.

"Distended abdomen, with dry, hard, insufficient stools."—G.

"Great difficulty in expelling the stools, which are insufficient."—G.

"Flatulent colic; worse towards evening, and from wine."—G.

"Constant trembling of the hands, with cold extremities."—RAUE.

"Impending paralysis of the brain."—HUGHES. (Hydrocephaloid.—F.)

Chronic sick headache; great weakness of sight; sticking in the right eye.

"Alternate redness and paleness of the face."

Somnambulism.

"Child cries out during sleep; when awakened expresses fear, and rolls its head from side to side."

Spasms, where old ulcers have disappeared.

"Frequent jerking of the whole body during sleep."

Infantile convulsions.

Articular rheumatism, with tearing pains and trembling.

## HELONIAS DIOICA.

*False Unicorn.*

Acts especially on the generative organs of women, and kidneys; also, "enriches the blood through its influence upon the nutritive processes;" and, lastly, it acts upon the glandular system of the digestive organs. Its characteristics are unknown.

## HYPOPHOSPHITES.

These valuable remedies deserve a careful investigation by the profession. Their characteristics are unkown.

## GROUP VIII.

| | |
|---|---|
| Lachesis, | Naja tripujians, |
| Crotalus, | Theridion curass., |
| Hydrophobinum, | Tarantula. |

THIS group represents our most powerful hæmatic and neurotic remedies; the influence exerted upon the blood and nervous centres is of a most malignant nature. Their action is similar to the most malignant fevers, gangrene, malignant pustule, pyæmia, phlebitis, putrid sore throat, &c.

### LACHESIS.

*Trigonocephalus Lachesis.*

Acts especially upon the blood, cerebro-spinal and ganglionic nervous systems; has a great influence over the pneumogastric nerve; also especially affects the outlets of the body, throat, and rectum; generative organs of woman, especially the left ovary; urinary organs, and intestinal canal.

#### *Grand Characteristics.*

Very unhappy and distressed after sleeping.

"She cannot bear any pressure, not even the clothes, upon the uterine region. She wishes frequently to lift them, not that the abdomen is so very tender, but that the clothes cause an uneasiness."—G.

"Very distressing aggravation after sleeping, as if the child was dying."—F.

"Throat greatly swollen internally and externally; discharge from the nose and mouth of an intensely fetid and excoriating fluid; fauces covered with diphtheritic membrane; pulse quick and small; extremities mottled and livid; swallowing almost impossible."—E. M. HALE.

"Sensation in the anus and rectum as if several little hammers were beating there."—DR. EGGERT.

"Especially suited to women at the climacteric period, with frequent uterine hemorrhages and hot flushes, accompanied with burning vertex headaches, and pains in the back."—HUGHES.

"Chills at night and flushes of heat by day."—G.

"Left ovary swollen, with tensive, pressing, stitching pains; inability to lie on the right side, on account of a sensation as if something were rolling over to that side."—G.

"Pain in the left ovarian region, increasing more and more until relieved by a discharge of blood."—G.

"Larynx and throat painful, when touched, and on bending the head backwards."—G.

"When anything touches the larynx, the latter is not only very sensitive, but it is as though it would suffocate him; it also increased the throatache behind."—S.

"During the heat, as if from ebullition of the blood, he is compelled to loosen his neck-covering; it seems to impede the circulation of the blood, with a feeling of suffocation."—SMITH.

"Pressure upon the larynx causes cough."

"On touching the throat, there comes a dry, hacking cough, also in the morning, after sleep, at night, and from tobacco-smoke."—SMITH.

Spasmodic cough, worse in the evening and at night, with tickling in the throat.

"The slightest pressure produces violent and long-continued cough."—SMITH.

Inflammation and ulceration of the left tonsil.

"A tormenting, constant urging in the rectum, without a stool; wanting to pass a stool, but the constant pain is increased by urging, and the patient is obliged to desist."—DR. BOYCE.

Traumatic gangrene; parts deep purple color.

"Jealous, proud, suspicious."—G.

Spasms come on during sleep.

"Thinks she is dead (in typhoid), and that preparations are made for the funeral, or that she is nearly dead, and wishes some one would help her off."—J. B. BELL.

"Want of ear-wax in the ears."—JAHR.

"Pain on swallowing going up into the ear; the course of the pain is along the parotid gland externally."—G.

"Earthy yellowness of the face."—RAUE.

"Deglutition painful, with regurgitation through the nose."—G.

"Nose bleeds a few drops before the menses."

"Diseases of the throat that commence on the left side."—G.

"Cannot put out the tongue but with difficulty; trying it, the tongue trembles."—H.

"Inability to bear anything tight about the waist."

The throat is so sensitive she cannot bear the least touch of the finger.

"Diarrhœa in warm weather, aggravated by acid fruits; worse at night and after sleep."

"Dark, almost black urine."—RAUE.

Frothy urine.

"Feeling of a ball rolling in the bladder, or abdomen, or in both."—RAUE.

Organic lesions of the stomach or bowels, with vomiting of bilious matter.

"Excessively offensive stools; the child always awakens in distress."—G.

"Tickling and jerking, extending from the thighs to the genital organs, with sexual excitement."—H.

"Pains in the uterine region, increase at times more and more, till relieved by a flow of blood from the vagina; after a few hours or days, the same again, and so on."—H.

"Catamenia at the regular time, but too short and feeble."—H.

Cough worse after sleep.

"Expectoration difficult; has to hawk, hem, cough and spit a good while before he succeeds in getting a little tough phlegm away."—H.

Fever worse afternoons.

"With every single cough, a stitch in the hemorrhoidal tumor."—H.

"Cannot lie; must sit up bent forwards."

"Suddenly something runs from the neck to the larynx, and interrupts breathing completely; it wakens at night; spasm of the glottis."—S.

"It has a remarkable power of allaying the sympathetic cough of cardiac disease."—Hughes.

"Much pain of an aching kind in the shinbones only."—H.

"Severe spasms of the legs."

Nightly pains in the limbs.

Spasms, with strange actions, such as "crawling upon the floor, spits often, trying to hide, laughing, or very angry."—RAUE.

Fright from seeing snakes.

Typhoid fever, with stupor, muttering, sunken countenance, dropping of the lower jaw, dry, red or black tongue, cracked on the tip and bleeding, trembles while protruding, dry lips.

"Is of great service in the fainting tendency of nervous women. In vesicular rashes, in pemphigus and eczema of the hands; but most of all in the flushes that occur at the critical age, with head symptoms of insomnia."—BAYES.

Bluish, livid ulcers, worse in the evening; the ulcer is surrounded by smaller ulcers, and burn where touched.

Traumatic gangrene, of an ash-gray color, emitting an exceedingly offensive odor.

This is one of our best remedies in all acute cases of gangrene.

"It is no less important in the worst inflammation of the fauces, malignant diphtheria, or gangrenous, especially of the left side."—F.

## CROTALUS HORRIDUS.

*Rattlesnake Poison.*

Acts especially on the blood, solar plexus, and pneumogastric nerves; also affects the cerebro-spinal system. This powerful remedy has not been used as much as it should be.

### *Grand Characteristics.*

"Hemorrhages from every orifice of the body, even from the pores of the skin."—RAUE.

"Sore pain from pit of the stomach to region of liver, with qualmishness, nausea, and vomiting of green bilious matter."—NEIDHARD.

"Mouldy smell from the mouth."—NEIDHARD.

"Tongue scarlet-red, or brown and swollen."—N.

Yellow, sallow face.

Vertigo and trembling of the whole body.

Violent frontal headache, with difficult deglutition, nausea, and bilious vomiting.

Very severe frontal headache, with coma and delirium.

Very foul breath.

"Hemorrhage from the gums, nose, stomach, lungs, urethra, womb, and bowels."—NEIDHARD.

Fetid diarrhœa.

Great prostration of the vital forces.

Most of the symptoms appear on the right side.

Fever of a low typhoid form.

Especially adapted to bilious remittent fevers, yellow fever, typhus and typhoid fevers, in their worst form; glanders, scurvy, gangrene, and all malignant blood diseases.

Prophylactic in yellow fever. The patient should be inoculated with the virus.—See C. NEIDHARD, M.D., on Crotalus.

## HYDROPHOBINUM.

*Saliva of Rabies Canina.*

Acts especially on the cerebro-spinal system, affecting most powerfully the nerves of sensation and motion. The sentient nerves of the mouth and pharynx are especially and peculiarly affected, also the salivary glands. There is great congestion and inflammation of the brain, medulla oblongata, spinal cord, tongue, throat, fauces, glottis, larynx, œsophagus, and stomach.

### *Grand Characteristics.*

"The desire for stool was immediately caused when he heard or saw the running of water." —LIPPE.

Spasms are excited at every attempt to drink water, or at the sound of water.

Wants water, but cannot drink it.

"Periodical spasms of the œsophagus, with constant painful urging to swallow, but impossibility of doing it."—H.

"Difficult and incorrect speech."—H.

"Profuse, watery stools, from six to twenty

a day, with pain in the lower part of the bowels; worse in the morning."—HALE.

"Frequent spitting."—H.

"Prophylactic in hydrophobia."—H.

"Dr. Hale, and others, have reported cures with hydrophobia, cases in which the stools were induced by sight or sound of running water."—F.

## NAJA TRIPUJIANS.

*Cobra de Capello Virus.*

The action of this serpent-virus is very similar to that of the Lachesis, excepting that "the neurotic symptoms predominate over the hæmatic." The pneumogastric nerve is so powerfully affected that respiration, in some cases, is completely suspended, causing death. The next organ which suffers the most (excepting the parts supplied by the pneumogastric nerve), is the head. It has a special influence over the heart and spinal cord.

PROMINENT CHARACTERISTICS are:

"Temporo-frontal headache, accompanied with great depression of spirits, and associated with spinal pain and palpitation of the heart."—DR. RUSSELL.

Pharyngo-laryngeal inflammation, with dark-red color of the fauces, and spasmodic irritable cough.

"To quiet chronic nervous palpitation, to aid in the restoration of a heart recently damaged by inflammation, and to assuage the sufferings of chronic hypertrophy and valvular disease, it is ranked by Dr. Russell as the chief remedy, and I think I can confirm his estimate."—Hughes.

## THERIDION CURASSAVICUM.

*Small Orange Spider of the West Indies.*

Acts on the cerebro-spinal and ganglionic nervous systems; especially affecting the pneumogastric nerve.

### *Grand Characteristics.*

"Time seems to pass very rapidly."—Lippe.

"Great aversion to work."—G.

"Vertigo and nausea increased to vomiting."

"Headache behind the eyes."

"Every penetrating sound and reverberation penetrates through her whole body, particularly through the teeth, and increases the vertigo, which then causes nausea."—H.

"Nausea and vomiting when closing the eyes."—H.

"Nausea increased to vomiting during vertigo."

"Nausea and fainting; after it, very pale, and sick at the stomach, as soon as she closed her eyes, with vanishing of her thoughts."—H.

"Violent stitches up high in the chest, beneath the left shoulder; are perceived even in the throat."

"Anxiety about the heart."

"Great inclination to be startled."

"Pains in all the bones, as if every part would fall asunder; feels as if broken from head to foot."

Most complaints are accompanied with vertigo.

"Adapted to scrofulosis, where the best chosen medicines do nothing. In phthisis florida, Theridion is indispensable, and effects an entire cure if given in the beginning of the disease. In cases of rachitis, caries, necrosis, I depend chiefly on Theridion, which, although it does not seem to affect the external scrofulous symptoms, apparently goes to the root of the evil, and effectually destroys the cause of the disease."—DR. BARUCH.

## TARANTULA.

*A Venomous Tropical Spider.*

Acts on the cerebro-spinal system and pneumogastric nerve.

### *Grand Characteristics.*

"Especially indicated in chorea-form affections, where the right arm and left leg are principally affected."

Neuralgia of the uterus, with many nervous symptoms, accompanied with sadness and despair.

## GROUP IX.

| | |
|---|---|
| Cantharides, | Asparagus, |
| Apis mel., | Urtica urens, |
| Chimaphila, | Petroleum, |
| Terebinth., | Erechthytes, |
| Copaiva, | Mitchella, |
| Cubebs, | Euphrasia, |
| Hydrastis, | Helleborus, |
| Kali chloricum, | Sambucus, |
| Borax, | Uranium, |
| Cannabis sat., | Eupatorium purpur., |
| Erigeron, | Sticta, |
| Apocynum can.; | Zingiber. |

The above group of remedies all act especially upon the mucous membranes, and may be called the mucous group. Many other remedies affect the mucous membranes, but none so especially as the above group, excepting Mercury.

### CANTHARIDES.

*Spanish Fly.*

Acts especially on the urinary mucous membrane, inflaming the whole tract from the kidneys to the urethra. This powerful irritation is more or less reflected upon the sexual organs. It also affects the mucous membrane of the alimentary canal, but not so specifically; and lastly, the cerebro-spinal system, especially affecting the cerebellum.

### *Grand Characteristics.*

"Constant desire to urinate; passing but a few drops at a time, sometimes mixed with blood."—G.

Great burning distress in the urethra, with constant desire to urinate.

Great desire to urinate, with complete strangury, and tenesmus of the cervix vesicæ.

Cutting, burning pains in the urethra, with ineffectual efforts to urinate.

"Stools like the scrapings of the mucous membrane, mixed with blood, with burning and scanty urine."—HEMPEL.

"Tremendous burning pain through the whole intestinal canal; unquenchable thirst, with disgust for all kinds of drinks."—RAUE.

"Vesicles and canker in the mouth."

"Vomiting, with violent retching and severe colic."—G.

"Thoughts of drinking, sound of water, or touching the larynx, reproduces the spasms." —G.

"Excessive desire for sexual intercourse." —G.

"Menses too early, and too profuse."—G.

"Membranous dysmenorrhœa."—G.

"Sterile females."—G.

"In vesicular erysipelas, burns and scalds, causing vesication, herpes zoster, &c., use a dilute tincture locally."—FRANKLIN.

## APIS MELLIFICA.

*Poison of the Honey Bee.*

Acts especially on the mucous tissues of the tongue, fauces, throat, and neck of the bladder; also slightly upon the mucous membranes of the eyes, kidneys, and lungs. On the serous tissues, it produces an inflammation which disposes to dropsical effusions. It especially affects the right ovary and tonsils, not so profoundly the salivary glands; also the ganglionic nervous system is especially affected; not so powerfully the sentient and motor nerves. And lastly, it causes an affection of the skin, similar to urticaria.

### *Grand Characteristics.*

"Stinging pains in the affected parts, similar to bee-stings."—G.

"Red spots on the skin, like bee-stings, with stinging, burning pains."—G.

"Stinging and burning pains in the face, throat, urethra, ovaries, piles, tumors, panaritium, carbuncles, induration, scirrhus, open cancers."—H.

Stinging pains in the right ovary, which is much swollen, and numbness of the right side.

"Red, and highly inflamed tonsils; dryness

of the mouth and throat, with stinging, burning pains when swallowing."—H.

"Sensation in the abdomen, as if something tight would break, if too much effort was made to void a constipated stool."—G.

"Could bear nothing to touch his neck; could hardly breathe from suffocation."—DR. C. W. BOYCE.

"Greenish, yellowish, slimy, mucous, or yellow, watery diarrhœa; worse in the morning." —J. B. BELL.

"Diarrhœa every morning; stools greenish-yellow."—H.

"Urine dark-colored and scanty."—H.

"Great soreness when touched in pit of stomach, under the ribs, in abdomen."—H.

"Enlargement of the right ovary, with pain in left pectoral region, with cough."—H.

Amenorrhœa, dysmenorrhœa, and menorrhagia, from acute congestion of the ovaries.

"Œdema, or dropsy, without thirst."—H.

"Child lies in a torpor; delirium; sudden, shrilling cries; squinting, grinding teeth, boring head in pillows; one half of body twitching, the other lame; head wet from sweating; urine scanty."—H.

"Very busy; restless; changing the kind of work; with awkwardness; breaking things."

"Much yawning and uneasiness."—RAUE.

"Œdematous swelling of the eyelids, with stinging and burning pains; lids turned inside out, with granulations on their edges; cornea much involved; falling out of the eyelashes." (Use a cerate made by triturating the poison-bags of the honey-bee: thirty bags to one hundred grains of lard. This is one of my favorite prescriptions.)

"Waxy paleness of the feet and legs, which are swollen."—RAUE.

"Skin unusually white, and almost transparent, with ovarian dropsy."—H.

"Incontinence of urine, with great irritation of the parts; worse at night and when coughing."—RAUE.

"Intermittents; 'chill about 4 P.M.; worse in a warm room, or near the stove; renewed chilliness from the slightest motion, with heat of face and hands.' Protracted cases; no sweat; falls into a deep sleep."—DUNHAM.

Ascites; urine scanty and dark-colored; great soreness of the abdominal walls, with stinging, burning pains.

"Diphtheria, with great debility at the beginning; the pseudo-membrane assumes at once a dirty, grayish color; puffiness around the eyes; numbness of the feet and hands."—RAUE.

"Inflammations, with burning and stinging."—LIPPE.

"Dropsical effusions."—LIPPE.

Bad effects from suppressed scarlet fever.

"Sensation as though he would not be able to breathe again."—P. P. WELLS. This may be a key-note for this remedy in cases of hydrothorax."—F.

"Rapid, painful, and spasmodic respiration; aggravated by lying down, and ameliorated by inhaling the fresh air in an upright position."—F.

"A most important remedy in hydrothorax, and also in basilar meningitis of children, after effusion."—F. (See Hah. Monthly, January, 1869, page 242; and U. S. Med. and Surg. Journal, vol. ii, pages 31 and 129.)

"Aggravation from heat, especially in a warm room."—F.

"Amelioration, from cold water, of the pain, and swelling, and burning."—F.

## CHIMAPHILA UMBELLATA.

*Pipsissewa.*

Acts especially on the mucous membrane of the urinary organs, particularly that of the bladder.

Its grand KEY-NOTES are:

Great quantities of mucus in the urine.

Vesical tenesmus, with frequent inclination to urinate.

"Chronic renal and vesical affections, with an enormous amount of thick, ropy, mucous sediment in the urine; sometimes it is mixed with blood."—HALE.

## TEREBINTHINA.

*Turpentine.*

Acts especially on the kidneys and urinary mucous membrane, and on the mucous membrane of the bowels, especially the colon. Affects especially the ganglionic nervous system, and slightly the cerebro-spinal system.

### *Prominent Characteristics.*

Blood is thoroughly mixed with the urine, like coffee-grounds sediment.

"Burning, drawing pains in the kidneys."

"Mind clear, then unconscious, followed by inability to concentrate his mind."—E. W. ROGERS.

"Exhilaration; steep hills were mounted without effort."—E. W. ROGERS.

Griping, pinching colic.

"Pressure in the bladder, extending up into the kidneys when sitting, disappearing when walking about."—HALE.

"Burning in the bladder when urinating."

Congestion and inflammation of the urinary organs, with scanty urination.

"Entero-colitis, with hemorrhages and ulcerations of the bowels, especially epithelial degeneration."—HALE.

"Stools of mucus and water; more in the mornings."—HALE.

"Tongue smooth and glossy, as if deprived of its papilla, in typhoid fevers."—WOOD.

Neuralgia and nervous headaches.

"Great languor and loss of strength."—HOLCOMBE.

Worms, with foul breath; choking sensation in the throat; dry, hacking cough, vertigo, &c.

"Dryness of mucous membrane of air-passages."—LIPPE.

"Burning in chest, along the sternum."—LIPPE.

"Burning in right hypochondrium."—LIPPE.

## COPAIBA.

*Copaiva Balsam.*

Acts especially on the urinary mucous membrane, particularly that of the urethra; and on the pulmonary mucous tissues.

### *Prominent Symptoms.*

Burning in the urethra.

"Yellow, purulent discharges from the urethra."

"Bloody urine, with constant urging to urinate, and tendency to chordee."—FRANKLIN.

Cough, with profuse discharge of greenish mucus.

Especially useful in gonorrhœa.

"Has cured numerous cases of hæmaturia in women."—F.

## CUBEBS.

*Piper Cubeba.*

Acts especially on the mucous membrane of the kidneys and urinary organs; also on the mucous lining of the air-passages.

### *Prominent Symptoms.*

Subacute inflammation of the genito-urinary apparatus, with ardor urinæ.

Retention of urine, and especially if the patient has had gonorrhœa.

"False membranes; thick and dark; principally in the larynx."—DR. HOUAT.

"Deglutition difficult and very painful, water and food often passing through the nose and into the larynx, causing cough, with blood."—DR. HOUAT.

Burning pains in every part of the neck.

"Incessant bronchial cough."—DR. HOUAT.

Barking, croupy cough; throat feels full and choked up.—DR. HOUAT.

For membranous croup, this remedy is being highly recommended, used in massive doses of the tincture.

## HYDRASTIS CANADENSIS.

*Golden Seal.*

Acts especially on the mucous membranes of the outlets of the body; as the mouth, nose, eyes, throat, rectum, vagina, uterine cervix, and urinary organs; also upon the glandular and lymphatic systems.

### *Prominent Characteristics.*

"After menstruation, leucorrhœa like the white of an egg."—DR. BOYCE.

"Dull, aching pains in the stomach, which cause a very weak, faintish feeling."

"Great sinking at the epigastrium, with violent and long-continued palpitation."

Cachectic condition, with loss of appetite, and fainting turns.

"Goneness in the epigastrium; acidity and constipation; after stool, for hours, severe pain in the anus and rectum."

"Old people, with debility."—HUGHES.

"Cough, with expectoration of thick, yellow, very tenacious mucus, stringy and profuse."

"Erosions and superficial ulceration of the cervix and vagina, with tenacious discharge." —HALE.

"Small-pox; great swelling; redness and itching, with great soreness of the throat."

Infantile excoriations in the folds of the neck and groins. (Use the dry powder.)

"Stomatitis, with simple ulceration of the buccal mucous membrane." (The Muriate of Hydrastia acts best.)—HALE.

In cancerous tumors it has of late enjoyed quite a reputation; but the characteristics are not known; probably of a hard, knotty nature.

Simple ulcers.

Simple constipation, of a hepatic origin.

Subacute inflammation of the mucous membrane of the penis and bladder.

## KALI CHLORICUM.

*Chlorate of Potash.*

Acts especially on the mucous membrane of the mouth and urinary organs; also upon the glandular system.

### *Grand Characteristics.*

This may be called a specific for aphthæ and stomatitis; it will cure almost every case.

Heat and dryness of the mouth.

Peeling off of the lips.

Burning, stinging blisters on the tongue and buccal cavity.

Gums inflamed; very sensitive; bleed frequently; sometimes salivation.

Very fetid breath.

Follicular ulcers on the inside of the lips, and dorsum of the tongue; mouth full of saliva; glands enlarged and tender. In cachectic conditions of the whole system.

## BORAX.

*Biborate of Soda.*

Acts especially on the mucous membrane of the mouth and intestinal canal; on the female generative organs, and lastly, on the skin.

### *Grand Key-notes.*

"Cannot bear a downward motion, as in a swing, in a rocking-chair, or in running down stairs."—G.

"Child cannot bear a downward motion, not even during sleep; the downward motion of putting it into the bed or cradle, will surely awaken it."—G. "Or lifting up its feet to put on diaper."—F.

"Very nervous; cannot sleep well; starts at the least noise."—G.

Child has much colic and indigestion, and is extremely nervous and excitable.

"Aphthæ; the child frequently lets go of the nipple; showing signs of pain in the mouth from nursing."—G.

"Very important in many cases of difficult

dentition, and catarrhal affections of little children."—F.

"Great heat and dryness of the mouth."—G.

"Pain from the stomach to the small of the back, before the menses."—G.

"Sterility, or too easy conception."—LIPPE.

"Menses too soon, too profuse, attended with colic, nausea, and pain extending from the stomach to the small of the back; with sharp pains in the groins."—G.

"Labor pains are accompanied by violent and frequent eructations."—G.

"White, albuminous leucorrhœa, with a sensation as if warm water was flowing down." —G.

"Frequent soft, light-yellow, slimy stools, with faintness and weakness."—G.

"Pain in the right pectoral region."—G.

"Acne, in plethoric young females, used locally."—HUGHES.

## PETROLEUM.

*Rock Oil.*

Acts especially on the mucous membrane of the digestive and genito-urinary organs, and upon the lymphatic glandular system and skin.

### *Grand Characteristics.*

"Brown or yellow spots on the skin."

"Red, raw, moist eruption, burns like fire." —J. B. Bell.

"Imagines that another person lies in the same bed."—J. B. Bell.

"Much diarrhœa through the day; none at night."

Stools slimy, with pain in the bowels.

"Nausea when riding."—G.

"Particularly applicable in all gastric trouble of pregnant females."

"Feeling as if there was a cold stone in the heart."—G.

"Labia majora perspire and itch much." —G.

"Gastralgia, with pressing, drawing pains; ameliorated by keeping on eating something constantly." (*Vide* Chelidonium.)

"Burning and stinging in the anus and rectum."—G.

"Raw hemorrhoids; scurf on the anus."—G.

"Impaired hearing; a large quantity of thick or thin wax, which is dry and hard, and of a brown-red color."—Raue.

"Bitter, sour taste; disgust for meat."—G.

"Cold feeling in the abdomen."—G.

"Great desire to urinate, with itching of the meatus."—Raue.

"Itching herpes on the perineum."—G.

"Profuse leucorrhœa every day, with lascivious dreams at night."—G.

"Menses cause an itching in the genitals."—G.

"Small wounds spread and ulcerate."

"Spots on the legs are painful to the touch."

"Heat in the soles of the feet and palms of the hands."

"Fetid sweat in the axillæ."—G.

"Tenderness of the feet when they are bathed in foul-smelling moisture."—HUGHES.

"Deep, fistulous ulcers."—G.

## CANNABIS SATIVA.

*Hemp.*

Acts especially on the mucous membrane of the bladder, urethra, and prepuce; on the lungs; slightly on the cerebro-spinal system, and lastly, on the generative organs.

### *Grand Characteristics.*

"Great swelling of the prepuce, approaching to phymosis."—FRANKLIN.

Severe pains in the kidneys, every few minutes passing bloody urine.

Inflammatory stage of gonorrhœa, with all its painful symptoms; especially, violent pain, of a burning character, in the urethra during and after micturition; strangury.

"Dark redness of the glans and prepuce."—FRANKLIN.

"Light red spots on the glans, of the size of a lentil."—TESTE.

Sensation as if drops of cold water were falling.

"Chordee, and mucous discharges."—TESTE.

"Frequent, teasing, hard dry cough."—TESTE.

Vomiting of green bile.

Opacities of the cornea; cataract.

## ERIGERON CANADENSE.

*Canada Fleabane.*

Acts especially on the genito-urinary organs; on the muscular coat of the arteries; on the glandular system; and lastly, on the mucous membrane of the colon and rectum.

Its KEY-NOTES are unknown. It is a splendid remedy for hemorrhages, from any organ in the body, and for many diseases of the kidneys and bladder.

## APOCYNUM CANNABINUM.

*Indian Hemp.*

Acts especially on the mucous membrane of the urinary organs, and pneumogastric nerve; also on the lymphatic glandular system of the intestinal canal, the skin, and cerebro-spinal system.

"Acts on the system in four different ways:

1. Nausea and vomiting; 2. Increased alvine discharges; 3. Copious perspiration; 4. Diuresis."—DR. GRISCOMB.

### *Prominent Characteristics.*

All kinds of dropsies, with a "sinking feeling at the pit of the stomach."—HALE.

"Irritable condition of the stomach, that cannot contain even a draught of water."—DR. FRELIGH.

"Obliged to sit up; lying down produces violent dyspnœa."—DR. FRELIGH.

"Urine excessively scanty, thick, yellow, and turbid."—DR. FRELIGH.

"Ardor urinæ."—PETERS.

"Watery diarrhœa, or constipation."—DR. ROGERS.

"Skin dry and husky."—HALE.

"Ascites, with bruised feeling in the abdomen."

Hydrocephalus; "sutures opened; forehead projecting; sight of one eye totally lost; the other slightly sensible; stupor; constant involuntary motion of one leg and arm; urine suppressed; vomiting, with stupor."—PROF. RENWICK.

"General œdema."

"In idiopathic, chronic, and asthenic forms of dropsy, connected with a watery, non-albuminous state of the blood, and general weakness of the system."—HALE.

"Hoarse, loose coughs."—HALE.

## ASPARAGUS OFFICINALIS.

*Asparagus.*

Acts especially on the convoluted tubes of the kidneys.

KEY-NOTES not known, but prominent symptoms for its use are:

"Countenance pale, wax-like, and bloated."

"General expression of anxiety and distress."

"Urine scanty and straw-colored, and offensive to the smell."—MARCY and HUNT.

"Palpitation of the heart at night."—MARCY.

"Fulness of the chest."—MARCY and HUNT.

"Rapid, laborious, and sighing respiration." —M.

"Feeble, irregular pulse."—MARCY and HUNT.

"Great languor, and disinclination to physical or mental labor."—MARCY and HUNT.

"Fretful and feverish."—MARCY and HUNT.

"Frequent, painful micturition."—MARCY.

"Pains in the kidneys just under the false ribs."

"Especially adapted to hydrothorax and

general dropsy, where the kidneys are more or less involved."—MARCY and HUNT.

## URTICA URENS.

*Stinging Nettle.*

Acts especially on the skin, producing inflammation of an urticarious and œdematous nature: on the mucous membrane of the digestive organs; genito-urinary organs; mammary glands; and slightly on the brain.

Its KEY-NOTES are not known, but prominent characteristics are:

Urticaria, "when the eruption looks pale, like the stings of nettles, and requires to be rubbed all the time."—G.

"The upper part of the body enormously swollen, pale and dropsical, and covered with confluent, small, transparent vesicles, filled with serum and sudamina."—KING.

"Sensation of soreness in the bowels while lying down, and on pressure, a sound as if the bowels were filled with water."—SHAW.

"Stools of mucus and blood."—LIPPE.

"Insufficiency, or entire want of secretion of milk after parturition."—LIPPE.

"Breasts swell, and fill with a serous fluid, and afterwards milk."—FIARD.

Hemorrhages from the womb, lungs, stomach, or bowels.

## ERECHTHITES HIERACIFOLIA.

*Fire Weed.*

Acts on the mucous membrane of the digestive and urinary organs, as an acrid emeto-cathartic; and on the bloodvessels.

Its KEY-NOTES are unknown; it is used in hemorrhages, dysentery, and diseases of the kidneys; especially useful in hemorrhages.

"This plant, sometimes called Senecio hieracifolia, has cured old ulcers on the legs. The bruised root was applied to the ulcer."—F.

## MITCHELLA REPENS.

*Partridge-berry.*

Acts especially on the genito-urinary organs; on the muscular system, producing an exhausted state of the muscles; and slightly on the nerves of motion and sensation.

Its KEY-NOTES are unknown. Is used in diseases of the uterine organs and kidneys.

## EUPHRASIA.

*Eyebright.*

Acts upon the upper portion of the respiratory

mucous membrane, especially that of the eye, and nasal organs.

Its grand KEY-NOTES are:

"Profuse lachrymation, tears acrid and burning."—G.

"Coryza, with burning tears."—HUGHES.

"Catarrhal inflammation of the eyes and nasal organs, with profuse secretion of acrid mucus from the eyes and nose, with pain in the frontal sinuses."—RAUE.

Chemosis.

## HELLEBORUS NIGER.

*Christmas Rose.*

Acts on the mucous membrane of the digestive and urinary organs; especially on the serous membranes, striking down their functional power, so as to prevent the separation of effete principles from the serum, producing the various forms of dropsy of the brain, thorax, bowels, and cellular tissue, with which it is *en rapport;* also affects the cerebro-spinal system. The ganglionic nervous power of the liver and generative organs is more or less paralyzed. Lastly, it acts on the skin.

### *Grand Characteristics.*

"Urine, after settling, looks like coffee-grounds."—G.

"Diarrhœa of jelly-like mucus."—RAUE.

"Slow comprehension."—RAUE.

"Shocks pass through the brain like electricity."

"Soporous sleep, with screaming and starting."—G.

"Face pale and puffed."—G.

"Nostrils, dirty and dry."—RAUE.

"Lower jaw sinking down."—RAUE.

"Chewing motions with the mouth."—RAUE.

"Frequent rubbing of the nose."—G.

"Squinting pupils dilated."—G.

"Easily made angry."—RAUE.

"Forehead drawn in folds, and covered with cold perspiration."—G.

"Automatic motions of one arm and one leg."—RAUE.

Various forms of dropsy, from simple paralysis of the functional power of the serous membranes, coming on suddenly. HYDROCEPHALUS.

## SAMBUCUS NIGRA.

*Common Elder.*

Acts on the skin as a powerful sudorific, and on the mucous membrane of the respiratory tract.

### *Characteristics.*

Profuse debilitating sweats.

Useful in catarrhal affections, whooping-cough, suffocative; expectoration by day, scanty, tough.

Suffocative attacks; asthma of Millar.

## URANIUM.

*Nitrate of Uranium.*

Acts especially on the kidneys, producing sugar in the urine.

Especially useful in diabetes, and incontinence of urine.

Excessive lacteal secretion.

## EUPATORIUM PURPUREUM.

*Queen of the Meadow.*

Acts especially on the urinary organs and ganglionic nervous system. Acts upon the digestive organs, but just how, is not known.

### *Grand Characteristics.*

"Much smarting and burning in the urethra during urination."—DR. DRESSER.

"Constant desire to urinate; passes but a few drops at a time, and is obliged to make the effort very often."—DR. B. L. DRESSER.

"Suppression of urine, with restlessness and moaning."—DR. DRESSER.

"Burning distress in the bladder."—DR. DRESSER.

Deep, dull, aching pains in the bladder.

Profuse urination.—DR. DRESSER.

Urine mixed with mucus.—DR. DRESSER.

"Dull, aching pains in the region of the kidneys."—DR. DRESSER.

Rheumatic pains in the lumbar region.

"Numbness of the legs."—DR. DRESSER.

Renal dropsy; body and extremities enormously œdematous; scanty secretion of urine, and distressing dyspnœa.—DR. DRESSER.

"The lower belly swollen and hot, in suppression of urine."—DR. DRESSER.

"Excessive irritation of the bladder, with large deposits of lithiates."—HALE.

"Catarrhus vesicæ, attended with ulceration."—HALE.

Intermittent fever; "chill commences in the back, and then spreads over the body."—HALE.

"Violent shaking, with comparatively little coldness."—HALE.

"No thirst during the chill, but much frontal headache."—HALE.

Fever for several hours; nausea and vomiting, with thirst.

"Not much sweat; in moving during the sweat, a chilliness would pass through the body."—DRESSER.

"Paroxysms come on at different times of the day, every other day."

Severe bone-pains.—DR. VON TAGEN.

"Weak, tired, unsupportable feeling."

Night sweats; hectic fever.

"Head feels light; cannot get rid of the sensation as if the head was falling to the left side."—DR. DRESSER.

"All symptoms are worse on left side of the body."—DR. DRESSER.

"A heavy, furred tongue; brown along the centre, and a bitter, pappy taste, with the chill."

## STICTA PULMONARIA.

*Lungwort.*

This lichen acts especially on the mucous membrane of the air-passages; also affects the fibrous tissues, and the nervous system.

### *Characteristics.*

Its great sphere of usefulness is in catarrhal affections of the air-passages, and rheumatisms.

"Excessive dryness of the nasal mucous membrane."—DR. BOYCE.

"The secretions are so quickly dried, that they are discharged after great effort, in the form of hard scabs."—BOYCE.

"The soft palate felt like dried leather."

"Deglutition painful, from the same cause."

"Cough at first dry and hacking, from tickling in the larynx, which finally extends to the lungs."—D. S. JONES.

"In sleeplessness of children, after surgical operations (setting fractured leg, *e. g.*), I have found it to act like a charm."—F.

"It is often useful in cases of insomnia from various causes."—F.

"The characteristic of Sticta in catarrhal affections (nasal), is a constant necessity of blowing the nose, but no discharge results; analogous to the well-known symptom of Nux vomica, futile calls to stool."—F.

## ZINGIBER.

*Ginger.*

Affects especially the mucous membrane of the intestinal canal.

### *Grand Characteristics.*

"Bad, slimy taste in the mouth, with acid stomach and diarrhœa."—M. N.

"Increased secretion of mucus, without fever."—STRUMPF.

"Complaints from eating melons."—EBN. NASAH.

"Vomiting of slime, especially with old drunkards."—STRUMPF.

"Nausea after stool in the morning."—FR.

28

Much flatulency.

Diarrhœa, especially in the morning.

"Diarrhœa from drinking impure water; often in the United States Army; relieved by a few drops of the tincture in water."—TAFEL.

"Smarting sensation below the larynx, followed by a cough, with rattling of phlegm."—FR.

"Urine, increased secretion of; thick, turbid; retention of after typhus."—LIPPE.

Menstruation too early, too profuse; blood dark, clotted.

Dry, hacking cough, with pain in the lungs and difficult breathing; in the morning, expectoration.

Dull aching in both kidneys (sensation of heat in the left kidney), with desire to urinate.

Great sleepiness; coma.

Chilliness beginning in the lower limbs, and going upwards.

Hot and chilly at the same time.

# GROUP X.

| | |
|---|---|
| Colocynth, | Scammonium, |
| Dioscorea, | Mezereum, |
| Collinsonia, | Gummi guttæ, |
| Plumbum, | Elaterium, |
| Jalapa, | Rheum. |

THIS group represents, in the Allopathic school, their most powerful drastic, hydragogue cathartics. In our school, their grand sphere of usefulness lies among the neuroses, affecting more particularly the abdominal plexuses of nerves, and various branches of the sentient nervous system. This may be called the colic group.

## COLOCYNTH.

*Bitter Cucumber.*

"Acts particularly upon the sentient nerves, especially upon those which go to make up the plexus cœliacus. It likewise acts upon the trigeminus or fifth pair, upon the sacral plexus, upon the lumbar and crural nerves, and upon the mucous and fibrous tissues over which these nerves are ramified. In affecting the cœliac plexus, it may give rise to inflammatory symptoms in the bowels; and, in affecting the crural nerve, its action may lead to paralysis of the extremity. Its action upon the trigeminus is manifested by various neuralgic affections of the face, eyes, and head. It may likewise cause sympathetic irritations in the lungs and heart, by its action upon the peripheral extremities of the pneumogastric nerve, through the connection existing between this nerve and the solar plexus, by means of the great sympathetic."—HEMPEL.

### *Grand Characteristics.*

"Terrible colicky pains, causing him to bend up double, with great restlessness, moaning, and lamenting."—G.

"Severe colicky pains, mostly around the navel; has to bend double, being worse in any other posture, but with great restlessness, and loud screaming, on changing it; worse at intervals of five or ten minutes."—H.

"Colic so distressing, that they seek relief by pressing corners of tables or heads of bedposts against the abdomen."—H.

"Child writhes in every possible direction; doubles itself up, and screams in great distress; it cries very hard."—G.

"Feeling in the whole abdomen as if the intestines were being squeezed between stones." —G.

"Cutting, as from knives in the bowels." —G.

Much distress and distension of the abdomen, with diarrhœa, which is aggravated by everything eaten or drank.

"Inflammation of the bowels, in consequence of violent indignation."—G.

"Affections from anger, with indignation, particularly vomiting and diarrhœa."—G.

"More cutting pain in the bowels than tenesmus; with great tenderness of the abdomen to contact; desire to bend double."—G.

"Intense boring or tensive pain in the ovary, causing her to bend up double, with great restlessness, moaning, and lamentations." —G.

"Dysentery, where the disease is located in the small intestines; stools slimy, bloody, like scrapings; during stool, sometimes tenesmus, at other times not; after stool, relief of the pain."—HUGHES.

"Bloody diarrhœa, with violent pain in the bowels, extending down the thighs."—G.

"Dysentery like diarrhœa, renewed each time after taking the least food or drink."

"Chronic, watery diarrhœa in the morning, with pain in the sides of the abdomen."—RAUE.

"Diarrhœa after indignation; stools green." —G.

"Urinates small quantities, with frequent urging; fetid, thickening, viscid, jelly-like urine."

"Dysuria; straining ineffectual; worse before, during, and after urination, which is scanty."—HEMPEL.

"Cephalalgic pain; tearing, screwing, together with great restlessness and anxiety."—R.

"Neuralgia of the face; tensive, tearing, with heat and swelling; especially left side; motion and touch increase the pain; better from rest and warmth."—RAUE.

"The nerves about the hip joint suffer most severely; the pain darting sometimes down the anterior crural, and sometimes down the sciatic trunks, even to the feet."—HUGHES.

"Great thirst."—RAUE.

"Bitter taste in the mouth."—HEMPEL.

"Constant heat and dragging pain in the vagina, with swelling of the labia."—G.

"Does not like to talk, to answer, to see friends."—H.

"Pains in the limbs; worse from slight touching, and then increasing gradually."—H.

"Improvement, from drinking cold water."—H.

Pains worse from motion.

Adapted to choleric temperaments.

"The grand sphere of Colocynth lies among the neuroses, especially where pain is the most prominent feature. It is in colic and sciatica that its greatest triumphs have been achieved."

Also in neuralgia of the fifth nerve, of the solar and other abdominal plexuses, and of the lumbar and femoral nerves.

## DIOSCOREA VILLOSA.

*Wild Yam Root.*

Acts especially upon the umbilical and cœliac plexuses of nerves; and upon the muscular tissues over which these nerves are ramified; also on the liver, and upon many portions of the sentient nervous system.

The grand sphere for the use of Dioscorea is among the neuroses of the bowels and stomach; where the cœliac and umbilical plexuses of nerves are in a great state of hyperæsthesia, the pain and spasm is unbearable.

Spasmodic stricture of the urethra.

"Disposition to paronychia (felons)."—J. B. Bell.

"Steady twisting pains in the bowels; worse when lying down."—Helmuth.

"Cramps of the stomach, with a tendency to eructate."—Helmuth.

"Spasmodic colic, with much flatulence."—Hale.

"Pulsating pain at the upper part of the sternum."

"Great burning distress in the stomach, with prickling pains in it."—B.

"Great faintness at the stomach."—B.

"Profuse, deep-yellow, thin stool, followed by a very weak, faint feeling, without relieving the pain in the bowels."—B.

Morning diarrhœa.

"Constant, heavy pain in the pit of the stomach; worse after eating, and which is relieved by copious eructations of air."—B.

"Spasmodic pains in the abdomen, with unusually severe tenesmus."—B.

"Distressing pyrosis."—HELMUTH.

"Dysentery, with violent, lancinating pains in the bowels."—DR. ROGERS.

"Just before and during stool a severe pain in the sacral region and bowels, of a writhing, drawing character; the pains radiate upwards and downwards, until the whole body and extremities become involved with spasms."—B.

## COLLINSONIA CANADENSIS.

*Stone Root.*

Acts on the abdominal plexuses of nerves, and through them on the whole intestinal canal, but more especially upon the rectum and small intestines. It also affects the liver, kidneys, and heart; but just how, is not yet understood.

The grand sphere for Collinsonia is in neuroses of the bowels, where pain is one of the most prominent symptoms; and especially in diseases of the rectum, such as constipation, hemorrhoids, diarrhœa, and dysentery.

"Obstinate and habitual constipation, associated with hemorrhoids."—DR. FOWLER.

"Severe weight in the rectum, with an intense irritation, itching, and a sensation in the rectum as if sticks, sand, or gravel had lodged there."—HALE.

"Constipation; stools lumpy, and light-colored, with straining, and dull pain in the anus."

"It is in constipation and hemorrhoids, from congestive inertia of the lower bowel, that Collinsonia proves such a precious remedy, especially in the latter months of pregnancy."—HUGHES.

"In large doses, it irritates the rectum so much as to set up a diarrhœa, soon running on into dysentery. It has not been used to any extent in complaints of this kind, but in proctitis and rectal dysentery it should rival aloes."—HUGHES.

"Pains in the epigastrium, in constipation and piles."—PROF. G. W. BARNES.

"Severe colicky pains in the hypogastrium every few minutes, with fainting; has to sit down to get relief."—B.

"Stools are all preceded and followed by severe pains in the hypogastrium."—B.

"Stools of mucus, or mucus and blood, or pure blood, with more or less tenesmus."—B.

"Copious, watery stools, with nausea and fainting."—B.

"Hemorrhages; blood dark and tough, enveloped in viscid phlegm; previous discharge of blood per anum; subsequent costiveness."—DR. LIEBOLD.

## PLUMBUM METALLICUM.

*Lead.*

Acts on the cerebro-spinal system, and especially upon the great sympathetic nervous system. Its action is so completely paralyzed, that nutrition of the various tissues, especially the muscular tissue, is nearly, or quite destroyed. The nervous centres are softened and indurated, and we have anæsthesia, atrophy, paralysis; the bodily and mental powers are completely prostrated; spasmodic pains in the abdomen; contraction of the colon, and obstinate constipation.

### *Grand Characteristics.*

"Sensation as if drawing in from the abdomen to the back, with great depression of spirits."—G.

"Obstinate constipation, the fæces composed of lumps, packed together like sheep's dung."—G.

"Constipation, with violent colic."—G.

"Sensation as if a rough body were traversing the rectum during stool."—G.

"Severe colic, with contracted abdomen, and bending backwards."—G.

"Much trouble with the urine, in not being able to pass it, apparently from want of sensation to do so; the will to do so cannot effect it, as if from paralysis."—G.

Complete paralysis of the urinary organs.

"A sensation in the abdomen, at night in bed, which causes the patient to stretch violently for hours together; sometimes she must stretch in every possible direction, or she feels that she must do so, and this inclination is so strong that it is almost uncontrollable."—G.

"Menorrhagia, with a sensation of a string pulling from the abdomen to the back."—G.

"Cessation of the menses, on the invasion of colic, but they reappear after the paroxysm, or not again until the next period."—G.

"Leucorrhœa, with a continual sense of drawing in from the abdomen to the back."—G.

"Complete impotence, with excessive emaciation, and great debility."—HEMPEL.

"Pale dry skin, with liver spots."—G.

"Badly smelling sweat of the feet."—G.

"Sciatica, with drawing, pressing pains."

"Hectic fever, with dry hacking cough, and great exhaustion."—HEMPEL.

"Chronic spinal meningitis, when the paralyzed parts soon fall away in flesh, and the limbs are painfully contracted."

"Fluids can be swallowed without difficulty; solids come back into the mouth again."—G.

"Long-continued stupid feeling in the head." —G.

General or partial paralysis, with atrophy and wasting away of the tissues.

## JALAPA.

*Jalap.*

Acts on the intestinal canal, augmenting its secretions, producing copious liquid stools; accompanied with more or less spasmodic action of the intestines; with fever, showing that the great sympathetic system is more or less involved; slightly affects the urinary organs.

Its KEY-NOTES are unknown, but prominent symptoms for its use are:

Watery, sour diarrhœa, especially in infants, with restlessness and crying, nausea and vomiting; with griping pains in the bowels, and watery diarrhœa.

Screams and nightly restlessness of infants. —HAHNEMANN.

Painful diarrhœa of infants, with violent restlessness and crying.—NENNING.

## SCAMMONIA.

*Scammony.*

Acts powerfully on the intestinal canal, producing copious watery stools, severe colicky pains, and inflammation of the mucous lining of the bowels. Its characteristics are unknown.

## DAPHNE MEZEREUM.

*Spurge Olive.*

Acts on the abdominal plexuses, and various parts of the sentient, nervous system. Increases the secretions of the intestinal canal; producing copious watery stools, with more or less griping pains; also nausea, vomiting, and gastro-enteritis. Especially affects the periosteum.

### *Grand Characteristics.*

"Periostitis, and swelling of the bones, especially on the tibia, with most violent nightly pains in the bones."—G.

"Boring, pressing pains, coming like lightning, which leave the parts numbed."—G.

Violent, nightly toothache.

"Great emaciation; muscles of the face tensely drawn like strings."—Hempel.

Violent pain and pressure in the stomach after eating most simple things, like broth, milk, bread, &c.

"Chocolate-colored vomiting, with hard lumps in the epigastrium."—HEMPEL.

"Prolapsed rectum, which remains strangulated; very painful when touched."—HEMPEL.

## GUMMI GUTTÆ.

*Gamboge.*

Acts especially on the gastro-intestinal canal, causing violent vomiting, purging, syncope, and death; all the symptoms very much resemble those of cholera. Important also in some affections of the eyes.

### *Grand Characteristics.*

Violent vomiting, with purging and fainting.

"Profuse watery diarrhœa, with colic and tenesmus."—HEMPEL.

Diarrhœa, of water and mucus, with colic in the umbilicus during stool.

The symptoms are aggravated while sitting, and in the evening.

## ELATERIUM.

*Fruit of Momordica Elaterium.*

Acts on the gastro-intestinal canal in a peculiar manner. Dr. T. K. Chambers says, "It causes an enormous flow of watery serum from the first mucous membrane that absorbs it. If its vapor be drawn up into the nostrils for a short time, it is a powerful errhine, and is followed by the secretion of floods of water from the Schneiderian membrane. If it is dissolved in the œsophagus it causes such a deluge of the gastric fluids, that the stomach cannot contain them, and they are rejected by vomiting. If it succeeds in passing the pylorus, a choleraic diarrhœa gushes forth, stripping the membrane of its epithelium, just like its morbid prototype."

Its characteristics are unknown.

## RHEUM.

*Rhubarb.*

Acts on the nervous plexus of the abdomen, and through it, on the muscles of the bowels, throughout the whole length of the intestinal canal; also on the liver, and urinary organs.

### *Grand Characteristics.*

Sour diarrhœa, with cutting pains about the navel.

"Much colic, with very sour stools."—G.

"Very sour smell of the child, which cannot be removed by any amount of washing and care in keeping it clean."—G.

Fetid, papescent diarrhœa, with high-colored urine and distension of the abdomen.

"Colic in children made worse, at once, by uncovering an arm or a leg."—Raue.

# GROUP XI.

| | |
|---|---|
| Asafœtida, | Platina, |
| Valeriana, | Moschus, |
| Valerianate of Zinc, | Chamomilla, |
| Scutellaria, | Castoreum, |
| Ambra grisea, | Cypripedium, |
| Nux moschata, | Agnus castus, |
| [illegible], | Mephitis. |

THIS group constitutes our main remedies for hysteria, and may be termed the hysterical group.

"The ovaries, as the head-centre of the sexual system, must now be regarded as the real *fons et origo*, the fountain-head of all hysterical affections. Hysteria extends its influence over the entire sexual apparatus; from its profound connection with the sympathetic system, may extend its influence to all the involuntary organs, and by its final extension to the cerebro-spinal nervous system, may involve also all the voluntary muscles; but its *original seat* and *constant source* must be found in the *ovaries*."

"Hysteria is as truly and as exclusively due to irritability of the ovaries, as irritable uterus and hysteralgia are to a similar condition of the uterus."

"Hysteria is a *purely nervous affection*, which, being to a great extent hereditary in its origin, finds its *primary seat in the ganglionic or great sympathetic nervous system*, which, in this extended development, occupies the *motor* rather than the *sensory* nerve-filaments, and which thus finally results in spasmodic contractions, rather than in poignant sensations."

"These spasms first appear in those parts of the body and muscular tissues which are in immediate relation with the abdominal, the cœliac, and the thoracic ganglia."

I have now given the true seat of hysteria, and from this the student can, at once, get an idea of not only the action of this group of remedies, but also the organs and tissues they affect.

## ASAFŒTIDA.

*Asafœtida.*

Acts especially on that portion of the great sympathetic nervous system that presides over the sexual organs of woman; especially the ovaries and mammæ. Through the great sympathetic, its action is extended to the cerebro-spinal nervous system, affecting more especially the motor nervous system. It also increases the secretion of the gastro-intestinal mucous membrane, and alvine evacuations. Especially affects the bones.

### *Grand Characteristics.*

"Hysterical spasms, with much trouble about the œsophagus."—G.

"Every excitement that brings on hysterical symptoms, points to the œsophagus."—G.

"Sensation of pressure, or as if a body or

lump were ascending in the œsophagus, obliging frequent deglutition to keep it down."—G.

"This feeling in the œsophagus causes great difficulty in breathing."—G.

"Soreness in the œsophagus, preceded by burning."—G.

"Darting upwards, towards the œsophagus, from the chest."—G.

Eructations, of a smell like garlic or fæces.

"Accumulation of gas, constantly pressing upwards; none downwards."—RAUE.

Pulsations in the pit of the stomach.

"Watery, liquid stools, of the most disgusting smell;" or constipation.

"Leucorrhœa; profuse, greenish, thin, and offensive."—G.

"Menses, scanty and too early."—G.

Mammæ become turgid with milk, in those who are not pregnant, as during the ninth month.

"Excessive sensibility of the vital organism."—G.

"Flushes in the face; constant change of mind; fits of great joy and laughter, or anxious sadness."—G.

Particularly adapted to nervous, hysterical, scrofulous individuals, with venous, hemorrhoidal constitution, and phlegmatic temperament.

Scrofulous caries of the bones; the ulcer has high, hard edges; bleeds easily; is sensitive; with a profuse, greenish, thin, offensive discharge, accompanied with an hysterical temperament.

"Most pains are accompanied by numbness in the affected parts."—RAUE.

"Important also in some forms of tertiary syphilis; especially mercurio-syphilitic affections of the bones and joints."—F.

## VALERIANA.

*Valeriana Officinalis.*

Acts especially on the great sympathetic, and, through it, on the cerebro-spinal system, especially affecting the nerves of motion.

### *Grand Characteristics.*

Excessive nervous excitability, in hysterical temperaments.

Especially suited to hysterical females, where the intellect predominates over the mind.

"Feels a sensation as if a thread was hanging down in the throat, with tickling deep in her throat."—G.

"Sensation of something warm rising in the throat, arresting breathing."—G.

White lips; body icy cold; with faintness.

"Vertigo in hysterical females."—G.

Hysterical spasms, with fearfulness and tremulousness, with palpitation of the heart.

Spasms of the stomach in lymphatic, hysterical women. (Sovereign remedy.)

Neuralgia; the pain is unbearable.

Sciatica; "the pain is unendurable while standing, with a feeling as if the thigh would break off."—RAUE.

Hysterical dyspnœa and chorea.

## VALERIANATE OF ZINC.

Affects the great sympathetic, and, through it, the cerebro-spinal system.

Of this precious remedy, I cannot give the key-notes; but among all the remedies for nervous, hysterical subjects, this is one of the best. I use it for almost every disease with great nervous irritability, with the best results; and hope the profession will develop its therapeutic properties.

## SCUTELLARIA.

*Skullcap.*

Acts on the great sympathetic, and, through it, on the cerebro-spinal axis; especially affecting the motor spinal nerves.

Its key-notes are unknown; but it is a most valuable remedy in many nervous diseases, especially hysteria, sympathetic irritation of the nerve-centres in children, tremors and twitching of the limbs, chorea, catalepsy, epilepsy, hydrophobia, and many spasmodic affections. It is especially adapted to the hysterical temperament.

I once cured a case of gastralgia, of a violent and obstinate nature, in a very fleshy, lymphatic, hysterical lady, with this remedy, after two days' trial with the usual remedies.

## AMBRA GRISEA.

*Gray Amber.*

Acts on the sympathetic and cerebro-spinal nervous systems, especially affecting that portion of the nervous system that presides over the sexual organs and motor nerves.

### *Grand Characteristics.*

Extremely nervous, hysterical subjects.

"Discharge of thick, bluish-white mucus from the vagina," only at night.

"Discharge of blood between the periods, at every little accident; for instance, after a very hard stool, or after a walk a little longer than usual."—G.

"Stitches in the ovarian region, when drawing in the abdomen, or pressing upon it."—G.

"Pain as from soreness and violent itching; the vulva is swollen."—G.

"During urination there is a burning, smarting, itching, and titillation of the vulva and urethra."—G.

Hysteria, with fainting fits, and dry spasmodic cough.

"Choking and vomiting can hardly be avoided when hawking up phlegm from the fauces." —RAUE.

Frequent micturition of copious, pale urine.

Spasmodic choking.

Great languor in the morning.

Cold feet and legs.

"Nervous vertigo, to which old people are subject."—HUGHES.

"Sleep disturbed by coldness of the body, and twitchings of the limbs."—G.

"Hastiness and nervous excitement when talking."—RAUE.

Spasms of the facial muscles.

## NUX MOSCHATA.

*Nutmeg.*

Acts on the great sympathetic and cerebro-spinal nervous systems, especially affecting the generative organs of women, and the motor nervous system.

### *Grand Characteristics.*

"Enormous distension of the abdomen after every meal."—G.

"Awakens with a very dry mouth; the tongue is so dry it sticks to the mouth."—G.

"Sudden change from grave to gay, from lively to serene."—G.

"Excessive tendency to laughter."—G.

"Nervous irritation of the intestinal tract; stomach and abdomen especially distended, and all her symptoms worse after every unpleasant emotion."

"At every menstrual nisus, the throat, mouth, and tongue become intolerably dry, particularly when sleeping."—G.

"Leucorrhœa in women, who always awaken with a very dry tongue."—G.

"Great pressure in the back, from within outwards, during the menses."—G.

During pregnancy has great fulness of the stomach, with difficulty in breathing.

Menses too early and too profuse, with discharge of thick, black blood; tongue and mouth very dry, particularly after sleeping.

"Fainting, with palpitation of the heart, followed by sleep."—H.

"Very sluggish flow of ideas."—H.

"Pains in the teeth, from inhaling cold air, or taking warm drinks."—H.

"Feeling as if the teeth were being grasped to be pulled out."—RAUE.

"Especially adapted to people with dry skin, and who do not perspire easily."—RAUE.

"Spasms of the head and forehead."

"All the ailments are accompanied by sleepiness and inclination to faint."—LIPPE.

"While eating, soon satisfied; headache from eating a little too much."—H.

"Chronic diarrhœa, caused by pregnancy."

"Antidotes the effects of too large doses of Calc. c., in children."—F.

"Diarrhœa, with disposition to faint."—F.

"Suppression of menses from exposure to the wet, with severe pains in the abdomen."—F.

"Sleepiness in some cases, disposition to faint in others, are remarkably characteristic of Nux moschata."—F.

"Diarrhœa, undigested, or like chopped eggs, with loss of appetite and great sleepiness; in summer, with children."—H.

"Menorrhagia; blood thick, dark, with such as have had catamenia very irregularly."—H.

"Pain in sacrum, when riding in a carriage."—H.

"Sudden hoarseness from walking against the wind."

"Cough when becoming warm in bed."—H.

Its great field of action is in diseases of an hysterical character.

## PLATINA.

*Platinum.*

Acts upon the great sympathetic, especially the abdominal and pelvic plexuses, and upon the cerebro-spinal axis, affecting both the motor and sensory nerves; and lastly, it especially affects the generative organs of woman.

The grand KEY-NOTES for platina are:

"Very nervous spasmodic temperaments."—G.

Hysteria, with much depression of spirits.

Melancholia in females with uterine diseases.

"Excessive sexual desire, particularly in virgin females."—G.

"Voluptuous tingling in the vulva, and abdomen, with depression of spirits, anxiety, and palpitation of the heart."—G.

"Mons veneris cold and excessively sensitive to the touch, cannot bear the napkins usually applied."—G.

"Labor-pains are suspended by the very painful sensitiveness of the vagina, and external genital organs; the pains are spasmodic and excessively painful."—G.

"Menses in excess; blood dark and thick, with chilliness and sensitiveness of the vulva."—G.

Metrorrhagic discharge of thick, black blood.

"Albuminous leucorrhœa, only in the daytime, with great sensitiveness of the vagina." —G.

"Stool exceedingly difficult; it adheres to the rectum and anus like soft clay."—G.

"Much threatening of the menses to come on."—G.

"Amenorrhœa, with painful pressure, as if the menses would appear, with pain in the small of the back."—G.

"Metrorrhagia, with sensation as if the body was growing larger every way."—G.

"Ovaritis; the pain in the region of the ovary is of a burning character, occurring in paroxysms, with stitches in the forehead, and excessive sexual desire."—G.

"Great bearing down to the genitals, with profuse menstruation."—G.

"Much anguish; she feels as if she would lose her senses and die soon."—G.

"Feeling of numbness, with trembling and palpitation of the heart."—G.

"Anxiety, weeping, palpitation of the heart, with a numb feeling in the malar bones, as if the parts were between screws."—RAUE.

"Self-exaltation and contempt for others." —G.

"The physical symptoms disappear, and the mental symptoms appear, and *vice versâ*."—G.

"Past events trouble her."—G.

"On entering a room after a walk everything looks small; she feels large and looks down upon them."—DOUGLAS.

Hysterical cough from stifling behind the upper fourth of the sternum.

Old syphilitic and sycosic affections.

Indurations of the uterus.

## MOSCHUS.

*Musk.*

Acts especially on the cerebro-spinal and sexual systems, and upon the motor nervous system.

### *Characteristics.*

"Especially adapted to hysterical paroxysms, and nervous palpitation, even when it has gone as far as unconsciousness."

Palpitation of the heart from nervous excitement.

"Violent sexual desire, with intolerable titillation in the genital organs."—G.

"Menses too early, too profuse, with intolerable titillation in the genital organs."—G.

"The sight of food makes her sick."—G.

"Eructations, with hot saliva in the mouth."

"Eructations tasting of garlic."—G.

"Vomiting of the food, then subsequent vomiting, and more vomiting."—G.

"Hysteric spasms, with fainting; crying one moment, and next moment bursts out in incontrollable laughter."—G.

"Nervous, suffocative constriction of the chest."—HUGHES.

## CHAMOMILLA.

*Chamomile.*

Acts especially on the sensory and excito-motor nervous system, and also extends its influence to the emotional nerve-centres. Also affects the pneumogastric nerve, and alimentary canal, especially the liver.

### *Grand Characteristics.*

"Becomes almost furious about the pains; worse in open air and nights."—G.

"Often gives vent to her ill-humor, in spite of all restraint."—G.

"Very impatient, can hardly answer one civilly."—G.

"Contrary to her condition in health, she is always out of humor, particularly at her menstrual period, when she is headstrong, even unto quarrelling."—G.

Can hardly speak a pleasant word.

"Child is excessively fretful; must be carried up and down the room all the time; is only quiet then."—G.

"Child starts and jumps much during sleep." —G.

"Child wants different things, and repels them when getting them."—H.

Inflammation brought on by a fit of passion.

One cheek red, the other pale.

"The epigastrium is painfully bloated in the morning, with sensation as if the contents were pressing into the chest."—RAUE.

"Severe colic; abdomen distended like a drum; wind passes off only in small quantities."—G.

"Colic, with green diarrhœa and restlessness."—G.

"Abdominal pains, with frequent emissions of large quantities of pale urine."—G.

"Diarrhœa: green, and watery, and slimy, or like chopped eggs and spinach."—G.

"Green, watery, corroding stools, with colic, thirst, bitter taste, or bitter eructations."—G.

Stools smell like rotten eggs.

"Bitter taste, with bilious vomiting."—G.

"Hot diarrhœic stools, smelling like rotten eggs."—G.

"Painless, green, watery diarrhœa; mixture of fæces and mucus."—RAUE.

"Nightly diarrhœa, with severe colic, causing the child to bend double."—G.

"Hot all over, with thirst."—H.

"Burning in the vagina, as if excoriated, with yellow, smarting leucorrhœa."—G.

"Frequent discharge of coagulated blood, with tearing pains in the veins of the legs, and violent labor-like pains in the uterus." —G.

"Frequent pressing towards the uterus, like labor-pains, with frequent desire to urinate; passes large quantities of pale urine."—G.

"Her pains are spasmodic and distressing; can hardly bear them; wants to get away from them; is very impatient."—G.

"Dry, hacking cough; one cheek red and hot, the other pale and cold."—G.

"Tickling in the pit of the throat; causes a scraping, dry cough; worse at night, even in sleep, especially with children taking cold in winter."—H.

"With the pains, hot and thirsty."—H.

"Over-sensitive to open air; aversion to wind, particularly about the ears."—H.

"Face sweats, after eating or drinking."—H.

"Warm sweat on the head, wetting the hair."

Excessive sensitiveness to pain.

"Sour-smelling sweat during sleep; mostly on the head."—H.

"Neither lying down, nor sleeping, nor sweating, lessens the pain; but it is relieved after sweat, or on rising."—H.

"Puts his feet out of bed; soles burn."—H.

"Violent rheumatic pains drive him out of bed at night, and compel him to walk about." —FREEDLY.

## CASTOREUM.

Acts on the nerves of motion and the sexual organs.

Its characteristics are unknown; is used in nervous, hysterical diseases (even in the form of paroxysmal cough, in chronic bronchitis. —F.)

## CYPRIPEDIUM.

*Large Yellow Lady's-Slipper.*

Acts on the great sympathetic, and especially on the cerebro-spinal nervous system, producing marked irritability, or hyperæsthesia of the nervous tissues.

A valuable remedy in hysteria, and many nervous diseases, where there is great hyperæsthesia and irritability of the nervous system.

## AGNUS CASTUS.

*Chaste-tree.*

Acts especially on the genito-urinary organs. There is no excitation of the sexual instinct, but complete prostration and impotence; semen watery and deficient, with utter absence of erections; promotes menstruation and the secretion of milk.

### *Characteristics.*

Impotence, with complete paralysis of the sexual organs.

"Gleet; yellow, purulent discharge; old sinners, with sexual inability."—HEMPEL.

"Induration of the testicles."—HEMPEL.

"Agalactia in young women; milk much diminished."—HEMPEL.

"Premature old age, which arises in young persons from abuse of the sexual powers, marked by melancholy, apathy, mental distraction, self-contempt, general debility, frequent loss of the spermatic fluid."—HUGHES.

Retention of urine, from paralysis of the bladder.

## MEPHITIS PUTORIUS.

*The peculiar secretion of the Skunk.*

Acts on the motor nervous system and generative organs.

### *Grand Characteristics.*

Adapted to neurotic diseases of an hysterical character.

In some forms of asthma it has a wonderful curative effect. "I have found it very useful in the asthma of an intemperate man."—F.

Cough worse at night, and causes great distress on inhaling.

Its characteristics are unknown. Dr. Holcombe says he has found it very useful in whooping-cough, and in many kinds of spasmodic, suffocating coughs.

Whooping-cough, at night and after lying down, with suffocation; convulsions; vomiting.

"Fine, nervous vibrations in bones."—LIPPE.

"Rheumatic, wandering pains, with much pressure to urinate, and shocks."—LIPPE.

Sensation in the head as if it became enlarged.

Headache, with pain in the eyes, and weakness of vision.

The letters become blurred; they run together.

"Wakens from sleep at night, with congestion of blood to the lower limbs."—LIPPE.

"Chilliness in the evening, with desire to urinate, and colic, as if diarrhœa would set in."—LIPPE.

# GROUP XII.

| | |
|---|---|
| Cina, | Cucurbita pepo semen, |
| Santonine, | Teucrium, |
| Spigelia, | Artemisia, |
| Filix mas, | Staphysagria, |
| Kousso, | Terebinth., |
| Mercury, | Sulphur. |

THIS group represents our main remedies for worms in the gastro-intestinal canal, and may be termed our anthelmintic or entozoic group. Worms most frequently occur in debilitated, scrofulous, cachectic children, in whom the assimilating powers are weak, the gastro-intestinal mucous membrane irritable, and in a low state of vital power. The partially digested food undergoes some other decomposition; this semi-assimilated matter in the digestive tube is the hot-bed for the formation of intestinal entozoa. Now, this group of remedies acts especially on that part of the ganglionic or great sympathetic nervous system that controls assimilation and nutrition in the intestinal mucous membrane and mesenteric glands, so renovating and improving digestion, that the whole gastro-intestinal apparatus is enabled to perform its natural functions, and the hot-bed for those parasites cannot exist.

Mercury, Sulphur, and Terebinth, will be found in their more appropriate groups.

# CINA.

*Wormseed.*

Acts especially on the ganglionic nervous system, that controls assimilation and nutrition in the gastro-intestinal canal, and, through it, on the cerebro-spinal axis, affecting more especially the motor nervous system; it also slightly affects the eyes and kidneys.

### *Grand Characteristics.*

Especially adapted to lumbricoides; not so much to ascarides.

Constantly picking and boring at the nose.

"Frequent swallowing, as if to swallow something down the throat."—G.

Scrofulous children are often ravenous for food.

"The urine turns milky after standing a little."—G.

"Exceedingly unamiable; nothing pleases the child."—G.

"Will not lie awake five minutes without crying; it must be rocked, carried, or dandled upon the knee constantly, day and night; the mother and nurses are all worn out taking care of the child."—G.

Tossing, during sleep.

"Short, hacking cough."—G.

Grinding of the teeth, and tossing during sleep; always cross when awake.

Belly hard and distended.

Diarrhœa always after drinking.

Pinching colic in the umbilical region.

Stools mixed with lumbrici.

Itching of the anus.

Spasms of children, resembling epilepsy.

*Santonine*, the active principle of Cina, will generally be found far more reliable than Cina. The characteristics are the same that call for Cina.

Lard, thoroughly applied to the anus, morning and night, for two weeks, is said to be a certain cure for ascarides.

## SPIGELIA.

*Pink Root.*

Acts especially on the sentient nervous system of the head, eyes, chest, and abdomen; irritates the intestinal mucous membrane, causing mucous papescent stools. The cerebro-spinal, or narcotic effects are, vertigo, dimness of vision, dilated pupils, spasmodic movements of the eyelids and facial muscles, and sometimes, general convulsions; affects, especially, the sclerotica and the heart.

### *Grand Characteristics.*

"Dyspnœa; can lie only on the right side, with trunk raised; the least motion produces great suffocation, with anxiety, and palpitation of the heart."—G.

Palpitation of the heart so violent, that the walls of the chest are raised.

"Waving palpitation; not synchronous with the pulse."—RAUE.

"Purring feeling over the heart."—RAUE.

"Trembling carotids."—RAUE.

Rheumatic pericarditis, with violent palpitation of the heart, and anxiety.

"Hemicrania; the pain is increased by motion, noise, and especially by stooping; one or both eyes are generally involved in the disorder."—RAUE.

Rheumatic sclerotitis; pains are sharp and tearing; with pressure on the eyeballs.

"Nausea every morning before breakfast."

Adapted to "anæmic and debilitated subjects;" and to scrofulous children afflicted with ascarides and lumbrici.

"Should be carefully studied in cases of chronic rheumatic affections of the eyes."—F.

## FILIX MAS.

*Male Fern.*

Its effects and characteristics are unknown, but it is considered almost a specific for tape-worm. (Given in large doses of an infusion of the root.)

## KOUSSO.

*Brayera Anthelmintica.*

This has extraordinary powers for the destruction and expulsion of the tape-worm. It appears to act exclusively as a poison to the worm.

## CUCURBITA PEPO SEMEN.

*Pumpkin Seed.*

This acts especially as a poison to tænia (tape-worm), and for the destruction of this parasite no remedy is more reliable.

## TEUCRIUM (Marum Verum).

*Cat-thyme.*

This is a remedy of great value for ascarides, where there is great itching of the anus, creeping, crawling at the anus. Also for *polypus narium*, as a snuff, with creeping, biting sensation in the vicinity of the polypus. Ingrowing toe-nails.

## STAPHYSAGRIA.

*Stavesacre.*

Acts on the cerebro-spinal system, gastro-intestinal canal, genito-urinary organs, and skin.

### *Grand Characteristics.*

"The teeth are black, or show dark streaks running through them."—G.

"Teeth turn black, and cannot be kept clean;" gums spongy, and bleed easily.

"The sound teeth, as well as those decayed, are very painful to the touch of food or drink." —G.

"She is very sensitive to the least impression; the least word that seems wrong, hurts her very much."—G.

"A feeling of weakness in the abdomen, as if it would drop."—G.

"Sensation, as if the stomach were hanging down relaxed."—G.

"Extreme hunger, even when the stomach is full of food."—G.

"The more trouble she has with her gums and teeth, the more constipated she becomes." —G.

"Much pain in the teeth, at the menstrual molimina."—G.

"Mercurial affections of the teeth and gums; caries in the former, suppuration in the latter." —F.

"Pot-bellied children, with much colic, and troubled with worms."—RAUE.

"Diarrhœa worse after drinking cold water." —G.

"Bad effects of chagrin."—G.

"Spermatorrhœa, in which the prostatic portion of the urethral mucous membrane is the seat of chronic inflammatory irritation, which sometimes extends into the ejaculatory canals, and seminal ducts."—HUGHES.

"Sensation of a round ball in the forehead, sitting firm there, even when shaking the head." —H.

"The least motion makes the heart beat." —H.

## ARTEMISIA.

*Mugwort.*

Acts on the cerebro-spinal system, and alimentary canal. Used for epilepsy in wormy children; also for chorea, catalepsy, and somnambulism.

# GROUP XIII.

| | |
|---|---|
| China, | Cedron, |
| Quinia, | Chanchalagua, |
| Ostrya vir., | Capsicum, |
| Polypori, | Salix alba, |
| Eupatorium perf., | Cornus florida, |
| Natrum mur., | Ptelea, |
| Arsenicum, | Nux v., |
| Ipecacuanha, | Carbo v., |
| Gelseminum, | Sulphur. |

The above group represent our true remedies for intermittent fever, and may be styled the anti-periodic group. All of them affect, prominently, the ganglionic nervous centres, producing symptoms similar to intermittent fever. They also affect, more or less, the cerebro-spinal nervous system. Arsenicum, Ipecac, Gelseminum, Nux v., Carbo veg., and Sulphur, have been treated of in their more respective groups.

## CHINA.

*Peruvian Bark.*

Affects especially "that portion of the ganglionic system of nerves which presides over the functions of the vegetative sphere; hence, the semilunar ganglion seems to be the chief focus for the action of Peruvian bark." The ganglionic nervous system is so influenced, that there are produced regular paroxysms of periodical fever. It also has narcotic powers; the cerebral nerves are greatly irritated, which leads to congestions of the cerebral vessels, as shown by the roaring, singing, buzzing, hissing, loss of hearing and vision, headache, flightiness, phantasms, and excessive activity of the sensorial functions. It also affects especially the spleen and genito-urinary organs, and, lastly, the liver.

### *Grand Characteristics.*

The system has been debilitated by the loss of vital fluids, especially blood, semen, by diarrhœa, leucorrhœa, or over-lactation.

Patient is worse every other day.

"Sensation of great distension of the abdomen, not relieved in the least by eructations or dejections."—G.

"Abdomen feels full and tight as if stuffed; eructations give no relief."—G.

"Offensive, painless, undigested stools, with much distension of the abdomen."—G.

Diarrhœa of yellow, watery, undigested stools, with much flatulence, and no pain.

"After eating fruit, undigested stools, sometimes involuntary."—H.

The liver is swollen, hard, and tender.

A good deal of colic every afternoon.

"Bitter taste in the back part of the throat; everything tastes bitter."—G.

"Craves dainties, but hardly knows what."

Ravenous appetite.

"Salivation (years after having taken mercury) uninterrupted day and night, with great weakness, particularly of stomach."—H.

"Menses too profuse, with sensation of great distension of the abdomen."—G.

"Cessation of labor-pains from loss of blood, singing in the ears, and fainting, skin cold and blue."—G.

"Hemorrhage after miscarriage (twins), with great loss of blood; placenta retained."—F.

"She cannot bear to be touched during labor-pains, not even her hands."—G.

"Leucorrhœa before the menses, with painful pressure towards the groins and anus; or bloody, fetid leucorrhœa, with contractions in the inner parts."—G.

"Hemorrhages from abuse of chamomilla; discharges clots of dark blood."—G.

"Heaviness of the head, with loss of sight, fainting, and ringing in the ears."—H.

"Intense throbbing headache, after excessive hemorrhage."—H.

"Headache improved by moving the head up and down."—H.

"Convulsions, with rush of blood to the head and chest, with throbbing of the carotids."—G.

"She thinks she is very unfortunate, and constantly harassed by enemies."—G.

"Full of plans, projects, and schemes, especially in the evening and at night."—H.

"Sleeplessness at night; he lies awake nearly all night, thinking, thinking, restless and uneasy, and miserable the next day."—HOLCOMBE.

Long-lasting, congestive headaches, affecting the whole brain, with deafness and noises in the ears, of a nervous origin.

Neuralgia, the pain is excited by merely moving the affected parts, and gradually rises to a most fearful height.

"The slightest contact causes darting, tearing pains."—RAUE.

"Neuralgia may have disappeared for the moment, but the touching of the affected parts brings on the most horrid and intolerable pains."—G.

Neuralgia of a periodical character in any organ of the body, aggravated by contact or motion.

Congestions of any part of the body, with well-marked periodicity; worse every other day.

"Weakly persons who have lost much blood, with singing in the ears, and fainting spells." —H.

"Weakening night sweats till morning." —H.

"Debility and other complaints, after loss of blood and other fluids, particularly by nursing or salivation, bleeding, cupping, &c., or the whites, night sweats, seminal emissions, &c." —H.

"Very debilitating morning and night sweats."—H.

"Heat over the whole body, with the veins greatly enlarged."—Raue.

Intermittent fever; paroxysms regular or irregular; retarding; thirst during the sweat; skin cold and blue; great congestion of the head; veins greatly enlarged; ringing in the ears, with dizziness and enlarged feeling of the head; sweats easily, especially at night; pain in the region of the liver and spleen, on bending or coughing; urine gives a voluminous, brickdust-like or fatty sediment, or contains crystals of urates; cachectic sallow yellowness of the skin; anæmia, and great debility, anxiety, and palpitation; in miasmatic districts.

"She often feels as if her garters were too tight and loosens them, and as if her waist were too tight and she must loosen that."—G.

"Can only distinguish the outlines of distant objects; when reading, the letters are surrounded with a white border; sees better after sleeping."—RAUE.

"Cough, with a granular expectoration during the day or in the evening; not at night or in the morning."—H.

"In swarthy persons, thin large stools, undigested or not, usually with passage of wind, and sometimes colic, but always worse in the morning; worst sleep after 3 A.M."—J. C. M.

Hypertrophy of the spleen from malaria.

In all affections that China or Quinine is homœopathic to, periodicity is one of the greatest symptoms.

I have included the characteristics of the Sulphate of Quinine among the China characteristics, it being the active principle of China.

## OSTRYA VIRGINICA.

*Iron Wood.*

Acts especially on the ganglionic abdominal nervous centres, and slightly on the cerebro-spinal system.

I deeply regret not being able to give the characteristics of this, the most valuable of all American drugs, for intermittent fever. It is the nearest known analogue to the Sulphate of Quinine, and to me it is the Quinine of North America. In sporadic and endemic intermittents, in my hands, for the last two years, it has been a specific. Have never used it in epidemic, malarial intermittents. I will give the method I have adopted to prepare the remedy, and urgently call on the profession to develop its therapeutic properties.

Take a tree, from four to eight inches in diameter, split off the outer, white sap, and leave the inner, red wood for use. Now saw this red wood into as thin pieces as is possible, so as to reduce as much of the wood to saw-dust, as you can. Then take the saw-dust and thin slips, put into a boiler of pure, soft water; boil it six hours; then strain, and boil it down until it becomes the consistence of cream. Now place it on plates and dry in the sun until you have a dark-red powder. When it is ready for trituration and use, I use the second and third decimal triturations.

## POLYPORUS OFFICINALIS.

*Larch Agaric.*

Acts upon that portion of the ganglionic nervous system that presides over the functions of the liver and chylopoietic organs. The solid constituents of the bile are increased, and the fluid portion diminished. The hepatic cells do not perform their functions, that of eliminating the excrementitious substances of the blood, consequently we have jaundice, with all the various symptoms that accompany it; with congestion, either acute or chronic; and, if pressed far enough, it will produce inflammation of the liver, with enlargement and other lesions of that organ; affects the whole intestinal canal and the urinary organs.

### *Grand Characteristics.*

The solar plexus and ganglionic nervous system are so influenced as to produce regular periodical fever; type, quotidian or tertian; better in quotidians.

Sporadic and endemic (not epidemic) disorders; and in the spring, summer, and winter.

During the apyrexia the patient is far from being well; has headache; bitter taste in the mouth; tongue coated white or yellow; loss of appetite, and more or less pains in the abdominal viscera, especially the liver.

Head feels light and hollow, with deep, frontal headache and faintness.

Chill alternates with the fever several times a day.

Not much thirst.

More or less organic lesions of the liver and abdominal viscera, with anæmia and sallow, jaundiced condition of the skin.

Intermissions very short; almost continued fever.

Urine thick and high-colored, or red and scanty.

Perfect loss of appetite; pale and anæmic.

Loose, papescent stools, without pain.

Ravenous appetite.

Lienteria; stools undigested.

Bowels inclined to be torpid, or loose, papescent, mucous stools.

Stools of pure mucus, or mucus and blood, and bile, with great faintness and distress in the solar plexus, after stool, from portal congestion.

Intermittent diarrhœa or dysentery.

Nausea, and sometimes vomiting.

Chill, light and short; fever, long, and followed by slight perspiration.

Great languor, with severe aching pains in the large joints and bones of the back and legs.

Great aching distress in all the large joints.

Hectic chills and fever, in consumptives.

Sick headache, from organic lesions of the liver.

Periodical headache and facial neuralgia.

Bilious temperaments.

The effects of the Polyporus Pinicola are so similar, that it is useless to take up more space with it.

## EUPATORIUM PERFOLIATUM.

*Boneset.*

Dr. Dunham says: "Its great action is upon the muscular system (or fibrous tissues), producing great *soreness* and *aching;* and upon the gastro-hepatic system, producing a condition resembling what is known as a bilious state." It affects the whole alimentary canal, producing green, bilious stools; it also affects the kidneys, skin, and bronchial mucous membrane.

### *Grand Characteristics.*

Its great field of action is in bilious intermittents, with the following characteristics:

"Intolerable aching in the back and legs, as if the bones were broken."—G.

Severe, aching distress, and soreness of the limbs.

"Painful soreness of both wrists, as if broken or dislocated."—G.

"Calves of the legs feel as though they had been beaten; soreness and swelling of the feet." —Dr. Dunham.

"These pains make the patient very restless; chill comes on in the morning; thirst several hours before the chill, which continues during the chill and heat."—Hale.

"Vomiting at the conclusion of the chill."

"Profuse perspiration."—F.

"Little or no sweat at any time during the disease."—HALE—DR. GRAY.

"Great deal of shivering and trembling during the chill."—DR. GRAY.

"Heavy chill early in the morning of one day, and a light chill about noon the next day."—DR. GRAY.

"Vomiting of whatever is taken into the stomach, and of bile."—DR. GRAY.

"Vomiting of a green liquid; several quarts at a time; with frequent, green, watery stools, cramps, and terrible thirst."—DR. GRAY.

"Vomiting of bile, with great tenderness in the epigastrium, and trembling."

Nausea; frequent efforts to vomit; extreme tenderness in the epigastrium, with fulness and tenderness in the hepatic region, from portal congestion.

Paroxysm terminates with vomiting.

Tongue coated thickly, yellow.

"Urine scanty; dark mahogany color."—HALE.

"Violent headache during the paroxysm."

Head very sore and painful, as if bruised.

"Soreness of the eyeballs."—DR. DUNHAM.

"Great weakness and faintness during the fever."—DOUGLAS.

"Dyspnœa very great, obliging the patient

to lie with his head and shoulders very high." —NEIDHARD.

"Influenza; great pain in the back and limbs; lassitude; skin bathed in perspiration; is pale and morbidly sensitive, and the excretion of a passive kind."—RAUE.

Coldness during nocturnal perspiration.

## NATRUM MURIATICUM.

*Chloride of Sodium.*

Salt acts especially on the blood, lymphatic vessels, and glandular system. On the blood, it causes a dyscrasia, resembling very closely a scorbutic disorganization, with disposition to angry eruptions, ulcers, and inflammations. On the lymphatic system, it deteriorates its fluid, leading to disintegration of the tissues. It increases the secretions of the glandular system. "Salt, which is a normal constituent of the animal body, especially of the blood, by which circumstance it is made evident that this agent is necessary to the animal body, is a local excitant, causing a very considerable degree of local irritation; a moderate quantity of it taken internally, excites the mucous membranes and muscular fibres of the primæ viæ, promotes their secretions, the peristaltic motions of the intestines, and the digestion; in a large dose, it causes burning and pain in the fauces and stomach, thirst, dryness, and redness of the mucous lining, desire to vomit; in still larger doses, it causes vomiting and diarrhœa, which may terminate in fatal inflammation of the mucous membrane of the stomach and intestines." It also produces vascular enlargement of the spleen; lastly, it affects the genito-urinary organs, and the skin.

### *Grand Characteristics.*

In inveterate, badly treated, or recent cases of intermittent fever.

"There soon appears an eruption of hydroa, or fever blisters, which cover, like pearls, the upper and lower lip."—RAUE.

"Lips dry, cracked; upper lip swollen; breaks out around the mouth."—H.

"Hard chill about 11 A.M., with great thirst, which continues through all stages; the heat is characterized by the most violent headache."—RAUE.

"White-coated tongue, or map tongue."——RAUE.

Sallow complexion.

Pressure and distension of the stomach.

"Scorbutic, putrid inflammation of the gums; bloody saliva, and difficulty of talking, as if the organs of speech were weak."—RAUE.

"Great complaints about the dryness of the tongue, which is not very dry."—L.

"Losing of flesh while living well."—H.

"When the throat and neck of children emaciate rapidly, particularly during summer complaint."—H.

"Great aversion to bread, of which she was once very fond."—H.

Bread is disgusting to the patient.

"Feeling of great hunger, as if the stomach was empty, but no appetite."—G.

"Very much nausea, particularly in females using much salt food."—G.

"She always has heartburn after eating." —G.

"Great longing for salt."—G.

"Excoriating diarrhœa like water, only in the daytime."—G.

"Constipation, with sensation of contraction of the anus."—G.

"Difficult expulsion of stool, fissuring the anus, with flow of blood, leaving a sensation of much soreness in the anus."—G.

"Ripping up sensation in the anus after stool."—G.

"Severe cutting pains in the urethra after micturition."—G.

"This remedy is indicated in females, whose menses delay and decrease more and more, and every morning they awaken with a violent headache."—G.

"Very sad and gloomy during the menses,

with much palpitation of the heart, and morning headache."—G.

"Terrible sadness during the menses."—G.

"At the menstrual nisus, sweet risings from the stomach, and spitting of bloody saliva."—G.

"Pressing and pushing toward the genital organs every morning; she has to sit down to prevent prolapsus uteri."—G.

"Greenish leucorrhœa, particularly when walking in the morning."—G.

"Uterine cramps, with burning and cutting in the groins."—G.

"Very sad during labor; pains feeble."—G.

"Chlorosis, chronic cases; cachectic individuals, with dead dirty skin; frequent palpitation and fluttering of the heart; oppression and anxiety in the chest."—G.

"Dryness of the vagina, which is painful during an embrace."—G.

"Much itching of the vulva, with pimples on the mons veneris."—G.

"Falling off of the hair from the mons veneris and labia majora."—G.

"Dreams at night of robbers being in the room, so vividly, that she will not be satisfied till the house has been searched."—G.

"Somnambulistic rising, and sitting about the room."—G.

"Headache, as if bursting; beating, or

stitches through to the neck and chest, with heat in head, red face, nausea and vomiting before, during, and after catamenia, or during the fever stage, decreasing gradually after the sweat."—B.

Awakens every morning with a violent, bursting headache.

"Great inclination to weep, with great debility and great thirst."—G.

"Thin, watery, excoriating discharges from the eyes, after the abuse of Nitrate of Silver."—G.

"Excessively sore, red, disgusting eyelids."—Raue.

"After great bodily exertion, an itching, nettle-rash appears."—H.

"Hangnails; skin around the nails dry and cracked."—H.

"Painful contractions of the hamstrings."—H.

"After all kinds of cauterizations with Nitrate of Silver."—H.

## CEDRON.

Acts especially on the cerebro-spinal system, and the kidneys; slightly on the bowels.

### *Grand Characteristics.*

Is considered a specific for the bites of the venomous serpents of South America.

Intermittent fevers, in low, marshy regions; in warm seasons, the paroxysms are accompanied by violent cerebral symptoms.

The paroxysms are quotidian, or tertian, in the afternoons, or evenings.

The chills and shivering generally very strong, with cramps, and tearing pains in the upper and lower extremities.

"Palpitation of the heart, and hurried respiration, with severe headache."—MARCY and HUNT.

Dry heat, followed by profuse perspiration.

"Numb, dead feeling in the legs; they feel enlarged."—MARCY and HUNT.

"Entire body feels numb."—MARCY and HUNT.

"Profuse secretion of urine."—MARCY and HUNT.

"Urine throws down a bran-like sediment."

"Urine very high-colored."—MARCY and HUNT.

"Great deal of pain in the kidneys."—MARCY and HUNT.

## CHANCHALAGUA.

*Chironia Chilensis.*

I know nothing specific about this remedy, but it is claimed to be a most valuable remedy in ague.

## CAPSICUM ANNUUM.

*Cayenne Pepper.*

Acts on the mucous membrane of the alimentary canal, especially the throat; also on the genito-urinary organs, and ganglionic nervous system.

### *Grand Characteristics.*

Burning and smarting, as though Cayenne pepper were sprinkled on the parts.

Throat smarts as if from Cayenne pepper, with sensation of constriction on swallowing.

"It has long been regarded as an efficient remedy in cynanche maligna and scarlatina anginosa."—MARCY and HUNT.

"It promotes the separations of the sloughs, and improves the constitutional symptoms."

"Equally efficacious in removing false membrane from tonsils, in torpid forms of diphtheria."—F.

"Its extraordinary power to control the capillary circulation, to bring excess of blood, and thence to scatter more than it has brought, enables it to remove congestions, to reduce swellings, as promptly and effectually as Belladonna."—MARCY and HUNT.

Excessive burning and soreness in the mouth and throat, with much congestion of the mucous membrane.

"Diarrhœa, with severe burning in the

lower part of the rectum, continued after stool."—G.

Intense burning along the urethral canal.

"Intermittent fever, in flabby, mucous constitutions; chill predominant; thirst in the chill, or during the chill and heat; much pain in the back and limbs; slimy, burning stools." —MARCY and HUNT.

Chilliness in the back.—G.

"Much flatulent distension of the abdomen."—G.

"Coldness of the scrotum, with impotence; atrophy of the testes, and shrivelled spermatic cord."—HEMPEL.

## SALIX ALBA.

*White Willow.*

Affects the ganglionic nervous system, similar to intermittent fever, and is a very efficient remedy in this disease. Its characteristics are unknown.

## CORNUS FLORIDA.

*Dogwood.*

Acts especially on the gastro-intestinal canal, producing nausea, vomiting, violent pain in the bowels, purging and general derangement of the digestive organs. Through the ganglionic system it causes chills, fever, colliquative sweats; depression of the vital forces and loss of tonicity of the heart, and of the muscular fibre in general.

***Grand Characteristics.***

Its main sphere of usefulness is in intermittent and bilious fevers.

"Paroxysms preceded for days by sleepiness, dull heavy headache, and sluggish flow of ideas."

"Chill, with cold clammy skin."—HALE.

"Fever, with hot, moist skin, cerebral fulness, stupor, and violent, dull headache."—HALE.

"Nausea, vomiting, bilious watery diarrhœa, and violent pains in the bowels."—HALE.

"General debility from loss of fluids and night sweats."—HALE.

"Indigestion, with distressing heartburn."—HALE.

Its action is very similar to that of China.

## PTELEA TRIFOLIATA.

*Wafer Ash.*

My friend, Prof. E. M. Hale, of Chicago, writes me the following, in regard to the action of Ptelea. I give his letter in full.

CHICAGO, November 14, 1868.

MY DEAR DOCTOR BURT:

It is quite impossible for me to give you the information you want relative to Ptelea.

I *think*, however, it acts mainly on the *skin* and

*mucous membranes*, and that a majority of its symptoms arise from that source.

It causes scaly eruptions, *ptyriasis versicolor.*

It causes the worst form of dyspepsia, with alternating *canine hunger*, and disgust for food.

Some of the provers think it causes *profound depression of spirits*, others *great exhilaration of spirits.*

The monograph will be published soon in the "Massachusetts State Transactions."

I think it will prove a valued polychrest, but needs confirmation.

Yours, truly,

E. M. HALE.

It has decided anti-periodic properties.—B.

(The full proving of Ptelea may be found in the Transactions of the American Hom. Institute for 1868.)

## GROUP XIV.

| | |
|---|---|
| Secale cornutum, | Senecio aurens, |
| Ustilago madis, | Cinnamonum, |
| Pulsatilla, | Millefolium, |
| Sepia, | Caulophyllum, |
| Kreosote, | Tanacetum, |
| Sabina, | Gossypium, |
| Hamamelis, | Belladonna, |
| Trillium, | Cimicifuga, |
| Cyclamen, | Platina, |
| Crocus, | Borax, |
| Thlaspi, | Calcarea. |

THIS group especially affects the female organs of generation: the ovaries and their appendages (Fallopian tubes, uterus, vagina, and mammæ), and may be called the female group.

### SECALE CORNUTUM.

*Spurred Rye.*

The toxical action of Secale is directed against both the blood and the nervous system. "Whether the toxication of the blood is prior to the violent irritation of the nervous system, or whether the disorganizing action of the poison reaches the blood from the nervous centres, seems, to some extent, immaterial in a therapeutic point of view." Acts most powerfully on the cerebro-spinal and ganglionic nervous system.

Wibmer says: "At first the patients only complain of languor, and of formication in the tips of the toes and fingers, which sometimes look blackish-blue in some places. Frequently it commences with nausea, violent vomiting, and pains in the stomach; the abdomen becomes distended and hard; the head feels heavy, dizzy; the senses become blunted. At a later period the patients are attacked with violent convulsions of the hands, feet, knees, shoulders, elbows, mouth, lips, and tongue. These shift from one side of the body to the other, and are generally accompanied by intolerable pains; at times by a burning heat, and at other times by chilliness; sometimes they abate periodically, and then return again; sometimes the spasms assume the form of emprosthotonos; at other times, that of opisthotonos. These convulsions most frequently terminate in epilepsy. They are very destructive to children. Between the paroxysms the patients lie in an uninterrupted sopor; after the paroxysms, most of them manifest a craving for food, without being able to satisfy themselves. They are exceedingly feeble and languid; complain of dizziness and hardness of hearing; their limbs are rigid and motionless. Sometimes they are attacked with violent diarrhœa; the tongue swells very much; the secretion of saliva is increased; the eyes frequently become covered with a thick mist, so that the patients become blind, or see double. Their mental faculties are disturbed; melancholy, madness, intoxication, set in; the vertigo increases; the pains now cease; sensibility is extinguished. The hands and feet are sometimes covered with spots resembling flea-bites; they dry up, as it were; the skin turns black, wrinkles; whole extremities sometimes become gangrened and fall off. In this way the patients sometimes escape death, dragging their mutilated bodies about for months and even years afterwards. Many, however, die within nine or twelve weeks. A number had relapses after the lapse of a year; most frequently in the months of January or February."

"It was observed, in various epidemics, that the convulsions and pain in the limbs, with stupor, would prevail; and, in other epidemics, gangrene of the extremities; hence the distinction between *convulsive* and *gangrenous* ergotism."

It will be seen by this, that Secale vitiates the reproductive process, in its very beginning, and poisons the very fountains of life, and is adapted to deep-seated, inveterate affections of the reproductive sphere.

The most remarkable feature of the physiopathological action of Secale, is upon the female sexual system.

Wibmer says of it: "Numerous experiments show that it excites the uterus to contract, and that, in ten to fifteen minutes after its exhibition, it causes the uterus to contract, and expels the fœtus and placenta, without injury either to the uterus or the fœtus, unless the drug is given in too large a dose, or at an improper period. It is especially during labor that it manifests this power of exciting uterine contractions. The continued use of this drug may, likewise, cause miscarriage. In animals that were killed by Secale, the uterus and its ligaments were found inflamed, and an effusion of blood had taken place in the uterus, as well as in the vagina; the fœtus was destroyed by asphyxia, in consequence of the excessive contractions."

"Diet found, in his experiments upon animals, blood was discharged from the uterus, even when unimpregnated."

Also, has a powerful action on the bloodvessels of the spinal cord; diminishing the amount of blood in the spinal cord, and its membranes.

Brown-Sequard says: "The two remedies most powerful in diminishing congestion of the spinal cord, are Belladonna and Secale."

"These two remedies are powerful excitants of unstriped muscular fibres in the bloodvessels, in the uterus, in the bowels, and in the iris."

### *Grand Characteristics.*

"This remedy is often indicated in thin, scrawny women, and in those who are afflicted with melancholy, anguish, dread of death; with constant sensation of pressure and bearing-down sensation in the uterus."—G.

"The patient is of a passive character; of thin, scrawny, cachectic appearance, and subject to passive hemorrhages."—G.

"Passive hemorrhages; in feeble, cachectic people, the corpuscles are dissolved, particularly when the weakness is not caused by previous loss of fluids."—G.

"Passive hemorrhages; everything seems

open and loose; no action in thin, scrawny, cachectic women."—G.

"Copious flow of black, liquid blood; worse from the slightest motion, with convulsive movements in abortion."—G.

"Strong tendency to putrescence; discharge of black blood; a kind of sanies, with tingling in the limbs, and great debility."—G.

"Hemorrhage, with spasmodic contractions; every discharge of blood is preceded by a violent, painful contraction of the uterus, or by distressing bearing-down pains."—G.

"Labor; the pain is much prolonged, as if pressing and forcing the uterus, especially in thin, scrawny, cachectic women."—G.

"She has a constant sensation of bearing down in the abdomen; it seems to her too constant and too strong to be effectual."—G.

"Labor-pains are weak, suppressed, or distressing; in weak cachectic women, use the 200th dilution."

Puerperal convulsions in scrawny, illy-nourished women, with too feeble labor-pains.

"Lochia very offensive and thin; discharge scanty or profuse; may be painless, or accompanied by prolonged bearing-down pains in thin, scrawny women."—G.

"The inflammation seems to be caused by suppression of the lochia or menses."—G.

Metritis, great prostration, extremities cold, frequent vomiting; the blood discharged from the uterus is fluid, mingled with dark, badly-smelling coagula.

"Failure of lactation in thin, cachectic, scrawny females; the breasts do not properly fill with milk; there is much stinging in them; she has been much exhausted with venous hemorrhage."—G.

"All her symptoms are worse just before the menses."—G.

"Menses too frequent, too profuse, last too long, with prolonged bearing-down pain; cutting colic; cold extremities; cold perspiration; great weakness, small pulse, and sometimes violent spasms."—G.

"Suppression of the menses in thin, scrawny married women, who suffer much at the menstrual nisus, with continual, long-lasting, forcing pain in the uterus."—G.

Leucorrhœa, jelly-like, alternating with metrorrhagia, in thin, scrawny women, with prolapsus uteri and excessive menstruation.

Moles, polypi, and morbid growths in the uterus, with prolonged forcing pains.

"Putrid, fetid, and colliquative diarrhœa."

"Painful diarrhœa, with great prostration."—G.

"Excessive, offensive perspiration."—F.

"Involuntary diarrhœa."—F.

"Cholera infantum, great debility, vomiting and diarrhœa; much thirst; pale face; sunken eyes; dry heat; quick pulse; restlessness and sleeplessness."—G.

"Very thin, scrawny children, with shrivelled skin, especially when there are spasmodic twitchings, sudden cries, and feverishness."—G.

"Twitching of single muscles; twisting of the head to and fro; contortion of the hands and feet, labored and anxious respirations."—G.

"Cholera, cramps, and cold, clammy perspiration; coldness in the back, abdomen, and limbs, with tingling in the limbs; cold, dry, livid tongue; serous vomiting; suppression of urine; vertigo and desire to sleep."—Raue.

"Hæmatemesis; patient lies still, with great weakness, but no pain; face, lips, tongue, and hands deadly pale, covered with a cold sweat; pulse frequent and thread-like."—Raue.

"Partial paralysis of the ciliary muscle, which renders it difficult or impossible to read or see any length of time."—Hughes.

"Quiet delirium, or grows wild with great anxiety, and a constant desire to get out of bed."—G.

"Anæsthesia of the limbs; paralysis of the

limbs, with convulsive jerks and shocks in the paralyzed limb."—HEMPEL.

"Violent pain in the sacral region; cannot bear the heat of the stove."—RAUE.

"The limbs become pale, cold, and shrivelled, or cold and lead-colored, losing all sensibility."—RAUE.

"Skin dry and brittle, not emitting a drop of blood when cut."—HEMPEL.

"Large ecchymosis; blood blisters on the extremities; becoming gangrenous; black suppurating blisters."—HEMPEL.

"Dry gangrene of the extremities, the parts are dry, cold, hard, and insensible, of a uniform black color, and free from fetor."—HEMPEL.

"Worse from warmth."—F.

"The ulcer feels as though it had been burnt; discharges a putrid bloody fluid, and is sometimes decidedly gangrenous and painless; in thin, scrawny, cachectic people."—G.

"Desire to be uncovered, even in cholera, with cold perspiration; worse from warmth." —F.

## USTILAGO MADIS.

*Smut-Corn.*

Acts especially on the skin and generative organs. On the skin, it produces an eruption similar to rubeola; rubbing any part of the body a few moments, it would break out with this fine red eruption; on the face it came in patches like ringworm (Herpes circinatus), but not vesicular. The eruption is about the size of a pin's head, itches violently at night, and constantly remains red and hard. The chest and joints are more affected than other parts of the body. The whole scalp becomes one filthy mass of inflammation, two-thirds of the hair came out, and what was left in, was mostly matted together. A watery serum kept constantly oozing from the scalp, so great as to keep the hair constantly wet.

"Shedding of the hair, both of man and beast, and sometimes even of the teeth."—ROULIN.

"Mules fed on it lose their hoofs."—ROULIN.

On the genital organs of man, it produces sexual dreams every night, without emissions; great depression of the sexual system for weeks, with great relaxation of the scrotum; constant aching pains in the testicles for days; severe, sharp, neuralgic pains in the testicles, more in the right; constant aching pains in the right testicle for days; spells of violent pains in the testicles, more in the right; every five minutes sharp pains in the testicles that produced faintness; two nights had a profuse cold sweat upon the scrotum, which was greatly relaxed.

On the generative organs of woman, it has a most powerful effect, but its true action has yet to be defined. I think the difference between the action of Ustilago and Secale on the uterus and tissues generally, is this: Secale acts on the striated or striped muscular fibres, which minister as a general rule to the animal functions. While Ustilago acts more on the smooth or unstriped muscular fibres and lymphatic glandular system, which preside over organic life; it also especially affects the ovaries. It causes in the uterus constant aching distress, referred by the patient to the mouth of the womb.

"In a cow-house, where cows were fed on Indian corn infested with this parasite (Ustilago), eleven of their number aborted in eight days; after their food was changed, none of the animals aborted."—ANL. (Med. Vetr. Belge and Rep. de Ph.).

"Six drachms to two bitch dogs with young soon caused them to abort."

"Fowls fed on this fungus lay eggs without shells."—ROULIN.

Also affects the urinary organs, and slightly the digestive organs.

Lastly, the lymphatic, glandular system, and skin are especially affected.

### *Grand Characteristics.*

I regret that I am unable to give its characteristics, but will give a few of what I think are characteristics.

Acts better on tall, slim, very fair complexions, and what might be called consumptive persons; also very lymphatic women, with clear, white skin.

Menstruation too frequent, too profuse, and lasts too long.

Suppressio-mensium from ovarian irritation, with much pain in the ovarian region, and flatulence and soreness of the bowels.

Vicarious menstruation from the lungs and bowels.

Scanty menstruation from ovarian irritation.

Menorrhagia at the climacteric period, with much pain on the top and side of the head; with burning distress in right ovary; goneness in the epigastrium; the flooding lasts for weeks; blood dark-colored, with many clots, and vertigo.

Active and constant flooding, with frequent clots of bright red blood, with bearing-down pains.

Passive hemorrhage; blood dark-colored, lasting many days, with anæmia, and dull, heavy headache.

Abortion, with bearing-down pains, as if everything would come from her.

Deficient labor-pains, where the os is soft, pliable, and dilatable.

Dysmenorrhœa of a congestive character, with much ovarian irritation; severe pain in the ovaries, uterus, and back, every few minutes.

Spasmodic pains in the left ovary, which is very sore and tender.

Ovaritis; constant pain in the ovary, with sharp pains passing down the leg with great rapidity; ovary much swollen, and very tender.

Intermittent neuralgia of the left ovary, which is large as a hen's egg, and very tender to the touch.

Between the menses, constant misery under left breast at the margin of the ribs.

Hypertrophy of the uterus.

Vertigo at the climacteric period, with too frequent and too profuse menstruation.

Nervous headache from menstrual irregularities.

Neuralgia of the testicles, and spermatorrhœa.

Urticaria, with intolerable itching at night.

Copper-colored spots on the skin.

Pustular ulceration of the skin.

(For all that is known about the Ustilago madis, *vide* my Monograph, printed by Dr. E. A. Lodge, Detroit, Michigan; and Hahnemann's Monthly, Ap. 1869.)

## PULSATILLA.

*Wind Flower.*

Acts especially on the vegetative or ganglionic nerves that govern nutrition, depressing and irritating their action, so as to produce a state similar to chlorosis, of a nervous character.

It especially affects the mucous lining of the sexual organs, the eyes, ears, gastro-intestinal canal, urinary organs, and skin. Causes a sub-acute catarrhal inflammation, with profuse mucous discharges, rarely going on to ulceration. If these discharges are suddenly arrested, the serous and fibrous tissues take on an active inflammation. Its effects are erratic in character; a blennorrhœa of one mucous surface may change to another; for instance, a leucorrhœa may change to a bronchitis or conjunctivitis. On the skin it produces an urticarious and vesicular eruption; also fetid sweat.

*On the motor nerves*, it causes a state of erethism, twitching, tremors, and the motion of the body is perverted.

*On the nerves of sensation*, it causes frequent chilliness, especially in the afternoon; hyperæsthesia, neuralgia, especially of the uterine and abdominal plexuses.

It also strongly affects the fibrous tissues.

*On the venous system*, it causes a state similar to varicosis.

*On the glandular system*, it affects the testicles, ovaries, mammæ, and tonsils.

Synovial membranes it affects, especially the small joints, the knee, hands, and feet, producing a rheumatico-gouty inflammation.

### *Grand Characteristics.*

Especially adapted to females with blue

eyes, very affectionate, easily excited to tears, and of a very yielding disposition.

"Very tearful; she weeps at everything, whether it is joyful or sorrowful."—G.

"She is timid and fearful, and yet extremely mild, gentle, and yielding; sometimes silent and melancholy, with bad taste in the mouth in the morning; nothing tastes good." —G.

"She weeps very easily about this or that; can hardly give her symptoms without weeping."—G.

"Craves fresh, cool air;" much worse in a close, warm room.—G.

"All her symptoms are worse towards evening; relieved in the open air, and worse on returning to a warm, close room."—G.

"The forms of her symptoms are very changeable; she is very well one hour, and very miserable the next."—G.

"Better from cold things; worse from warm."—G.

"She cannot sleep in the early part of the night, but sleeps late in the morning."

"Chilliness, even in the summer, when warmly clad, with vertigo, throbbing headache; pressure in the stomach; pain in the uterus, and dysuria, caused by nervous debility or from wet feet."—G.

"Semilateral headache, with bad taste in the mouth in the morning, without thirst, with nightly diarrhœa and scanty urination." —G.

"The blood is very changeable in its appearance; more apt to flow during walking in the daytime, and intermittent."—G.

"Catamenia too late and scanty, or suppressed, particularly by getting feet wet." —H.

"Menstrual colic, with great restlessness; tossing in every possible direction."—H.

"Menses suppressed, or flow intermittently, with evening chilliness."—G.

"Metrorrhagia, profuse at times, at other times intermittent, and mixed with clots; most profuse in persons given to reveries; in mild, tearful females."—G.

"Scanty, slimy menses, appear too late."—G.

Delayed menstruation, with much chilliness, and bad taste in the morning.

"Dysmenorrhœa, with pains so violent that she tosses in every direction, with cries and tears; the blood is thick and dark, or pale and watery, flows by fits and starts, and worse in a close, warm room."—G.

Amenorrhœa, in tearful, yielding dispositions; pale face; difficulty in breathing; much pain in the small of the back; much chilliness in the afternoon, and very bad taste in the mouth in the morning.

"Burning leucorrhœa, thin and acrid."—G.

"Milky leucorrhœa, with swelling of the vulva, particularly after the menses."—G.

"Leucorrhœa of thick, white mucus, especially when lying, or before and during the menses, with cutting in the abdomen."—G.

"Labor, the pains excite palpitations; suffocating and fainting spells, unless the doors and windows are open; she feels as though she must have them open."—G.

"Labor-pains alternating with hemorrhage and restlessness."—G.

"The breasts are much swollen, and rheumatic pains extend to the muscles of the chest, shoulders, neck, axillæ, and down the arms; she is fearful, tearful, but not thirsty."—G.

"She weeps at every nursing; the pain from nursing often extends into the chest, up into the neck, down the back, or changes from place to place."—G.

"Tension and contraction in the abdomen, as if the menses would come on, with nausea, and sometimes vomiting of mucus."—Raue.

"Labor-pains grow worse towards evening, in mild, tearful temperaments; no thirst."—G.

"Mild, tearful women, who have but little milk."—G.

"She can hardly find an easy position through the night, owing to the pain in the pelvic articulations."—G.

"Flying rheumatic pains, with much chilliness, especially after getting the feet wet." —H.

"Very sluggish circulation, manifested by constant chilliness, coldness and paleness of the skin."—RAUE.

"Dizzy when rising from a chair, with chilliness."—G.

"Drawing, rheumatic pains, frequently shifting from one part of the body to another; constant chilliness; worse nights."—G.

"Retention of urine, with redness, heat, and soreness of the vesical region externally."—RAUE.

"Involuntary emissions of urine, when sitting, coughing, or walking."—JAHR.

"After urinating, spasmodic pain in the neck of the bladder, extending to the pelvis and thighs."—G.

"Frequent and almost ineffectual urging to urinate, with cutting pain."—G.

"Constant pressure on the bladder, without desire to urinate; desire to urinate, with drawing in the abdomen."—G.

Scanty urine and no thirst.

Orchitis, the testicles and spermatic cord

swollen and painful; caused from cold or suppressed gonorrhœa.

Thickly coated white or yellow tongue, with bad taste in the morning.

"Morning sickness, vomiting of mucus; pulsations in the pit of the stomach; bad taste in the mouth every morning on awaking; she has to wash it out soon, it is so bad she cannot bear it; nothing tastes good to her; absence of thirst, and nightly diarrhœa."—G.

"She always has a very bad taste in the mouth early in the morning."—G.

"Disordered stomach; nausea; vomiting; repugnance to food; colicky pains in the abdomen, and dizziness from looking up."—G.

Cholera morbus caused by fat, rich food, with violent pains in the bowels; worse in the evening and night; drawing, cutting pains around the navel.

"Sour, bitter vomiting after fat, rich food." —G.

"Gastric disturbance from rich, fat food; she cannot sit long at a time, must walk about to relieve her pain."—G.

"Loathing, nausea, and retchings after greasy food, with sour eructations."—G.

"Pressure in the abdomen and small of the back, as from a stone, with disposition of the lower limbs to go to sleep when sitting, and attended with ineffectual desire for stool."—Raue.

"Obstinate constipation, in mild, gentle, tearful females, with very nauseous bad taste in the mouth in the morning, so very bad she has to wash her mouth out immediately on awaking."—G.

"Discharge of blood and mucus during stool; pallid countenance, and disposition to faint, with bad taste in the morning."—G.

"Watery diarrhœa, usually at night, with very bad taste in the morning."—G.

"Dysentery; stools mucus and blood; much chilliness towards evening; bad taste in the mouth in the morning; bruised feeling in the abdomen."—G.

Nausea, vomiting; thick yellow coating on the tongue, caused from cold, or rich, fat food.

"Stools of mucus streaked with blood; worse in the evening, and through the night, without thirst."—G.

"Diarrhœa always worse at night; no two stools alike, they are so changeable; for a time the child seems much better; then it gets worse again without any appreciable cause; always seems better in the open air."—G.

"Greenish, mucous diarrhœa at night."—G.

Hiccough at night.

"Coryza, fluid or dry, with loss of taste, sore

nostrils; later, a yellowish-green discharge." —H.

"Coryza, much worse every evening; the cough is very loose, and with all the fever, there is little or no thirst."—H.

"Child has difficulty of breathing when it lies on its side; worse evenings."—H.

"Wetting the bed; particularly little girls." —H.

"Cough very loose, with vomiting of mucus, and nightly diarrhœa."—G.

"Morning cough."—F.

Asthma, from deranged menstruation or suppressed urticaria.

Menses; the eruption is slow in making its appearance, with loose catarrhal symptoms.

Catarrhal ophthalmia, especially of the lids, with profuse lachrymation and secretion of mucus.

The eyes are always worse towards evening.

Weak eyes, with frequent styes.

"Much pain in the ears, with deafness; the meatus is red and swollen."—G.

Catarrhal otitis, with much pain.

Chronic otorrhœa, with discharge of pus.

"Toothache, relieved by cold water in the mouth."—F.

"Toothache on one side of the face; always ceases on going into the open air, but returns in a warm room, and gets worse; the pains are throbbing, or shooting, accompanied with much swelling; worse evenings; in mild, tearful females."—G.

Urticaria; worse nights, with diarrhœa from greasy food.

Rheumatism; pains shift rapidly from one part to another, unattended with any great swelling or redness; chronic cases, with weakness, rigidity, coldness, and weight in the diseased tissues.

Intermittents, with long chill, little heat, and no thirst.

"Very often needed in MEASLES."—F.

Worse in a warm room; from fruit, ices, pork, pastry, warm food.

Bad effects of Quinine; chlorosis from abuse of Iron; bad effects from suppressed menstruation; from Mercury, Sulphur, Chamomile tea, watering-places, and rich food, pork, pastry, &c.

## SEPIA.

*Cuttle-fish Juice.*

Acts especially on the nervous and vascular system, producing passive congestions, connected with dyscrasial suffering. The reproductive system must be involved. The grand sphere for the action of Sepia is upon the genito-urinary apparatus, especially affecting their mucous surfaces, their lymphatics, and vascular system.

Dr. Meyer, says of Sepia:

"1. It has its sphere of action on the portal system, in which it causes obstructions.

"2. Most of its symptoms indicate a higher degree of venous congestion.

"3. It is characterized by torpidity and depression, often ending in perfect exhaustion of the vital powers.

"4. Hence it is suitable in mild and easy dispositions, therefore especially for women.

"5. The affections arise and increase in severity, mostly in the evening and at night, during, and immediately after a meal.

"6. The affections either disappear during, or are alleviated by active exercise, and by pressure of the painful parts.

"7. The affections are often accompanied with chilliness.

"8. Great sensitiveness of the skin to cold air."

Lastly, it has a powerful influence on the skin, and lymphatic system.

### *Grand Characteristics.*

"Fetid urine, depositing a clay-colored sediment, which adheres to the chamber with great tenacity."—G.

"The urine is so putrid that it cannot be suffered to remain in the room."—G.

"The urine deposits a reddish clay-colored

sediment, which adheres to the bottom and sides of the vessel, as if it had been burnt on like burnt clay."—G.

"The bed is wet almost as soon as the child goes to sleep; always during his first sleep." —G.

"Gonorrhœa in the female, after the acute symptoms have subsided."—HUGHES.

Intense burning and cutting pain when urinating.

"Sensation as if everything would come out of the vagina; she has to cross her limbs to prevent it."—G.

"Burning, shooting, and stitching pains in the neck of the uterus."—G.

"A painful stiffness in the uterine region." —G.

"Pressing in the uterus oppressing breathing."—G.

"Prolapsus of the uterus and vagina; she has to cross her limbs, to prevent everything coming out of the vagina."—G.

"Leucorrhœa, with stitches in the neck of the uterus, and much itching in the vagina." —G.

"Profuse mucous leucorrhœa, having a fetid smell, or like pus, with drawing pains in the abdomen."—G.

"Leucorrhœa of a sanguineous, mucous, yellowish, watery character, worse after urinating."—G.

"Discharge of a green-red fluid from the vagina during pregnancy."—G.

"A putrid, excoriating discharge from the uterus, with shooting, stitching, and burning in the neck of the uterus."—G.

"Lancinating pain from the uterus to the umbilicus."—G.

"One of the most frequently indicated remedies for painful coition; contractive pain in the vagina; almost continual stitches in the vagina."—G.

Induration of the cervix uteri, with stitching pains in it, extending upwards.

"Troublesome and severe itching of the vulva, with pimples all around; painless vesicles in the outer parts of the vulva."—G.

"Severe itching of the vulva; the labia are swollen, with a humid eruption."—G.

"Menorrhagia, with a painful sensation of emptiness at the pit of the stomach; urine very fetid, and a sediment like burnt clay upon the bottom of the vessel; yellow saddle across the nose, and spots on the face."—G.

"Chronic metrorrhagia, when it is excited from the least cause; she has icy-cold paroxysms; icy-cold feet, and flushes of heat; great sense of emptiness at the pit of the stomach;

constipation, with great sense of weight at the anus, not relieved by stool."—G.

"Before the menses, violent colic, shuddering all over the body the whole day; acrid leucorrhœa; sensation as if the vulva were enlarged, and soreness in the perineum."—G.

"During the menses, tearing in the tibia; toothache; obscuration of sight, and violent pressure in the forehead, with discharge of plugs from the nose."—G.

"Amenorrhœa in feeble constitutions, with delicate thin skin; menstruation always irregular; sweats profusely when walking; particularly sensitive to cold air; repeated shuddering the whole day during the menstrual nisus; constipation and sense of weight in the anus; painful sensation of emptiness at the pit of the stomach; swollen and puffy appearance of the whole body; face puffy, pale, or yellow." —Marcy and Hunt.

"Between the menses a peculiar offensive perspiration, sudor hystericus, with a pungent, offensive perspiration in the axilla and soles of the feet."—G.

Sense of weight or ball in the anus not relieved by stool.

"Constipation; stools hard, difficult, and knotty, with sense of weight in the anus, not relieved by an evacuation."—G.

"The stool is very difficult, covered with mucus, and sometimes impossible to pass, even with the most terrible straining, with much burning at the anus and rectum, and sense of great weight at the anus."—G.

Piles; the portal circulation is retarded, causing an overloading of the portal vascular system with venous blood, plethora venosa; protrusion of the piles and anus; continual straining pain in the rectum; heat, burning, and swelling of the anus; discharge of black venous blood.

"Labor pains, with shuddering; rather wants to be covered up more, because she can bear the pains easier; spasmodic contractions of the neck of the womb."—G.

"Offensive, excoriating lochia."—G.

"The nipples crack very much across the crown; in various places deep cracks."—G.

"Morning sickness; she cannot take her accustomed ride in the morning, on account of nausea and painful feeling of hunger in the stomach."—G.

"In the morning, nausea, as if all the viscera were turning inside out; inclination to vomit in the morning when rinsing her mouth out."—G.

"Vomiting of milky water, or milky mucus,

with sense of emptiness of the pit of the stomach."—G.

"The thought of food sickens her, with sense of great weight in the anus."—G.

"Eructations tasting like spoiled eggs, or manure, with aversion to meat."—G.

"Pot-belliedness in women, with yellow saddle across the nose; very irritable and faint from the least exertion."—RAUE.

"Paroxysms of something twisting about in the stomach, and rising towards the throat; her tongue becomes stiff; she becomes speechless and rigid like a statue."—G.

"Sudden faintness, with profuse sweats and undisturbed consciousness, without being able to speak or stir."—G.

"Involuntary fits of laughter."—G.

"Sensation of coldness between the shoulders, followed by general coldness, and convulsive twitching of the right side, and difficulty of breathing."—G.

"Icy coldness of the feet."—G.

"Yellowness of the face, particularly across the bridge of the nose, like a saddle."—G.

"Very sad and fearful about her health; often weeps about it."—G.

Hemicrania from an affection of the reproductive system; countenance pale; face dirty yellow; especially in young females in which the cerebral nerves have excited the sympathetic; producing a long train of hysterical symptoms; the pain is stinging, aching, throbbing, tearing, and piercing.

"Great indifference to her own family."—G.

"Loose cough in the morning, with efforts to vomit."—G.

"Eruption very moist, almost constantly discharging pus-like matter; the child often jerks his head to and fro."—G.

"The least injury tends to ulcerate in thin, delicate skins."—MARCY and HUNT.

"The dandruff comes in circles like ringworm."—MARCY and HUNT.

"Specific in Herpes circinatus."—F.

"Worse in dry weather; during rest; when lying, sitting, and standing; on expiration; from uncovering, lying on back, and when scratching."—GROSS.

It is especially adapted to chronic diseases, affecting the female sex; especially when the sexual organs are in trouble, during the period of ovario-uterine activity.

Should never be used below the 30th, and more frequently the 100th and 200th dilutions.

## KREOSOTE.

*Creasotum.*

Acts through the vegetative nervous system, upon the digestive organs, teeth, bones, and especially upon the generative organs of women.

This remedy affects the organism very much like Pulsatilla, but more powerfully and deeply. As a remedy for female diseases, it rivals Pulsatilla.

### *Grand Characteristics.*

"Menses too early, too profuse, and last too long; inclined to be intermittent; she thinks she is almost well, when the discharge returns afresh."—G.

"She always feels chilly at the menstrual period."—G.

"Difficulty of hearing, before and during the menses, with buzzing and humming in the head."—G.

"The menses are usually too frequent and too profuse, succeeded by an acrid-smelling, bloody ichor, with corrosive itching and biting of the parts, and more or less pain during the flow, but much aggravated after it ceases."—G.

"Acrid, bloody ichor from the womb, with corrosive itching and biting of the parts; stitches in the vagina."—G.

"Stitches in the vagina, coming from above, causing her to start."—G.

"Putrid, acrid, corrosive leucorrhœa."—G.

"Leucorrhœa, with great debility, particularly of the lower extremities; it may be mild or acrid, causing much itching."—G.

"Very offensive, excoriating lochia, almost ceasing; then it freshens up, and again almost ceases, to freshen up again."—G.

"Her hemorrhage seems to pass into a corrosive, ichorous discharge, and then to freshen up again, and go on."—G.

"Continual hemorrhage from the tumor; at times becomes pale, and almost entirely ceases, and then recommences afresh."—G.

"Cancer of the uterus, with profuse discharge of dark, coagulated blood, or of a pungent, bloody ichor, preceded by pain in the back."

"Corrosive itching within the vulva, and biting between the labia and thighs, with soreness and burning after urinating."—G.

"Voluptuous itching, deep in the vagina."

"Burning and swelling of the external and internal labia."—G.

"In cancer, the whole mamma is hard, bluish-red, and covered with little, scurfy protuberances."—G.

"Awful burning, as of red-hot coal in the pelvis, with discharge of clots of blood, having a foul smell."—G.

"Sympathetic vomiting, where the irritation

starts from some other organ besides the stomach."—HUGHES.

"Teeth decay as soon as they appear."—G.

"When dentition is so badly performed as to become a disease, comprising general irritation of the teeth themselves, especially when the child is constipated," with great irritability and sleeplessness.

"Constipation in cachectic, delicate children."—G.

Caries of the teeth, when the pain is accompanied by turgescence of the gums, and facial congestion.

"Paroxysmal, moist cough, apparently caused by something crawling behind the sternum."—PROF. WALKER.

Spasmodic, moist cough.

"Buzzing and ringing in the head, with deafness during the menses."—G.

"Wretched, livid complexion."—G.

"Complexion livid; disposition sad and irritable."—G.

Œdema of the feet.

Fetid sweat of the feet.

"Herpes: humid, scaly, pustulous; on ears, eyelids, cheeks, mouth, elbows, fingers, malleoli; or large, greasy, pox-shaped pustules all over the body."—LIPPE.

Especially adapted to putrid diseases.

## SABINA.

*Common Savin.*

Acts especially on the generative apparatus of woman, and urinary organs. On the uterus it produces great congestion, violent inflammation, great pain, dreadful hemorrhage, abortion, and death. On the urinary organs it produces congestion, inflammation, and great strangury.

Also, has a most powerful effect on the gastro-intestinal canal; producing violent inflammation, vomiting, intense pain in the abdomen, purging, strangury, and death.

Portal congestion is a prominent effect of Sabina.

Also produces an arthritic diathesis.

### *Grand Characteristics.*

"Especially adapted to plethoric women, whose menses are habitually profuse, with drawing and tearing pains, from the back through to the pubis."—G.

"Metrorrhagia of clotted and fluid blood, with pain extending from the sacrum, or lumbar region, to the pubis."—G.

"Suppression of the menses is followed by a thin, fetid leucorrhœa."—G.

"Especially useful in protracted uterine hemorrhages, arising from a loss of tone in the vessels of the uterus, whether from previous disease, or the weight and pressure of the fœtus in utero; blood dark and clotted."—G.

"Hemorrhage after abortion or parturition; the blood is dark, having blackish clots, mixed with thin, watery blood; the pain extends from the back through to the pubis."—G.

"Dysmenorrhœa, with violent pain extending from the back through to the pubis."—G.

"Excessive debilitating menses, with abdominal spasms; the blood is partly fluid and partly clotted, and the pain runs from the back through to the pubis."—G.

"Yellowish, ichorous, fetid, leucorrhœa, and painful discharges of fetid blood every two weeks."—G.

"Leucorrhœa, after suppression of the menses; inclining to be corrosive, with itching of the vulva."—G.

"Severe stitching in the vagina, from before backwards."—G.

"An almost insatiable desire for an embrace."—G.

"Copious, starch-like leucorrhœa, with drawing pains in the small of the back through to the pubis."—G.

"This is one of the very best remedies we have to prevent abortion, at about the third month. Should be given in the 200th."—G.

"She is very nervous and hysterical; and

if she becomes pregnant, she is almost sure to abort about the third month."—G.

"Dystocia; pain of an uneasy, bad feeling, extending from the sacrum to the pubis; a slight sensation as of motion in the abdomen." —G.

"A quivering, as if something were alive in the abdomen."—G.

"Ardor urinæ, and profuse discharge of dark blood, with abdominal spasms."

"Diarrhœa, with pains extending from the back through to the pubis."—G.

"Constipation; stools difficult and painful; pain from the back to the pubis."—G.

"Piles; discharge of bright red or dark venous blood, with pain from the back through to the pubis."—G.

"Frequent urging to stool; finally a liquid portion is discharged, followed by a hard portion."—G.

"The cysts become swollen, red, and painful to the touch, or there are tearing pains during rest."—G.

"Music is intolerable to her."—G.

"Much irritability of temper."—G.

"Fig warts, with intolerable itching and burning in them."—G.

"Broad condylomata."—F.

Bœnninghausen says, "He found Sabina

the most efficient remedy in gout; and since it produces condylomata, it may be suspected that this malady, so much dreaded by our fathers, may have a sycotic anamnesis."

"Chronic arthritis; cannot bear a heated room; better in cool air."—G.

Use the 30th and 200th dilution; very seldom the 6th and 3d.

## HAMAMELIS VIRGINICA.

*Witch Hazel.*

Acts especially on the venous system, and on the generative organs of man and woman.

*On the venous system*, it produces venous congestion, inflammation, hemorrhage, and varicosis.

*On the generative organs of man*, it produces most intense neuralgia and inflammation of the testicles; amorous dreams, with emissions; great prostration of the animal passions; profuse cold sweat on the scrotum, with great relaxation of the genital organs, and varicosis of the spermatic veins.

*On the generative organs of woman*, it produces great irritation, congestion, inflammation, and neuralgia of the ovaries; passive hemorrhage from the uterus, and irritates the venous capillaries of the mucous membrane of the vagina and uterus.

### *Grand Characteristics.*

Dr. Hughes says: "I have the greatest confidence in Hamamelis, in phlebitis, in the various forms of varicosis, and in venous hemorrhages. In varicose veins of the leg, I conjoin its external with its internal use, laying strips of calico, soaked in a weak solution of one part to twenty, along the enlarged vessels, and supporting all with a bandage."

"In passive hemorrhages from all parts, whether from nose, stomach, lungs, or bowels, I have the utmost confidence in its use."—HUGHES.

"I think that the hemorrhages it cures depend rather upon the state of the bloodvessels, than on that of the blood."—HUGHES.

"Passive hemorrhages and venous congestion."—B.

"Epistaxis, either active or passive; long-lasting; blood venous."—DR. PRESTON.

"Hæmatemesis, with vomiting of large quantities of dark-colored blood."—DR. PRESTON.

"Dysenteric stools, loaded with dark, black blood."—DR. DUNN.

"Bleeding hemorrhoids, with burning soreness, and, at times, rawness of the anus, from portal congestion; the hemorrhage is generally very profuse; use it locally as well as internally."—HALE.

"Hæmaturia of dark, black blood."—DR. PRESTON.

"Varicose veins of the leg and foot, and phlegmasia alba dolens."—Dr. Preston.

"Varicose veins during pregnancy, with painful stiffness of the leg, and great weakness; sometimes burst and bleed profusely."—Dr. Preston.

"Great pain in the right leg, from the knee to the hip; leg much swollen, and sensitive to the touch; the cutaneous veins hard, knotty, swollen, and painful; veins of the abdomen hard, like cords, red and painful; skin erysipelatous; pulse small and wiry; urine red and scanty; much thirst; no appetite."—Dr. Preston.

"Hæmoptysis, active or passive; blood venous, and comes up into the mouth without coughing, or scarcely any effort."—Dr. E. W. Payne.

"Hemorrhage from the bowels, from portal congestion; stools dark and grumous, with great faintness, and cold sweat."—Dr. L. Pratt.

Long-lasting hemorrhage from extracting teeth.

"Discharge of blood per ani, in large quantities, of a tar-like consistency; hence, a specific in typhoid fever, with a bloody crisis."—W. H. Guernsey.

"Orchitis, with much pain, and great tumefaction of the testicles." Use internally and locally.

Neuralgia of the testicles; worse nights, and during rainy weather.

Impotence; organs much relaxed, with cold sweat on the scrotum.

"Varicosis of the spermatic veins; testicles much swollen, with drawing pains in the spermatic cord. Use locally and internally."—Dr. Preston.

"Ovarian diseases, accompanied with much swelling and tenderness. Locally and internally."—Dr. R. Ludlam.

"Ovaritis, from mechanical injury; ovarian region much swollen and tender; much pain, extending over the whole abdomen."—Dr. Okie.

"Frequent paroxysms of pain in the left ovary, passing down to the uterus, with anæmia, and every day or two the ovarian region much swollen."—B.

Cutting, tearing pains in the ovary, which is swollen, and very tender.

Dysmenorrhœa, from ovarian irritation.

"Vicarious menstruation, from ovarian irritation."—Dr. Kenyon.

"Passive, venous, uterine hemorrhage."

"Leucorrhœa, with much relaxation of the vaginal walls."—Hale.

Conjunctival inflammation, especially of the lids; also styes. Locally.

"The pains are often unbearable, with great sensitiveness to the touch, and fear of exciting new pain on moving."—B.

Use the tincture, 3d, 6th, and 30th dilutions.

## TRILLIUM PENDULUM.

*Beth Root.*

Acts especially on the generative organs of women, affecting the motor nerves of the capillary bloodvessels, producing relaxation of the muscular fibre, and mucous coats, causing passive hemorrhages.

Also affects the kidneys and mucous membranes.

### *Grand Characteristics.*

Its great field of usefulness lies among the hemorrhages, especially from the uterus and kidneys.

"Excessive flooding, with fainting; face pale and anxious; extremities cold; no pain."
—Dr. E. G. Wheeler.

In passive, uterine hemorrhage, with occasional clots, and much fetor, it is extremely valuable.

"Profuse uterine hemorrhage, at the climacteric period, with prostration, vertigo, dimness of sight, palpitation of the heart, and painful sense of sinking at the pit of the stomach."—HALE.

"Menses every fourteen days, lasting seven and eight days; in the intervening time, profuse leucorrhœa, of a yellowish color and creamy consistence; the blood is at first bright red, but owing to anæmia, grows pale."—RAUE.

"Profuse exhausting leucorrhœa, with atony, prolapsus, and chronic engorgement of the cervix."—DR. COE.

"Profuse lochial discharges."—DR. COE.

"Profuse yellowish leucorrhœa."

"Passive hemorrhages, from nearly all mucous membranes, especially the kidneys and nose."—HALE.

"Chronic diarrhœa, of bloody mucus."

Use the tincture, to the 6th dilution.

## CYCLAMEN EUROPÆUM.

*Sow Bread.*

Acts especially on the cerebro-spinal system, gastro-intestinal apparatus, and female sexual organs.

*On the head*, it produces sudden stupefaction; vertigo, and dull pressing headache; obscuration of sight; dilatation of the pupils; sleepiness; sleep disturbed by bad dreams; excessive sadness and melancholy.

*On the gastro-intestinal canal*, it causes violent vomiting and purging; sometimes vomiting of blood, with cold sweats; singing in the ears, and swimming of the head.

*On the generative organs of women*, it causes menstruation, increased in quantity, black and lumpy, and attended with hard labor pains.

### *Grand Characteristics.*

"Menorrhagia, with stupefaction of the whole head, and obscuration of sight, as if a fog were before the eyes."—G.

"Scanty, painful, or suppressed menstruation, with headache, vertigo, swollen eyelids, pale face, lips, and gums, loss of appetite, no thirst, and palpitation of the heart."—G.

Dr. Eidherr says, "He found it very efficacious, with blonde, leucophlegmatic subjects, in whom, besides retarded, suppressed, or scanty menstruation, or complete chlorosis, there was disinclination for any kind of labor; fatigue from slight causes; continual sleepiness, and chilliness all over the body, which no amount of covering would relieve."

Menses every two to four months, with excessive labor-like pains; vertigo; pressive pain in the forehead; anæmia; fits of fainting, and constant chilliness of the whole body.

Suppression of the menses, with melancholy; dizziness and headache; wants to be alone; weeping does her good; swelling of the eyelids; pale lips and gums; heart's action violent; always tired; loss of appetite, and constipation.

"Constant chilliness, with great desire for fresh air."—G.

Vertigo, diplopia, and strabismus.

Periodical, semilateral headache, with dizziness; diplopia; skin, eyelids, lips and gums very pale; much chilliness.

"After eating the least quantity, disgust and nausea in the palate and throat, with much dimness of vision; fiery sparks before the eyes, and intermittent thirst."—G.

The symptoms are aggravated in the evening, during rest, sitting, lying and standing.

Use the 30th, occasionally the 6th or 3d.

## CROCUS SATIVUS.

*Saffron.*

Acts especially on the generative organs of women, and on the sympathetic nervous system. On the uterus it produces congestion and hemorrhage of dark-colored blood. On the sympathetic nervous system it causes an extraordinary laughing mania.

### *Grand Characteristics.*

"Menorrhagia, of dark, stringy blood; as it is discharged, it forms itself into long strings." —G.

Menorrhagia, blood dark and clotted.

"Black, stringy discharge from the uterus, with rolling and bounding in the abdomen, as from a fœtus."—G.

Passive uterine hemorrhage; blood dark and stringy, in nervous hysterical women.

Flooding worse on motion.

"Dysmenorrhœa, with dark, stringy blood, and sensation in the stomach of great commotion, upwards and downwards, hither and thither."—G.

Miscarriage at third month.

False, or nervous pregnancy, with sensation as of something alive in the abdomen.

"Epistaxis of black, stringy blood."—G.

"She is worse every evening, with alternations of excessive, happy, affectionate tenderness, and rage."—G.

Chorea every seven days, with great hilarity, dancing, singing, &c.

"Spasmodic contraction of single muscles; jumping, dancing, laughing, whistling, wants to kiss everybody, with congestion of the head."—G.

Sings during sleep.

"Great mental dejection; menses suppressed, or blood dark and stringy."—G.

"Yellowish, earthy color of the face."—G.

"Great debility and palpitation of the heart on going up stairs."—G.

Use the 30th and 200th.

"Stitches in the abdomen arresting respiration."

"Feeling of nausea in the chest and throat, as if she would vomit."—G.

"Long, dull stitches near the anus; from time to time continuous, and painfully affecting the whole nervous system."—G.

"Feeling as if there were a gauze before the eyes."—G.

Use the 30th, 200th, and occasionally the 3d, and tincture.

## THLASPI BURSA PASTORIS.

*Shepherd's Purse.*

Acts especially on the generative organs of women, causing congestions and hemorrhage.

Its characteristics are unknown, but from what I can learn from the United States Medical and Surgical Journal, it is adapted to menorrhagia, too frequent, degenerating into a real hemorrhage, lasting many days; blood clotted with uterine colic.

Premature menstruation; "first day she barely had a show, but on the second day there was a real hemorrhage, with severe colics, vomiting and expulsion of clots; the flow continued very long, eight, ten, and even fifteen days, and then left the patient in a state of exhaustion, from which she had not time to recover, before another period; one period very profuse, the next less so."

Profuse hemorrhages from all parts of the body.—LIPPE.

Mr. Jousset says, "I have met with special success in hemorrhages, with violent uterine colic, with cramps consequent on abortion, at the critical age, and even where there was cancer of the neck."

Hemorrhage from cancer of the uterine neck, without pains.

It has given good satisfaction, in tincture, and at the 12th dilution.

## SENECIO AUREUS.

*Life Root.*

Acts especially on the generative organs of women, the urinary organs, and on the vaginal, intestinal, and pulmonary mucous membranes.

Its characteristics are not known.

Its effects resemble, very closely, Pulsatilla; and it has been found very useful in amenorrhœa, profuse leucorrhœa, catarrhal inflammation of the kidneys, and catarrhal affections of the lungs.

## CINNAMON.

*Cassiæ Cortex.*

Acts on the generative organs of women, and on the gastro-intestinal canal.

### *Grand Characteristics.*

"Menses too early and too profuse, particularly in females troubled with itchings of the nose and nightly restlessness; profuse flow of red blood."—G.

"She is constantly tossing, even during sleep."—G.

"Diarrhœa always worse after drinking." —G.

"Uterine hemorrhage, threatening or following miscarriage, especially if from a strain." —F.

"After a false step, or strain in the loins, the chief symptom is a profuse flow of red blood, in abortion."—G.

Much flatulence.

Use 3d and 6th dilution.

## MILLEFOLIUM.

*Yarrow.*

Acts especially on the vascular system, motor nervous system, and mucous membranes.

### *Grand Characteristics*

Are unknown; but it is especially adapted to all hemorrhages; more especially from the nose, lungs, kidneys, bowels, and sexual organs.

"Hæmoptysis, and other hemorrhages, in consequence of violent exertions."—F.

It stands at the head of the long list of our remedies for hemorrhages.

Use in low dilutions.

## TANACETUM VULGARE.

*Tansy.*

Acts especially on the generative organs of women, and on the motor nervous system; also, upon the kidneys and sympathetic nervous system.

*On the uterus*, it causes profuse menstruation, uterine hemorrhage, with labor-pains, and abortion.

*On the motor nervous system*, it causes cramps and clonic spasms.

*On the kidneys*, it causes congestion.

*On the sympathetic nervous system*, it causes symptoms resembling hysteria.

Also affects the digestive apparatus similar to Helminthiasis.

Its characteristics are not known.

It is recommended by Dr. Lippe as "especially suitable in St. Vitus's dance."

## GOSSYPIUM HERBACEUM.

*Cotton Plant.*

Acts on the generative organs of women; affecting, especially, the motor nerves of the uterus, producing uterine cramps and abortion.

Characteristics are unknown.

In the South, the green root, in decoction, is used in lingering cases of labor, with feeble pains; and to produce abortion.

Also, useful in dysmenorrhœa.

## CAULOPHYLLUM THALICTROIDES.

*Blue Cohosh.*

Acts upon the cerebro-spinal system; affecting, especially, the motor and sentient nervous system, and the female generative organs.

It also affects the muscular system, and small joints; metacarpal, tarsal, metatarsal, and all the phalangeal joints.

### *Grand Characteristics.*

"Especially affects the uterine motor nerves, so as to cause painful contractions and menorrhagia, and metrorrhagia.

"Menstrual irregularities; the pains and sufferings are of a spasmodic character; scanty flow; sympathetic cramps and spasms of neighboring organs: as the bladder, rectum, and bowels."—HALE.

"The motor power of the uterus seems almost entirely gone."—HALE.

"The menstrual flow is retarded, from a simple lack of the excito-motor force, either in the Fallopian tubes, or the parietes of the uterus itself."—HALE.

"Hemorrhage; due to deficient contractility, or deficient involution of the uterine tissues." —HALE.

Passive hemorrhages; an oozing from the lax uterine vessels, from debility of the excito-motor nerves of the uterus.

"Deficient, spasmodic labor-pains."—HALE.

Abortion; the pains are irregular and spasmodic.

"Protracted lochia, from atony of the uterus."—DR. KREBS.

"Reflex paraplegia, from an abnormal state of the uterus."—HALE.

"Complete insomnia."—LUDLAM.

"In hysterical women, with rheumatism of the uterus, and many spasmodic symptoms."—HALE.

Articular, inflammatory rheumatism of the small joints, in women.

"Rheumatism of wrists and hands."—F.

Hysterical spasms of the chest and larynx.

## GROUP XV.

| | |
|---|---|
| Acidum sulphuricum, | Acidum carbolicum, |
| Acidum nitricum, | Acidum fluoricum, |
| Acidum phosphoricum, | Acidum benzoicum, |
| Acidum muriaticum, | Acidum oxalicum. |
| Acidum hydrocyanicum, | |

M. TARTRA considers that "four varieties may be observed in the effects of the mineral acids. 1. Speedy death, from violent corrosion and inflammation. 2. Slow death, from a peculiar organic disease of the stomach and intestine. 3. Imperfect recovery; the person remaining liable ever after to irritability of the stomach. 4. Perfect recovery."

This group may be called the corrosive or escharotic group.

### ACIDUM SULPHURICUM.

*Sulphuric Acid.*

Acts especially on the ganglionic nervous system that presides over nutrition of the digestive apparatus; upon the cerebro-spinal system; upon the genito-urinary organs; and upon the skin.

#### *Grand Characteristics.*

"Much debility, with sensation of tremor all over the body, without trembling."—G.

"Coldness and relaxed feeling in the stomach; loss of appetite and great debility." —G.

"Diarrhœa, with great debility; sensation of tremor all over the body, without trembling."—G.

"Hard stool, consisting of small black lumps, mixed with blood, accompanied with such violent prickings in the anus that she has to rise up on account of the pain, with sensation of tremor all over the body, without trembling."—G.

Valuable for lead colic. (Also Alumina.)

"Hemorrhages of black blood from all the outlets of the body."—HUGHES.

Acidity of the stomach.

"Aphthæ; the mouth appears very painful, and the child is very weak; ecchymosis." —G.

"When some general deep-seated dyscrasia prevails, and the child is weak and exhausted, with no other symptoms."—G.

"She always gets a distressing nightmare before the menses."—G.

"Menses too early and too profuse; always preceded by a distressing nightmare; much general debility, and tremulous sensation in the whole body, without trembling."—G.

"Metrorrhagia, with tremulous sensation all over the body, without trembling."—G.

"Leucorrhœa of sanguineous mucus, with a sensation as if the menses would come on."—G.

"Milky or transparent leucorrhœa, without sensation."—G.

"Climacteric age, with constant flushes of heat, and a tremulous sensation all over the body, without trembling."

Profuse perspiration, with great debility.

Chronic headaches in leucophlegmatic temperaments, and relaxed muscles, with great debility in women subject to leucorrhœa.

Dose, 30th, 200th, and occasionally the 3d dilution.

NOTE.—There are so many chemical symptoms in the pathogenesis of the Acids, which are perfectly worthless to us as to their therapeutic value, that it is exceedingly hard to pick out their characteristics.

## ACIDUM NITRICUM.

*Nitric Acid.*

Acts especially on the mucous outlets of the body, where the mucous membrane merges into skin; the rectum and anus; vagina and mouth. It also affects the whole alimentary canal, especially the liver, the glandular system, the cerebro-spinal system, genito-urinary organs, the skin, and, lastly, the blood.

### *Grand Characteristics.*

Especially adapted to diseases depending upon the presence of some virulent poison, such as syphilitic, mercurial, and scrofulous miasms.

Salivation and ulceration of the mouth, from abuse of mercury.

Spreading ulcers in the mouth and throat.

Swelling of the parotid and submaxillary glands, with bleeding of the gums.

Putrid-smelling breath; mouth full of fetid ulcers; bloody saliva; mouth very dry.

Sore throat, extending up into the nose; discharges profuse thin purulent matter, with intermitting breathing.

"Much nausea and gastric trouble, relieved by moving about, or riding in a carriage."—G.

"Constant nausea, with heat in the throat."

"Fat food causes nausea and acidity, the urine smelling like that of horses."—G.

"Hard, difficult, and scanty stool."—G.

"Diarrhœa; great pain during and after stool, as though the anus was fissured."—G.

"Inclination to looseness of the bowels; most violent cutting pain after stool, lasting for hours."—G.

"Acute pain in the abdomen during stool; worse in the morning; stools brown and slimy."—G.

"Very painful stools, with profuse discharge of blood; the pain lasts so long, it is very exhausting."—G.

"The patient is worse after twelve at night; violent cramp-like pains, as if the abdomen would burst; with constant eructations."—G.

"Old hemorrhoidal tumors, secreting much slime, and bleeding profusely after stool."—G.

"Proctalgia."—F.

This is the best remedy we have for fissures in the anus.

"Fissures of the anus, on going to stool; pain in the rectum, as if something were torn away, or twitchings in the rectum, and spasmodic contraction of the anus, many hours after stool."

"Smarting more in the rectum than in the anus, immediately after stool, and continuing two or three hours; sometimes prolapsus ani, or discharge of much blood, accompanies these symptoms."—G.

Prolapsus ani, with much pain and smarting in the rectum and anus.

"Typhoid hemorrhages; great sensitiveness of the abdomen; green, slimy, acrid diarrhœa, with tenesmus."—HUGHES.

"Chronic hepatitis; gland enlarged; acts

favorably, even if it is of a fungoid disorganization."—HUGHES.

"The urine has an intolerably strong smell, like that of horses."—G.

Extremely offensive urine.

"Active hæmaturia; urging after micturition, with shuddering along the spine."—G.

"Small blisters on the orifice of the urethra, and inner surface of the prepuce, forming chancre-like ulcers."—G.

Balanitis and fig-warts, after abuse of Mercury.

"Easily bleeding ulcers; look like raw flesh, with zigzag edges; exuberant granulations on its base."—G.

"In syphilis, its particular sphere is the mucous patches, mucous tubercles, and general weakness of constitution, denoting that the system has been poisoned by Mercury, or shattered by the disease itself."—FRANKLIN.

"Mercurio-syphilitic inflammations of the fauces."—F.

Secondary affections of syphilis, especially in broken and cachectic constitutions, accompanied with emaciation, debility, caries of the bones, unhealthy ulcers on the surface, and great derangement of the nervous system.

"Menses too early, too profuse, and the urine emitting an intolerably strong smell."—G.

"Violent pressure, as if everything were coming out of the vulva, with pain in the small of the back, through the hips, and down the thighs."—G.

Leucorrhœa, consisting of mucus, which can be drawn out.

Flesh-colored or greenish leucorrhœa.

"Cherry-brown, and fetid leucorrhœa."—G.

"Leucorrhœa, where a syphilitic taint is the basis of the affection."—G.

The inguinal glands are sympathetically affected with the leucorrhœa.

"Stitches in the vagina, from without inwards, when walking in the open air."—G.

Hard knots in the mammæ.

"Eyelids swollen, hard, livid; copious yellow discharge running down the cheeks."—RAUE.

"Old people, with great weakness and diarrhœa."—RAUE.

Sleeps badly in the latter part of the night.

Herpes, condylomata, tubercles, ulcers, and syphilitic eruptions, with sore, prickling, itching pains.

One of the best known antidotes for all diseases of a mercurial origin.

"Very often useful in affections occurring after typhoid fever, especially if allopathically treated with calomel."—F.

## ACIDUM PHOSPHORICUM.

*Phosphoric Acid.*

Acts especially on the great sympathetic and cerebro-spinal nervous system; through it, it has a powerful influence on the generative organs, the urinary organs, alimentary canal, bones, and skin.

### *Grand Characteristics.*

"The chief sphere of the curative action of Phosphoric Acid, is the nervous system; and in this it influences less the functional than the organic diseases, when these latter are not very grave and deep."—HUGHES.

"Suited to individuals of originally strong constitutions, but which have become weakened by losses of animal fluids, by excesses, violent acute diseases, chagrin, or a long succession of moral emotions."—TESTE.

"Trinks looks upon Phosphoric Acid, Iron, and China, as the three leading restorers of the sinking vital energies."

"Is very weak, and indifferent to the affairs of life; listless; apathetic."—G.

"Indifferent to those things that used to interest her the most."—G.

"Conscious, but apathetic and indifferent in typhoid fever."—F.

Great sense of weakness, with a remarkable

state of indifference, from which she cannot arouse herself.

Diseases caused by debilitating influences, with excessive emaciation, and great prostration.

"In children and young persons, who grow too fast, after self-abuse, or long grief."—G.

Chronic consequences of grief, chagrin, care, anxiety, and disappointed love.

"Dreadful pain on top of the head, as though the brain were crushed, after long-continued grief."—G.

"Delirium, drowsiness, and sopor."—G.

Hypochondria, from sexual abuse.

"It is probably through the nervous centres that it affects the male sexual organs, on which its influence is very powerful."—HUGHES.

"Impotence, especially when the sensibility of the parts is excessive, and the semen is discharged shortly after an erection, or without an erection."

Bad effects from sexual excesses, with debilitating night sweats.

"Too early and too long menstruation, with pain in the liver; has to rise frequently at night, to pass large quantities of colorless urine."—G.

"Pain universally in the liver, during the menses."—G.

"Profuse leucorrhœa, with itching, some days after the menses."—G.

"Leucorrhœa, after the menses."—G.

"Uterine ulcer; has a copious, putrid, bloody discharge, with itching or corroding pain, or entirely destitute of pain."—G.

"Meteoristic distension of the uterus."

"Metritis; great debility, with indifference to all about her; slow fever."—G.

"Irritable uterus; it is distended with gas."

"Scanty milk; debility and great apathy."—G.

"She must often rise at night, in order to pass large quantities of colorless urine."—G.

"Urine like milk, mixed with jelly-like, bloody pieces, with pain in the kidneys."

"Phosphatic deposits, when these depend upon excess of Phosphoric Acid, from waste of nervous tissue, or upon alkalinity of the urine, from nervous depression."—HUGHES.

Diabetes mellitus.

"Gluey matter on the tongue, in choleraic diseases."

"Bread tastes bitter."—G.

"Mercurial, syphilitic ulceration of the lips, gums, and soft palate, with swelling of the bones; condylomata."—HEMPEL.

"Nausea, as if in the palate."—G.

"Sensation as if the stomach were being balanced up and down."—G.

"Children, with pale, sickly look; great debility; painless diarrhœa, and tottering gait." —G.

Meteoristic distension of the abdomen.

"Clammy, sticky tongue; abdomen much bloated; great rumbling in the bowels, and painless, watery diarrhœa, in cholera epidemics."—RAUE.

"Often specific in the diarrhœa which precedes epidemic cholera."—F.

"Copious, watery diarrhœa, with rumbling in the bowels."—RAUE.

"Stools, yellowish, and very offensive; the child is very listless; wants nothing, and cares for nothing."—G.

"The diarrhœa, although of long continuance, does not seem to debilitate much; the mother wonders that the child remains so strong with it all."—G.

"White, gray diarrhœa."—RAUE.

"The stools are hard and in pieces; she is obliged to rise frequently at night to void large quantities of colorless urine."—G.

"Intense pain in the periosteum of all the bones, as if scraped with a knife."—G.

"Hysteric affections of young women, with irritable fibre, excessive sensibility and irritability, accompanied by extreme delicacy and sponginess of the organic tissue; vascular orgasm, or atonic debility."—G.

Cerebral weakness from brain fag.

Use from the 1st to the 30th.

## ACIDUM MURIATICUM.

*Muriatic or Hydrochloric Acid.*

Acts especially on that part of the ganglionic nervous system that presides over the gastro-intestinal canal and the blood.

Also, affects the cerebro-spinal axis; but I think this is a secondary affection, from the great irritation of the ganglionic centres.

Affects particularly the mouth and anus; also, the genito-urinary organs and skin.

### *Grand Characteristics.*

"Cannot bear the slightest touch upon the anus, which often itches violently, and is not relieved by scratching."—G.

"Exceeding tenderness of the anus; she cannot bear the least touch, not even of the sheet."—G.

"Largely-protruding piles; bluish, and extremely sensitive and painful."—G.

"Varices of the anus, which are exceedingly sore to the touch; much prostration."—G.

"If the anus be very sensitive, either with

or without hemorrhoids, Muriatic acid is sure to be the remedy."—G.

"Diarrhœa, with intolerable itching of the anus, which is sometimes so sore that it cannot be touched."

"Watery diarrhœa; stools and urine involuntary."—G.

Adapted to low fevers, where there is putrescence of the fluids.

"Febris stupida; constant sliding down in bed; groaning and moaning in sleep; muttering and unconsciousness whilst awake."—Raue.

"Excessive dryness of the mouth and tongue; it is heavy and paralyzed; the patient cannot move it at all, even if conscious."—Raue.

"Pulse intermits every third beat."—Raue.

"Scarlatina maligna; intense redness rapidly breaking out all over the body, with coma; great anxiety and restlessness; dark, bluish-red fauces."—Raue.

Aphthæ, and ulceration of the mouth and throat, with extremely foul breath.

"Discharge of thin pus from the nose."—Raue.

Inflamed, swollen, and tender salivary glands; ulcers in the mouth and throat slough and extend together.

Sighing, great debility, and sliding down in bed.

"It is one of the few medicines which have a specific action on the tongue; it has been used successfully for many affections of that organ."—HUGHES.

"Leucorrhœa, with exceeding soreness of the anus, either from piles or from fissures."

"Uterine ulceration; putrid discharge very sensitive, and attended with a great sense of weakness."—G.

"Stitches and pain in the vagina."—G.

"Very sad and silent during the menses, as if she would die."—G.

"Menses too early and too profuse, with extremely sore hemorrhoids, which sometimes itch terribly."—G.

Profuse urination, with small stool.

Paralytic inability to void urine in low fevers.

Use particularly the 30th and 200th, and sometimes the 3d.

## ACIDUM HYDROCYANICUM.

*Prussic Acid.*

"Professor Jones, of Nashville, has made some very interesting experiments with this poison upon alligators, with a view of ascertaining its *modus operandi.*

" From these experiments he concludes that Prussic acid acts primarily, directly, and chiefly upon the medulla oblongata, and spinal cord; and that its ability to produce sudden death is dependent upon its action upon the medulla oblongata.

" Derangements in the relations of the medulla oblongata and spinal cord to the muscular system generally, and especially to the respiratory, are the first phenomena manifested in the action of Prussic acid.

" Prussic acid acts also upon the blood, the muscular fibres, and sympathetic nervous system; but the most marked phenomena, those disturbances of the respiration which induce death, are due to the direct action of the poison upon the medulla oblongata."—HOMŒOPATHIC INDEPENDENT.

It also affects the heart in a special manner. The sentient nervous system of the abdominal viscera is very prominently affected; it is a very close analogue of Nux vomica; and many diseases which Nux vomica fails to cure, will be cured by Prussic acid, especially the neuroses of the bowels.

### *Grand Characteristics.*

" Spasms, when the muscles of the back, face, and jaws, are principally affected, and the body assumes a bluish tint."—G.

Cholera, with marble coldness of the whole body; pulselessness, and rapid progress of the disease towards asphyxia.

Involuntary stools.

"Cessation of diarrhœa and vomiting; hiccough; paralysis of the œsophagus, the fluid runs gurgling down the œsophagus."—G.

Long, fainting spells, with trismus and tetanus.

Scarlatina; eruption dark-colored, and soon becomes livid; rapid feeble pulse; sinking at the stomach from prostration of the solar plexus.

Heart disease; violent palpitation, with fainting spells.

Use the 30th and 200th.

## ACIDUM CARBOLICUM.

*Carbolic Acid.*

The organs and tissues affected by Carbolic Acid are not known; it probably resembles the action of Kreosote very closely, with which it is very nearly identical, chemically.

Its great sphere of usefulness, so far has been, as a local remedy for the surgeon.

Three preparations of Carbolic Acid are used by surgeons:

1. Carbolic Acid and boiled linseed, or other fixed oil, in the proportion of one to five.

2. Carbolic Acid and water, in proportion of one to thirty.

3. Carbolic Oil and whitening, in the proportions requisite for the consistence of soft putty.

Also the dentists prepare a collodium of Carbolic Acid, and use it locally in odontalgia, with remarkable curative effect.

The results of the employment of these preparations in surgery are almost to be called wonderful, and promise to remove and prevent an immense amount of human suffering.

In all amputations, the cut surfaces are bathed with the Carbolic Acid lotion, the edges coaptated, and a paste of the Carbolic Acid applied, so as to prevent the air from coming in contact with the wound, and it all unites by the first intention.

In all forms of abscess, after opening it, and evacuating all the pus, wash with the lotion, and then seal it up with the carbolic paste. The antiseptic properties of the acid destroy and exclude those "atmospheric germs, or infusori, which keep up putrefaction."

In putrefactive sloughing wounds, the lotion destroys all fetor, facilitates the separation of the slough, and causes healthy granulations to spring up. "It has the power of arresting fermentation produced by organized matter."

Dr. Lemar says, "that the vapor of Carbolic Acid proves fatal to flies, ants and their eggs, lice, bugs, ticks, centipedes, acari, butterflies, earwigs, wood-lice, cockchafers, and other insects of their size, and their bodies resist putrefaction for a long time."

"For the extermination of mosquitoes and flies, a small piece of cloth, saturated with the acid, and hung up in the room."

Fish or infusori can be killed by dropping a

little of the acid into the water which contains them.

"Worms and larva in wood are killed by this acid; and all insects are also kept away from dead animals and vegetables, as grain in barns."

Animal parasites on the human body, such as lice, acari, fleas, chigo, harvest bugs, &c., may be destroyed by the lotion.

In pin-worms in children and adults, use injections of the lotion.

Many cases of itch have been cured by the Carbolic Acid lotion.

Its powerful antiseptic properties make it a valued agent for disinfection.

It does not act on putrid gases, but kills the living germs developed in the process of putrefaction, striking directly at the cause, and not the effect.

Its medical uses have been but few. It is reported to have cured two malignant cases of glanders.

Dr. Hornby, of Poughkeepsie, has cured catarrhal croup with it.

Dr. J. P. Connely, of Des Moines, thinks it one of the best remedies for whooping-cough.

Good in purulent conjunctivitis; used locally (but must be much diluted) as an injection in fetid leucorrhœa and ulceration of the uterus.

## ACIDUM FLUORICUM.

*Fluoric Acid.*

This acid is the most caustic and highly corrosive substance known. It readily dissolves silica and silicic acid. As a solvent of silex in the animal economy, it is especially useful. Glass is energetically acted upon by this acid; its transparency is instantly destroyed, and heat is evolved. "Its vapor is more pungent than chlorine, or any of the irritating gases." The organs and tissues it especially affects, I am not fully able to make out, but believe its greatest therapeutic action is upon the teeth, bones, cuticle, hair, faucial and pharyngeal mucous membrane, thyroid gland, genito-urinary organs, venous system, and ganglionic nervous system.

### *Grand Characteristics.*

Its main sphere of action is in diseases of the vegetative tissues, of a chronic suppurative character. In action it closely resembles Silicea.

Great loss of memory.

Falling off of the hair, with congestion of blood to the head.

Baldness.

Rapid caries of the teeth.

Ptyalism.

Dental and lachrymal fistulæ.

"Pains in the bones, with numbness and

powerlessness of the hands, and itching of the skin."—G.

"Pains from below upwards."—F.

Excessive moisture of the hands and feet.

Caries of the bones.

Chronic inflammation of the pharynx and fauces.

Hemorrhoids, with much congestion of blood in the rectum.

Much congestion of the sexual organs, "with menses too early and too profuse; thick and coagulated; an uncommon buoyancy of mind; she fears nothing, and is well satisfied with herself."—G.

"Enlarged and indurated liver, from abuse of whiskey."—RAUE.

Syphilitic erosions, mucous tubercles, exostoses, and nightly bone-pains.

"Squamous eruptions on the body."—HUGHES.

"Tubercles on the forehead and face, even when ulcerating."—RAUE.

"Caries in consequence of syphilis, or abuse of mercury, especially of the temporal bone."—RAUE.

Varicose veins. Typhus, with decubitus.

"Better able to endure fatigue; heat and cold."—F.

Whitlow, externally, solution of one-eighth

of a grain to an ounce of water; the compress kept constantly moist; give the 30th or 200th internally.

Bronchocele is said to be rapidly cured with it.

## ACIDUM BENZOICUM.

*Benzoic Acid.*

Acts upon the urinary organs, joints, fibrous tissue, and skin.

### *Grand Characteristics.*

Especially adapted to rheumatic or gouty subjects.

The urine is high-colored, with an exceedingly strong smell; "dark-colored, and much heavier than normal." (See Nitric Acid.)

Shifting rheumatoid pains in the joints.

Concretions in the joints, from rheumatism or gout, with strong-smelling urine.

Articular rheumatism, with strong-smelling urine.

Symptoms and pains appear first on the left side; then on the right.

## ACIDUM OXALICUM.

*Oxalic Acid.*

Acts especially on the spinal cord, and also upon the brain. "Its main sphere of action is on the nervous centres, which it paralyzes from below upwards." "The loss of power in the lower extremities—which is very characteristic—is accompanied with numbness, and neuralgic pains in the back and legs. As the poison advances up the spinal cord, paroxysms of spasmodically suspended respiration and palpitation of the heart manifest its influence."—HUGHES.

It also acts upon the pneumogastric nerve, the mucous membranes, and the joints.

### *Grand Characteristics.*

"Pain in the back is often relieved by Oxalic Acid, better than any other remedy."—PETERS.

Excessive lassitude of the body.

"Great lassitude and weakness of the limbs."

"Spinal neuralgia, with acute pain in the back, extending down to the thighs; numbness, tingling, and pricking in the lower portion of the spine."—HUGHES.

"Numbness, approaching to palsy."—HUGHES.

"All the pains seem to occupy only a small spot, half an inch to an inch in length, viz.: in the Eustachian tube, right wrist, right hypochondrium, region of navel, knee, &c."—NEIDHARD.

This acid has been used so little, that we know not its characteristics. It ought to be a remedy of great value.

"It has been found useful in severe gastric sufferings of pregnant women, especially with ptyalism."—F.

# INDEX.

D.



E.



F.



G.



H.

I.



J.



K.



L.



M.



N.



O.



P.



R.

S.



T.



U.



V.



Z.

www.ingramcontent.com/pod-product-compliance
Lightning Source LLC
LaVergne TN
LVHW021121110826
845150LV00005B/906

* 9 7 8 1 4 2 5 5 6 0 4 5 4 *